ALSO BY KEN CORBETT

Boyhoods: Rethinking Masculinities

A MURDER OVER A GIRL

A MURDER
OVER A GIRL

JUSTICE, GENDER, JUNIOR HIGH

KEN CORBETT

HENRY HOLT AND COMPANY   NEW YORK

Henry Holt and Company, LLC
Publishers since 1866
175 Fifth Avenue
New York, New York 10010
www.henryholt.com

Henry Holt® and ® are registered trademarks of
Henry Holt and Company, LLC.

Library of Congress Cataloging-in-Publication Data

Corbett, Ken.
  A murder over a girl : justice, gender, junior high / Ken Corbett.
    pages cm
  ISBN 978-0-8050-9920-1 (hardback)—ISBN 978-0-8050-9921-8 (electronic copy)
  1. McInerney, Brandon David.   2. Murder—California—Oxnard—Case studies.
3. School shootings—California—Oxnard—Case studies.   4. High school students—
California—Oxnard—Case studies.   5. Transsexual students—California—Oxnard—
Case studies.   6. Transsexual youth—California—Oxnard—Case studies.
7. Transgender youth—California—Oxnard—Case studies.   I. Title.
  HV6534.O96C67 2016
  364.152'3092—dc23   2015023835

Henry Holt books are available for special promotions and
premiums. For details contact: Director, Special Markets.

First Edition 2016

Designed by Kelly S. Too

Printed in the United States of America
1 3 5 7 9 10 8 6 4 2

You are not one of us.

—CHARLES DICKENS

A MURDER OVER A GIRL

PART ONE

———

MURDER

1

Behind Me

Have you tried not to think about this at all until today?

Yes.

Is this really hard for you?

Yes.

Did you see Brandon when he came into the courtroom this morning?

Yes.

You saw the same person that you saw shoot Larry King?

Yes.

Yes? Where is he sitting?—I know—I'm not going to ask you to look at him. But can you tell me where he is sitting?

Behind me.

Deep breath. Where?

Behind me.

Mariah Thompson had come to testify in *The People of the State of California v. Brandon David McInerney.* Three years earlier, on February 12, 2008, fourteen-year-old Brandon shot fifteen-year-old Lawrence "Larry" Fobes King twice in the back of the head, during their first-period English class at E. O. Green Junior High in Oxnard, California.

On this, the second day of the trial, July 6, 2011, Brandon stood accused of first-degree murder, lying in wait, and a hate crime. The hate was said to be gender hate. Larry King had begun referring to himself as a girl a few days before he was killed, and it was alleged by the Ventura County district attorney that Brandon killed Larry "because of his perceived gender or sexual orientation."

The bailiff, Los Angeles district deputy sheriff Mike Anton, met Mariah at the main door to Courtroom F51 of the Superior Court of the State of California, Los Angeles County, Chatsworth, California. Room F51 was a windowless, though brightly lit, sage-green box. It had been built for wear: plastic wood veneers, poorly padded folding seats, concrete floors. Even the sparse carpeting was made to endure, not bounce.

Mariah had been a classmate of Larry King and Brandon McInerney, and an eyewitness to the shooting. Sheriff Anton offered his hand to guide her to the witness stand. She did not look up as she walked past the visitors' gallery toward the well of the court. Sheriff Anton opened a small gate in the waist-high wall that divided the gallery from the well, and gently directed Mariah between the tables used by the prosecution and the defense teams.

Wearing a white cotton sundress and black ballet flats, she recoiled, even as she advanced, walking with her head bent forward, her shoulders rounded into her round frame. She made no eye contact. She stopped a few feet before the judge's bench. She tugged at the edge of her salmon-colored cardigan sweater.

The judge, the Honorable Charles W. Campbell, sat at his imposing bench, above Mariah. The clerk of the court, the record keeper, and her assistant sat at a long desk, perpendicular to the judge's bench, on the right. The court reporter sat just below the judge, not far from where Mariah stood. The jury was seated on a three-row riser, to Mariah's left.

Sheriff Anton instructed Mariah to raise her right hand and face the clerk. Mariah did not turn, nor did she look toward the clerk. She did, though, raise her hand barely above her hip.

Holding a Bible, Madame Clerk asked, "Do you solemnly swear that the testimony you are about to give in the case now pending before this court is the truth, the whole truth and nothing but the truth, so help you God?"

Mariah nodded and was sworn in.

With Sheriff Anton's help, she made her way up a single step to the witness stand, a small perch sandwiched between the judge's bench and the jury box.

Mariah sat hunched on the edge of the brown upholstered chair, the sort one might see in an office cubicle. Sheriff Anton, the unerring butler of the courtroom, ran his hand over the rail, as if to demonstrate that Mariah was protected. She stated her first name and spelled it. She looked, for the first time, out at the room.

FIFTY-SEVEN PEOPLE HAD GATHERED. THE judge, businesslike and patrician, could have just as easily been sitting at the head of a conference table in a corporate boardroom, his wavy silver hair carefully combed. Joining him at the front of the room were the patient women who ran the proceedings: the clerk, her assistant, and the court reporter.

There were twelve jurors. Nine women, three men. Eight wore wedding rings. Nine were white. Three were brown. During jury selection, three had indicated that they were retired; they were formerly a businessman, a career military man, and a social worker. Seven, all of them women, had reported that they were of middle age: three housewives, two nurses, one teacher, one office worker. Two of the jurors were younger: a female college student and a young man who worked in his family's business. Two were fathers. Seven were mothers.

The prosecution and the defense teams also sat in the well. Leading the prosecution was Deputy District Attorney Maeve Fox, a petite woman who wore the kind of suits women wear to formal lunches in fashion magazines. She was focused on her notes and did not look up as she stacked folders and arranged three-ring binders. Her habit of order comically collided with the disorganization of her investigator, Robert Coughlin, who sat next to Ms. Fox and seemed to be looking for something that had gone missing.

Heading up the defense was Scott Wippert, whose belt was as tight as he could cinch it, yet he still had to hitch up his pants. (I would later learn that he had lost ten pounds as he prepared for the trial.) Mr. Wippert was leafing through a yellow legal pad, making notes. Like Ms. Fox, he did not look up.

Robyn Bramson, the defense co-counsel, a freshman litigator, looked around the room. She squinted and squirmed. Kathryn Lestelle, the defense investigator, sat at the edge of the table, struggling to gather the tangled nests that were her hair and her notes.

Just before Mariah entered the room, Brandon had been escorted from a door on the right-hand side of the courtroom, a doorway that led to the holding cell in which he had been waiting. Two deputy sheriffs, broad men in khaki uniforms, had walked alongside him as he took his seat. Brandon was wearing civilian clothing: gray slacks, a light blue oxford-cloth shirt, and square-toed black shoes. He did not look toward the visitors' gallery. It was difficult at first to see his face, although it was not hard to see that he was taller than the sheriffs who accompanied him. Brandon now sat between Mr. Wippert and Ms. Bramson.

In the gallery, the press sat in a row of four single-file seats. Each chair was full: two local print journalists (Zeke Barlow from the *Ventura County Star* and Catherine Saillant from the *Los Angeles Times*) and two local television reporters (Christina Gonzales, FOX LA; and Amy Johnson, KCBS/KCAL).

The main visitors' gallery comprised five rows of eight seats each. Three retired attorneys, with three bald spots, sat in the front row. Four members of the McInerney family sat in the second row, behind the defense team: Kendra McInerney, Brandon's mother, tall like her son, wore a black-and-white sundress, with sandals. Her long blonde hair was streaked with gray and looked perpetually wet, as if she had just come from the beach. Seated to her right was her friend Nancy who dressed in men's work clothes and wore her black hair in a tight braid. She could have been the handsome Indian in a Hollywood movie from the 1940s, save for the fact that she had PAYASO GUETO (ghetto clown) tattooed on her neck. Shannon Mulhardt, Brandon's aunt, his father's sister, also sat close to Kendra. A family friend sat next to Ms. Mulhardt. Both of them looked like the settled suburban sisters of the less domesticated Kendra and Nancy.

The King family sat in the third row: Greg King, Larry's adoptive father, sat in the aisle seat, a red-faced man who looked over his glasses toward the well of the court. Whenever there was a break in the proceedings, he was the first out of his seat, reaching for his cigarettes as he hit the door. Dawn King, Larry's adoptive mother, struggled to settle in her seat, fiddling with her handbag and adjusting her necklaces. Dawn sat next to her mother, Sharon Townsend, Larry's adoptive maternal grandmother, a trim, unadorned contrast to her daughter. Larry's biological brother, Rocky, a long-limbed thirteen-year-old, sat still next to his grandmother. And next to Rocky sat Larry's adoptive uncle, Greg's brother. I never heard him speak, and I never learned his name.

The fourth and fifth rows were unofficially reserved for various family members and friends who had accompanied witnesses to the court. Witnesses were required to wait in the outer hallway until they were called into the courtroom. Today, the second day of the trial, Mariah's father and stepmother were in the fourth row, along with three other mothers who had come with their children, all of whom had been eyewitnesses to the shooting and would testify later that day. The back row included five more family members who had come to support their kin.

I sat in the second row of the visitors' gallery, two seats to the left of Kendra McInerney. I was one of three people who were there to observe the proceedings, for various projects on which we were working. I am a psychologist and had come to observe the trial as part of my research for writing this book. Sitting to my left was my friend Gayle Salamon, a professor at Princeton University, who was researching a book about how gender and sexuality were emobied at E. O. Green and in the courtroom. Marta Cunningham, a documentarian who was collecting data and interviews for her film *Valentine Road*, sat behind us, in the third row.

Sheriff Anton and his two deputies were stationed at a small desk near the jury. Two other deputies were stationed in the back of the courtroom, near the main entry.

AS MARIAH LOOKED OUT UPON the room, I doubt that she took in all the different people, for as quickly as she looked up, she lowered her head again, and began to weep. Fear illuminated Mariah's pale skin and blue eyes.

Deputy DA Fox, leading the prosecution, instructed Mariah to breathe. Ms. Fox offered to delay the questioning. She asked if Mariah might like to have one of her parents join her on the stand. Judge Campbell reiterated those offers. Mariah caught her breath, and said that she could go on.

Led by Ms. Fox's questions, Mariah described Larry King as a "skinny-ish" brown boy who was "out there" but "seemed happy." She smiled warmly when she said this. It was as if the smile had escaped. Then she explained that a month before Larry was killed, he had begun "dressing up." He wore high heels, makeup, and earrings to school. By Mariah's account, Larry was often teased and called names like "gay" and "fag." Yes, Larry would react to the teasing, sometimes taunting in return, but Mariah thought such rejoinders were always provoked.

Ms. Fox shifted her questions, and her focus, to the accused murderer. Mariah told us that she shared two classes, PE and English, with the defendant, Brandon McInerney. Mariah recounted how she had observed Brandon, along with her other classmates, teasing Larry. Careful to include Brandon in a group, Mariah did not name Brandon as a lone bully. She did not even have a clear recollection of seeing Larry and Brandon interact, one-to-one.

Mariah glanced at Brandon. Just as quickly, she returned her gaze to her hands, worrying a tissue in her lap. She smiled. Again, the smile quivered, and was quickly checked. Ms. Fox asked if kids said things to Larry like "You're so gay. Why do you dress like a girl?" Mariah quietly said, "Yes." She dared another glance at Brandon.

Moving quickly, as we would learn was her style, Ms. Fox turned to the day of the murder, February 12, 2008, and the classroom at E. O. Green Junior High School, where the murder took place. Using an aerial diagram of the school, Ms. Fox asked Mariah to identify the classroom and to confirm where she had been sitting on the morning in question. Mariah hesitated, and Ms. Fox repeated the question. As Mariah pointed at the diagram, she began to cry.

Sheriff Anton offered tissues and water. Mariah took the tissues, leaving the water bottle unopened on the edge of the witness stand. Calmed, she went ahead to describe how twenty-eight students had started off the school day together in their homeroom, where they stayed for about fifteen minutes before walking together to the computer lab to work on research papers. Mariah's paper was about Anne Frank.

Twenty minutes after the class had settled into the computer lab, Mariah turned away from her computer to ask a friend a question.

"What did you see? What happened?" Ms. Fox asked.

Mariah looked sidelong at Brandon, then back at Ms. Fox, who repeated the question. Mariah lowered her head. Her shoulder-length red-blonde hair fell forward. She attempted to push it back, but strands of hair caught in the corners of her mouth.

Mariah was by then seventeen years old. It was not difficult, though, to see her at fourteen, her age when she watched fourteen-year-old Brandon become a murderer and fifteen-year-old Larry leave life. Flush with emotion, caught in the magnifying lens of the witness stand, Mariah began to tremble. Terror emerged from her eyes and unfurled across her body.

She was not alone. When Mariah entered the room, she brought murder with her. It was with us all. One juror, a trim, elderly man, leaned forward and put his head in his hands. Two jurors wept.

To my right, Brandon's mother, Kendra, sobbed. She held a tissue to her nose, but it had given way, and her hands were wet. She struggled to breathe. As her gasps accelerated, I began to think through the medical response to a panic attack. (We might need a small brown paper bag for her.) Someone in the visitors' gallery said, "No!" not loudly enough to fill the room, but loudly enough to breach the court's instructed silence. The court reporter bowed her head. Larry's grandmother, Dawn King's mother, Sharon Townsend, put her hand on her forehead and then reached out to touch the shoulder of Larry's younger brother, Rocky.

Ms. Fox offered Mariah a break. She asked if Mariah might wish to move her chair so that her back would be turned to Brandon. Mariah did not respond.

Judge Campbell ordered a twenty-minute recess. Time would be reset. His order was kind but firm. He was not going to be insensitive to emotion. There would, however, be a limit to its interference and to his willingness to indulge it. Judge Campbell explained that when the proceedings reconvened, one of Mariah's parents would join her on the stand. The judge excused her, and Sheriff Anton helped her exit the witness stand and walk to her parents, who met her at the gate that separated the well from the visitors' gallery. Looking frightened, Mariah's father put his arm around her and led her from the room.

Brandon had remained motionless throughout Mariah's testimony, head down, shoulders loose. He'd stared at the edge of the table and at the water bottle he occasionally tipped on its side. After the recess was called, he rose from his chair with his defense team. He turned to face the visitors' gallery as the jurors filed out. He stood with his hands folded, as if he were in a receiving line. The pose looked coached. So, too, had Brandon's long brown hair been coached and combed in the manner of an Eton schoolboy. His social performance was as new and stiff as his shoes. The following week, Samantha Criner, Brandon's girlfriend, would testify that she had never seen him with long hair. "Gosh! He's never looked like that," she exclaimed. "I always wanted to see him with long hair, but he never would, you know. Buzzed, it was always buzzed."

Brandon was "a handsome boy." Most everyone said so. He was pale, prison porcelain, with gray eyes shadowed by a strong brow. His small chin, his thin mouth (it could have been drawn with two quick pencil strokes) were just the right element of flaw. At six foot three, he towered over his lawyers. His muscles pushed against the seams of his extra large shirt that sought to cover the evidence.

Two deputies escorted Brandon from the courtroom to his holding cell.

I walked to the bathroom. I went to the sink and began splashing my face with cold water. I put my glasses back on and looked in the mirror, taking in my short gray hair and the bags under my eyes. A thin man, I am often taken to be younger than I am. But as I looked at my reflection, I did not see much that spoke of youth. I thought about my father's father, who was fifty-seven years old when I was born. In my eyes, he had always been old. I myself was fifty-seven as I stood in front of the mirror. I was ten when my grandfather died. His death was my first. I had had to be ushered from the funeral, in tears.

As I stood at the sink, Zeke Barlow, the reporter from the *Ventura County Star*, came in, used the urinal, washed his hands, and began to pace. Zeke, whom I had met the day before, looked at me and asked, "Dude, you all right?"

"Barely," I said.

An elderly gentleman, unknown to me, walked to the urinal. And, as if he were speaking to himself or rhetorically to the room, the stranger said, "How could he?"

JUDGE CAMPBELL RECALLED MARIAH TO the witness stand. During the recess, her chair had been turned so her back was to Brandon. Mariah's angry-eyed stepmother joined her on the witness stand, sitting behind her, looking out over Mariah's right shoulder.

Ms. Fox asked Mariah more questions about the shooting, questions that would be asked over and over during the first few days of the trial. Mariah's answers were similar to the answers that would be given by all the eyewitnesses. Each would report the same basic sequence of events, the same baseline perceptions, and the same matters of fact. Their perceptions, however, gathered and diverged in distinctive ways. Their reports were unique, in detail and in torment.

Mariah, for example, told us that she made eye contact with Brandon as he dropped the gun and turned to leave the computer room. Together, they were the first to see who he had become.

Along with her classmates, Mariah heard both gunshots, but, unlike most, she saw the gun. "It was black, and it was like . . . I don't know how to explain it. It was like a little hand. It was little. It was black."

She could not recall seeing Larry slip from conscious life. Asked if she saw Larry fall, as she had reported to a police officer on the day of the shooting, she said, "I don't remember that much." Mostly she remembered "looking at Brandon, then running."

Mariah had come to the witness stand unprepared to see what she was going to see. In an e-mail exchange following the trial, she wrote to me, "Testifying alone wasn't easy because I never talk about it." "Alone" certainly captured what we saw: a terrified young girl, cornered in her own mind.

Forced to talk about that which she never talked about, Mariah brought us her unformulated, unarticulated experience. She took us outside of words. Language gave up. We moved with her into a frantic suffering that overtook what she saw. She did not so much describe the murder as relive it.

BY THE TIME MARIAH CAME before us, we had listened on the first day of the trial, July 5, 2011, to the opening statements by the attorneys and a half day of testimony. We had heard from grown-ups: authorities, well-groomed men in suits and ties. Each in turn took to the witness stand with three-ring binders and answered the attorneys' questions with sober precision.

We heard first from Detective Bernard Chase, a man with white hair and a goatee, who had worked homicide cases for thirty years. He calmly described the crime scene, point by point, showing us photos of a cluttered corner of a classroom. Blood pooled on a black-and-white checkerboard floor. There was an overturned blue plastic chair, as well as an upright but askew red plastic chair. (Or was that the blue chair? I struggled to recollect, even as I saw.) Strewn across the floor were a brown backpack, blood-soaked paper towels, three books (one green, one tan, one red), and some scattered papers. What seemed to be a pile of rags were in fact Larry's clothes, cut and torn in the haste of emergency. His black-and-orange sneakers had come to rest along the baseboard. Blood smeared on the floor had begun to dry and turn brown. The gun was an indistinct black blur on a bookshelf. Detective Chase explained that a first responder, concerned about safety, had picked up the gun from the floor and put it on the shelf.

We heard next from the lead detective, Jeff Kay, a studious young man with close-cropped hair and close-set eyes. Detective Kay carefully arranged his four large three-ring binders on the edge of the witness stand and answered Ms. Fox's questions about the gun. Detective Kay told us that the gun had been fired twice and had then jammed. It was not clear if it jammed as Brandon attempted to fire it a third time or if it jammed when he dropped the gun on the classroom floor.

Referring to his notes, Detective Kay went on to explain that the gun was an "RD 23, a small caliber handgun, that was made in Florida in 1979, the same year that it was sold to a Mr. George Gay." Beyond that, "no history" was known; efforts to trace the gun "through the ATF went cold," Detective Kay said. "The gun has been around for a long time" he continued, "and clearly, the defendant took the gun from his home; he told us that. But we do not know whose it was, or how long they had it."

"Well, how did Mr. McInerney get it?" Ms. Fox asked.

"We don't know. He has not said. But there were a lot of guns in that house," Detective Kay said.

He went on to detail the search of the McInerney home on the day of the shooting. His officers seized fifteen guns, mainly from an unlocked gun closet: handguns and rifles. Throughout the house, the officers found guns, gun paraphernalia, firearm references, gun-related resource materials, boxes and plastic bags filled with ammunition of different calibers, gun-cleaning supplies, a newspaper clipping of the Virginia Tech shooting, a DVD titled *Tactical Readiness: Shooting in Realistic Environments*, a loaded handgun in a bedside table drawer, a gun holster inside a laundry bin.

Following Ms. Fox's questions, Detective Kay told us about finding three notebooks that contained drawings, along with cutout drawings that had been wedged between pages of the notebooks. A drawing of an "image of the iron cross caught my eye," Detective Kay said, "but then, I saw that it was inscribed with the phrase White Pride World Wide."

Detective Kay explained that after seeing the drawing, he began to look differently at other materials his officers had found in the McInerney home, especially in the bedroom Brandon shared with his father. Detective Kay said, directly to the jury, "We found a lot of stuff, we found a lot of stuff that was Nazi related, or, I thought, maybe white supremacy related."

What his officers found included German maps, T-shirts (one with a sparrow on it and the word *Aufweiten,* a word he did not recognize, which led him to look on the Anti-Defamation League Web site, where he learned that it is a word and symbol employed by white supremacists), and computer printouts of several of Hitler's speeches. The officers also found a copy of *The 12th SS: The History of the Hitler Youth Panzer Division*, volume 2. This book, Detective Kay reported, was a companion to volume 1, found in Brandon's backpack at the murder scene.

"I quickly understood that I was beyond my depth," Detective Kay told Ms. Fox. On the afternoon of the shooting he called Detective

Dan Swanson from the Simi Valley Police Department, a local expert on matters related to white supremacy. By the evening of the murder, Detective Swanson had begun working on the case. In the course of the trial he would take the stand for six days, longer than any other witness.

But on the first day of the trial, Ms. Fox was setting the scene of the murder, noting the facts. Matters of motive, which would come to dominate, were not under question yet. Instead, along with the detectives, we heard from the coroner, Dr. Ronald O'Halloran, a pathologist who spoke with measured clinical objectivity about the cause and course of death: "gunshot wounds to the head." One shot was "dead center," he told us. We studied his close-up photo of the wounds: two small patches of flesh where hair had been shaved from the back of Larry's head. We lingered over the bullet holes: so precise, so small.

We had seen a picture of murder. But it was not until the second day, until Mariah's traumatic response, still caught in the murder, that the madness of murder cracked into the room.

On the second day, when it came time for the defense to cross-examine Mariah, Scott Wippert, the lead defense counsel, rose from his seat and said, "Mariah, I'm sorry that you had to come here and go through this, and I have no questions for you. Thank you very much."

Uncertain about what she was to do, Mariah looked first at Mr. Wippert and then toward the judge, who told her that she was free to go. The bailiff approached. Mariah bowed her head and walked from the room.

THE TRUTH HAD ALREADY HAPPENED. Larry was dead. Brandon had killed him. Those undisputed facts were parsed, and that story was told in the first four days of the trial.

Why Brandon killed Larry was the unsettled question: What was his motive? What drove him to shoot a fellow student in front of his homeroom teacher and twenty-six of his peers?

In response to the central matter of motive, Prosecutor Fox and

Defense Attorney Wippert set about to build their cases. They worked to tell the story they wanted the jury to see. They presented evidence, they called upon experts, they questioned witnesses, coaxing and confronting.

Ninety-eight witnesses were called to the stand, almost all to talk about motive. Some dressed as if for church and some with no nod to the courtroom's solemnity. Susan Crowley, Larry's seventh-grade special resources teacher, lifted the shoulders of her navy serge dress, too hot for the day, with her fingertips, and said, "This is my weddings and funerals dress." Tattooed straight-razor blades served as muttonchops on the inked face of Kyle Benavidez, who came to speak as a character witness for Brandon. Abiam Martinez, an eyewitness to the murder, was pressed into black pants and buttoned up in a starched long-sleeve shirt, his hair soberly combed into place. Samantha Criner, Brandon's girlfriend, tucked her mirrored sunglasses into the V of her tangerine T-shirt, after the bailiff had handed her a tissue for her gum.

As witnesses took the stand, they found it hard to follow customary courtroom restraint. Lawyers asked questions, and the witnesses were instructed to give brief answers, preferably "yes" or "no." But simple agreement or assent would not do. Some choked with fear. Some were hostile. Some were solemn. Some were brokenhearted. Their emotions were as much the story as the facts that were being argued.

Not only did witnesses contest the custom of attorney/witness exchange; they regularly talked over the attorneys, resisting the attorneys' reasoning or their tactics. The court reporter eventually fashioned a small sign and put it on the rail of the witness stand, to coach people: PLEASE LET THE ATTORNEY COMPLETE THE QUESTION BEFORE STARTING YOUR ANSWER. THANK YOU. THE COURT REPORTER.

Questions of trust reside at the heart of any trial. But they come to life with particular relevance when the matter before the court is motive. Motive is a story of emotion: not only is the story told with emotion; it is also deliberated with emotion. Jurors and we observers were left to determine whose story, whose facts, were to be believed. The jurors were explicitly instructed to do just that. Jurors and observers alike either joined a witness in belief or empathy, or discredited a witness as unbelievable and unsympathetic.

In the courtroom we lived often, as we did with Mariah, in a single, brief interlude, in a space flooded by feelings, as they saturated memory. The way Mariah described the gun as a "little hand" stayed with me, because the gun was personified, felt, and—in the way of living, especially in the wake of trauma—distorted. In Courtroom F51, while the story was under way, the certainty of knowing was in constant doubt.

Memory is cast by allegiance and recast by contradictory feelings and experiences. Memories and beliefs also follow on social customs or norms; our beliefs build and solidify our memories. None of us can claim a pristine memory-house.

Telling the story of a murder is not simply a recitation of facts or a pragmatic account of the living and the dead. The trauma of murder speaks beyond what we can see and understand. And it was this incomprehension—this departure from the story—that often allowed witnessing to begin.

ON FEBRUARY 23, 2008, I read a short account of Larry's memorial service in the *New York Times*. I was living then, as I do now, in New York City, where I am a clinical psychologist in private practice and an assistant professor of psychology at the New York University Postdoctoral Program in Psychoanalysis and Psychotherapy. In the winter of 2008, I was doing the final edits on a book about boys and boyhood, a subject I have studied for over twenty-five years.

I have a particular interest in examining the ways in which boys are various. No two boys are the same. No one boy is invariable. I have worked with and written about gender-expansive boys, as well as aggressive and hypermasculine boys, who are often called "normal." The story about the killing of a boy who had begun to identify as a girl, by a boy who was referenced in the early reporting as a "regular kid," naturally caught my attention.

On February 29, 2008, Ellen DeGeneres opened her daytime

television talk show by making a "personal statement." I did not see the original broadcast, but by the following day the clip was rebroadcast on a variety of social media outlets. Backed by a projected photograph of Larry holding a caterpillar in the palm of his hand, Ms. DeGeneres reported the plain fact of the shooting. Then she held that "Larry was killed because he was gay" and detailed what had, in short order, become the accepted motive-story: "Days before he was murdered, Larry asked his killer to be his Valentine."

This declaration of romance and gay identity, according to Ms. DeGeneres, led to Larry's death. She choked with emotion as she said, "Somewhere along the line, the killer, Brandon, got the message that it's so threatening and so awful and so horrific that Larry would want to be his Valentine that killing Larry seemed to be the right thing to do. And when the message out there is that it is so horrible to be gay, that to be gay you can be killed for it, we need to change the message."

Ms. DeGeneres did not mention anything about Larry's gender identity, a point that was subtly emphasized by Rebecca Cathcart, who wrote the *New York Times* account of Larry's memorial. Ms. Cathcart quoted various sources on the subject of gay teens, but she turned most of her attention to Larry's gender expression.

Ms. Cathcart did not specifically delineate the difference between sexual identity and gender identity. She did not spell out the difference between our sexual wishes—the objects of our desire and how we long for them (typically tagged as straight or gay, more rarely bisexual or polyamorous)—and our fantasies and convictions about our gender, or how our bodies come to matter (masculine, feminine, transgender, more rarely nonbinary). Nor did Ms. Cathcart explain that gender identity and sexual identity are generally conflated by social convention. For example, a masculine boy is presumed to be straight, while a feminine boy is presumed to be gay. It does not always work that way.

Ms. Cathcart did introduce the idea of Larry as a gender-expansive boy. She emphasized how Larry had begun to question gender as he began wearing makeup and feminine accessories: "Lawrence had started wearing mascara, lipstick, and jewelry to school, prompting a group of male students to bully him."

As I followed the early reporting of the case, I wondered about the "gender trouble" Larry had set into play (to borrow the philosopher and gender theorist Judith Butler's felicitous phrase). How was he to be named? Gay? Transgender? What category applied? What consequences would this category crisis have on how the story would be told? How would Larry's mixed racial identity, African American and Caucasian (he self-identified as "black"), be considered, as it intertwined with his gender? And what account would be offered, if any, of Brandon's gender? Would his "regular kid" boyhood go unquestioned or unexamined, as is often the case? Similarly, would his race be considered, or his whiteness be seen as a matter of race at all?

Soon I found myself imagining my way into Larry's and Brandon's lives. One way to think about what a psychologist does is to consider how psychologists imagine their ways into the minds of others. A strange business, to be sure, as the nineteenth-century English romantic poet John Keats took note. In the published edition of Keat's marginalia on his copy of Milton's *Paradise Lost*, Keats wrote, "One of the most mysterious of semi-speculations is, one would suppose, that of one Mind's imagining into another." I like the way the transitive action of "into" captures the reach and force of finding another. On another page, Keats wrote simply, "we imagine after it." We search. We look in multiple places.

Sitting in the courtroom, I sought to imagine my way not only into Larry's and Brandon's lives but also into the emotions of the storytellers, the witnesses. And tried to learn from what I thought and felt, in my position of imagining. Psychologists ponder and sift. We get lost. I followed my own mind as it got lost. The minds of others and the stories they tell are often best understood if we slip beneath the surface and follow their misstatements and contradictions. If we are willing to follow the other, even making wrong turns, we may discover that we are lost, but, left to find our way back, we may learn along the way.

The national press coverage of the shooting, thin to begin with, quickly died down. I began to follow the story in the *Ventura County Star*. I started collecting data in a Bankers Box on the floor next to my desk. I taped pictures of both boys, school portraits taken a year before the murder, on the side of the box. Even as other boxes have gathered, those black-and-white images, which I cut out of the *Ventura County Star*, have remained on the original box and have accompanied me throughout this project.

Larry looks over his right shoulder. His dark eyes peer out from under a shelf of black hair. He looks hesitant and smiles gently. Brandon smiles brightly, youthfully. His hair is buzzed. He looks as if he is in on the joke of school portraits.

The pretrial process dragged on and on, over three years in total, and the news cycle rolled on; little about the story found its way into the national media. Still, in the spring and summer after Larry's death in February 2008, there were, in addition to Ellen DeGeneres's widely viewed plea, two national magazine cover stories about the crime that began to frame the story.

The *Advocate*, a national gay and lesbian newsmagazine, ran a cover story in April 2008, and *Newsweek* ran a cover story in July 2008. Both focused on how young people are coming out as gay and transgender at younger ages, and how these kids are growing up caught between "messages of tolerance," on one hand, and often stringent and violent social norms, on the other.

It is a struggle to keep up with gender these days and to follow the gender-expansive ways in which many people are living. Facebook now offers more than fifty custom gender options, from cisgender (a person's experiences of their gender lines up with the sex they were assigned at birth), to gender fluid (a person may at any time identify as masculine, feminine, or nonbinary, or some combination of identities), to transgender (a person who does not identify with their natal body, but rather with the body and mind of the other sex), to gender queer (a person who does not subscribe to conventional gender distinctions and does not identify with either femininity or masculinity).

Grappling with gender is something of an ongoing debate that circulates among biology, ideology, and psychology. Gender-expansive bodies come to matter through challenges to social customs: wearing a dress instead of trousers. They also come alive with the help of biological interventions: hormone blockers, cross-hormone therapies, and sexual reassignment surgeries. A gender-y kid might play softball and knit in the dugout while the other team is up to bat. A gender-y kid might shave her head and wear her father's old jeans. A gender-y kid might begin hormone blockers and change his name.

Despite modernity's expansion, social convention routinely rounds up and quashes the complexity and variety that is gender. One is a boy or one is a girl, period. Boys will be boys, the saying goes, and we don't look very closely at their behaviors. Indeed, we often idealize boyishness. "Normal" boys are prized even though, sometimes, their boyishness (their aggression, their stoicism) can contain other meanings that go unnoticed until they are in trouble.

Race, too, as it shapes boys' lives, has often escaped our attention, and at a deadly cost. How was race going to show up in this story, especially given the vulnerability faced by black and brown boys on a daily basis? Or the racial hatred directed at transpeople of color, particularly transwomen and -girls?

We adults are behind the world in which our children live. They are running ahead. And in failing to catch up, we neglect them. We fail kids daily by not taking a more active hand in examining their lives, including the fossilized norms that no longer account adequately for their lives. Perhaps, if there is anything good to be taken away from a tragedy, it is the way in which an act like murder shatters any reasonable expectation and warns us not to fall back on reductive moral relativism, lest the tragedy be left to replay again and again.

One way that tragedy lets us in, and teaches us, is through trauma. Such a proposition may seem paradoxical at first, because traumatized minds and communities shut down. Lines are drawn. A story is told, retold, and, so, remembered.

During the trial, every witness had a story, and after the trial, over coffee at their kitchen tables or a drink in a sports bar, or in their offices, each of them stuck to his or her story. The memory, the story, was stowed. As people spoke from the witness stand, or to local reporters or documentarians, or as they answered my questions in one-on-one interviews, or in casual conversations, their positions, their stories, sometimes gained details, but rarely did they change.

Not always, though. Sometimes the stories veered, and at those moments—there were many—I experienced, as I did early on, with Mariah, the way in which trauma resurfaced. In those moments, in those flashes, the stories unformulated, and truth lay fractured. In these instances, terror became my teacher. As it did in moments (and, again, there were many) when emotion spoke outside of words, and emotions of the storytellers drew me into looking anew at what had happened.

In such moments, we make choices. Take Mr. Wippert and Mariah: the gentleman offering his sympathy to a traumatized girl. Did I think his gesture was sincere? I did. Did I think that it was also a masterful turning away from the gravity of murder? I did. In declining to cross-examine Mariah, Mr. Wippert succeeded in shaming the assistant district attorney, Ms. Fox, for questioning an eyewitness, which is the brick and mortar of prosecutorial labor. And, more important, Mr. Wippert succeeded in turning us away from the dead boy Mariah could not see, and onto the boy who was alive, the boy at whom she could not look.

Therein began Mr. Wippert's strategy to shift what we saw, apprehended, and recognized. He understood that what was going to matter was whose life was going to matter. Who would get recognized? Whose story was going to get told?

2

Thrown Through the Cracks

When I was not at the courthouse, I lived at the Extended Stay America, a hotel that offered one-room efficiency suites, in Chatsworth, California. Not only was my room a temporary guest quarter; it was materially temporary as well. The molded plastic bathroom door was misaligned with the lock-latch and would not close. One of the two stovetop burners had given up. The carpeting turned away from the corners of the room. I attempted to adjust a lamp that was affixed to a wall, only to have it give way, fall out of the wall and into my hand. In slow motion, chalky plaster dust sifted to the floor.

Crawford Mortuary stood on the adjacent corner, outside the hotel's front door, along with a string of putty-colored industrial buildings, car repair shops, and a school for the blind. To the left was Tampa Avenue, lined with big-box stores and chain restaurants. Like my room, all of these structures seemed to have been built with indifference to longevity.

The haste of prefab was showing. Dust was everywhere. The baked exteriors of the surrounding buildings buckled and split. Seams were separating. Corners were dinged and crumbling. Siding peeled.

On the morning of July 5, 2011, the first day of the trial and my second at the Extended Stay, I rose early, showered, made breakfast, burned the eggs, and broke the handle of a knife as I tried to cut an orange. I gathered my things and headed out the door to the parking lot, where a large man sat atop an ice cooler, reading a newspaper. It was seven thirty, and already he was attempting to cool himself with a wet towel around his neck. The heat, like the dust, would become a constant. Nearly every day, the temperature climbed into the nineties. It never rained.

The courthouse was a short drive from the hotel. I steered my rented compact from one four-lane road to the next. The Superior Court of the State of California, Los Angeles County, located in Chatsworth, was nestled in a cul-de-sac at the end of a small business park. The trial was being held in Los Angeles County instead of Ventura County, where the murder had taken place, because of concerns about finding a non-biased jury. The courthouse, a neo-Federalist building, looked more like a small corporate headquarters or a shopping mall than a civil court.

I entered through the main doors, which led to a two-story portico, and a central bay filled with security scanning equipment. I asked the security guard for directions and found my way to Courtroom F51 on the second floor. I took my seat in the second row of the visitors' gallery, and there I would sit for the next forty-three working days.

THERE WAS NO GAVEL. THERE was no "All rise!" The clerk of the court announced the case and introduced the judge, the Honorable Charles W. Campbell.

The judge called the jury in. Briefly, he spoke with them about the daily schedule, a few took notes, one looked out upon the gallery, while another fumbled with her large pink purse.

With that, the prosecution began.

As Deputy District Attorney Fox gathered her papers to deliver her opening statement, James Bing, Brandon's older half brother (Brandon and James share the same mother), rose from the visitors' gallery and shouted toward the jury, "My brother's fate is in your hands!" Cinematic

James was thrown out of court, and would not return until twenty-nine days later.

The room resettled. Ms. Fox led with a large-scale projected color photograph of the victim, saying, "This was Lawrence Fobes King. He was fifteen years old at the time of his death. He was five feet four inches tall and 111 pounds. What the Defendant did was take a handgun, and shoot him."

Larry looked out at us. His tentative beauty held our gaze. Mixed-race—Caucasian and African American—he glowed olive; Cézanne could have captured his color. Larry's blue-black hair was combed forward with care. He wore a red sweater. He smiled. A red glass sat on a table behind him. It looked as if he might have been at a party.

Our glimpse of Larry was brief. Ms. Fox turned off the projected photo as she turned to the defendant and explained that Brandon McInerney stood accused of the cold-blooded killing of one human being by another, without justification or excuse. She charged that Brandon had planned the murder and had skillfully carried it out, including concealing his purpose by secreting a handgun into school and waiting until he had the opportunity to accomplish the shooting with proper range and aim.

She said Brandon acted with "expressed malice aforethought," and that he had spoken openly of his hatred for Larry, as well as of his intent to kill him. She held that Brandon acted with premeditation, deliberation, will, and planning—the hallmarks of first-degree murder. Brandon was also charged with a hate crime. Ms. Fox specified, "The People must prove that the Defendant committed the crime in whole or in part because of the alleged victim's actual or perceived gender or sexual orientation."

Ms. Fox did not include race as a factor in the hate-crime charge. The fact that Larry was brown and Brandon was white, which often factors into hate-crime charges, was absent from the charges brought against Brandon. In a pretrial hearing, Judge Campbell had ruled there was insufficient evidence that the crime was committed because of Larry's race.

Larry's gender identity, his femininity, along with his perceived sexual identity, were deemed by the court to be the focuses of Brandon's alleged hate. Ms. Fox emphasized that the matter before the court was the perception of Larry's gender, the perception of a boy who had begun to identify as a girl, a boy Ms. Fox described as "shy and very effeminate," and "extremely effeminate, like a girl."

Larry had been identified as feminine throughout his short life, although it was only in the last few weeks of his life that he had begun to speak openly of his feminine identity. Ms. Fox explained, "As opposed to the shy, very quiet, closed-up kid, he started becoming a little more out—a little more open, a little more flamboyant."

He started practicing femininity. He got a pair of brown suede high-heeled boots and pounded out a walk. He created a look using makeup, nail polish, and hair spray. His special skill with hair spray led many people to comment on the magnificence of the swoop he could create. He also began to embellish his school uniform with feminine accessories—a scarf, some jewelry. All in all, it seems he may have worn the high-heeled boots, the scarf, and the jewelry on as few as nine days or for only parts of those days.

In that same short period of time, Larry asked a couple of kids and a teacher to call him by a new name, Leticia. This request was met with taunting (his classmates treated his bid as a joke) or resistance (Dawn Boldrin, his homeroom teacher, told him she would not call him Leticia until he legally changed his name). Leticia's efforts seem to have enjoyed more life and liberty at Casa Pacifica, the residential center where Larry had been living since late November of 2007, seventy-six days prior to his death. Found in his backpack on the day of his murder was a small gift box that held a pair of earrings and a note that said, "To Leticia, From All of Us."

But in school, at E. O. Green, "Leticia" was denied. Quoting one of his teachers, Ms. Fox suggested that "flamer" was the name more readily applied to Larry. And he had burned with passion for his femininity in the last month of his life. Everyone agreed that he was more intent on finding femininity than taking up his schoolwork. Larry had always struggled to learn. His mind wandered, his attention fled. His motives led him elsewhere. In the last month of his life, his grade-point average had fallen from failing to failing worse.

But the rush of living femininity brought Larry toward a different "attitude" and "confidence." Ms. Fox said, "He started reacting to the taunting and to the teasing and to the pushing and the shoving and the taking of the backpack. He started pushing back."

Larry began to forcefully lay claim to a feminine identity. The girl had some fight.

As Larry "started changing," tensions began to erupt at E. O. Green. Teachers went to the administration at the school, maintaining that Larry was not following the rules. Was there a place in this junior high for a boy who maintained that he was a girl? Had there been appropriate guidance? Wasn't the answer to the school community's discomfort to be found in the dress code? Ms. Fox emphasized that the teachers' questions about the dress code may have missed the point: it was the change in Larry's attitude that had really mattered. Larry was making a claim; he was accounting for himself in new ways, and he was pushing back when he did not get the response he wanted.

The anxiety and suppression regarding Larry's femininity at E. O. Green reemerged in the courtroom, where Leticia was rarely mentioned. Larry remained "Larry." He remained "he." Ms. Fox spoke of Larry asking to be called Leticia, but she did not call him by that name. Nor, in her opening statement, did she tell us that Leticia had begun to speak of herself as transgender.

It was difficult to know much about Leticia; she was so short-lived. What happened at E. O. Green happened quickly: a month or less, only a handful of days. Emphasizing this point, Ms. Fox kept punctuating her statements with the tag "very short period of time." The same could be said of Larry's time with us in court. Ms. Fox drew a broad outline of Larry. Then she turned to her case against Brandon.

Brandon lived with us day to day. He was physically present, and his identity became known to everyone in the courtroom through his gestures, posture, gait, facial expressions, and from the emotions of others that gathered around him.

He gave no account of himself. He did not take the stand. We heard Brandon speak only five times, always when answering a question posed by Judge Campbell. All of Brandon's utterances were one- or two-word assents: "Yes." "Yes, sir." "Yes, sir." "Yes." "Yes." His voice was surprisingly thin, the voice of someone who didn't much like talking.

Brandon was noticeably, consistently, still, with one ongoing exception: each and every time the door at the back of the courtroom clicked open, Brandon would turn and look over his left shoulder.

He remained motionless as Ms. Fox made her charge: "Ladies and gentleman, the evidence in this case will prove to you that this killing was an execution." He did not look at Ms. Fox as she straightened her arms out in front of her and put her hands together, as if aiming a gun. He remained still as she described the second shot, saying, "Larry King is completely and utterly incapacitated, and he slumps down in his chair and he's coming out of his chair as the Defendant is now standing and readying that gun to fire another round into his completely incapacitated victim."

Kendra McInerney, Brandon's mother, buried her face in her hands. Panic, anguish, and confusion overtook her. Kendra's suffering permeated the room. It filled in and around her silent son. Like Brandon, Kendra never took the stand. But her steadfast and often anguished presence, day in and day out, was arguably the strongest presentation of her son's case. It could be said that she made him.

What was felt in the courtroom was felt around Brandon. What was said was said about him. The avoidance that untold Larry was distinct from the abundance of feeling that told Brandon. Even Ms. Fox, the prosecutor, as befits her job—in theorizing about the hate that drove him to murder—turned her attention to Brandon.

Debating Brandon's hate would come to dominate the trial. Larry's position as the object of hate was essential to that story, and in that way he remained with us. Otherwise, Larry was gone. As Tolstoy instructs,

"Death is gone." In the courtroom, Larry's death became more than a material reality. His psychological residuum, his character, his way of being, were closeted, hushed. He was never psychologically met.

LARRY WAS BORN ON JANUARY 13, 1993, in Ventura County, California. His mother was fifteen and addicted to crack cocaine and alcohol. She turned tricks to support her habit and to provide what she could for Larry. She was seventeen when the state intervened and took custody of Larry and his newborn brother, Rocky.

When I inquired about Larry's early life, I was almost always told that his "records were sealed." When the state intervenes and removes a child from a parent, it "seals" the record of that adjudicated process. This kind of record-keeping is intended to protect the child. But I also took these "sealed" responses to my questions about Larry's early life to demonstrate how the adults in Larry's world were either ashamed of his past or willfully ignorant of what had taken place. In a way they were saying to me, "It is better not to know."

With time, though, people I spoke with—Larry's adoptive parents, his teachers, his school friends—began to tell me more and more about what they knew. Larry's early life came alive in these conversations or through nods and hints in response to my speculations. Larry's early life also leaked into court records, investigative records, teacher reports, and police reports. His past escaped less often in the courtroom itself and more often in the courthouse hallway.

Still, a past was conjured. A story was told, in ways not so different from the ways in which all life stories are recounted: facts (some true, some distorted) combine with memory (some melancholic, some self-serving) to collect, sort, assemble, and narrate.

Several people, including Dawn and Greg King, Larry's adoptive parents, told me that he and his younger brother, Rocky, were found abandoned at a busy intersection. Rocky was said to be listless, sitting in a stroller. Larry was described as screaming, holding the stroller's edge.

Surely Larry had screamed before. Surely there had been other times when his mother had not heard him, or so we are left to imagine. As we are left to imagine Larry in the arms of an electrified mother, convulsing and transmitting her euphoria, edginess, paranoia, and hostility into her child. We are left to imagine and consider that Larry's early world was one of madness. Trauma soldered his circuits.

Was there anyone to hold him together? Was there anyone to lend a hand as he tried to sit up, stand up, reach for a cup? His fledgling efforts to relate, communicate, ambulate were likely rarely met or inconsistently met at best. Similarly, did anyone help him as he sought to organize his perceptions, to learn what he was seeing, hearing, and feeling?

People came and went. They thrashed and moaned. We do not know who came and who went. We do not know exactly how they behaved. We do not precisely know their states of mind. But one can imagine a man, even a man in the crank of lust, lending his hand to a baby as he took his first steps, or a friend of Larry's mother fussing over a babbling toddler. Mindless neglect and willful cruelty, though, are more likely.

In the courtroom, Larry's biological mother was mentioned only once, as a "drug addict." Even when people would tell me things they knew about her, they would not name her. Every cop I spoke to knew Larry's mother. Still, they would not name her. Nor would the Kings.

But that did not stop all of them from telling stories. The Kings believed Larry's mother had run away from home and gotten involved in an East LA gang. The cops never mentioned anything about gangs. They tended to focus more on the times they arrested her for soliciting and/or drug possession. They laughed, recalling her as scrappy, small, fiery, and abundantly curvy. She put up a fight. She kicked out a hotel window with a high-heeled shoe and threatened a cop's car window with the same heel.

We know little to nothing about where Larry and his mother lived, or with whom. We know nothing about how Larry's mother may have loved him. We do not know how she may have tried to soothe him or when she gave up. We know that she died not long before Larry was killed. We know that HIV helped to kill her.

We know that the state intervened when Larry was two and a half years of age, because, at the very least, he was physically injured by other than accidental means. We know he was living without adequate food, clothing, shelter, or medical care. Larry was not rocked, soothed, or bathed. He was left wet, hungry, fevered, thirsty, vomiting, soiled, anxious, screaming. He was beaten and burned.

In my first conversation with Dawn King, Larry's adoptive mother, she described meeting Larry when he was two and a half. He was frantic, thrashing and screaming. She tried to hold him, but he would not calm down. Desperate, Dawn drew a bath, thinking perhaps that would help, and besides, "he was filthy." It was only as she set him in the tub that she understood it was not dirt: "Bruises! Burn marks! That baby was covered in bruises!" She attended as best she could to his tender skin and dressed him in clean clothes.

Larry remained in a state of panic. Dawn tried to feed him, thinking that perhaps he was crying because he was hungry. But he would not eat. It took her a few days to figure out that the only foods that he knew to eat were ketchup and Coke.

DURING THE SECOND WEEK OF the trial, I sat down with Greg and Dawn King, a white couple who had adopted brown Larry when Dawn was forty years old and Greg was thirty. We went to a local bagel shop, sat outside at a small café table, and chased the shade offered by an umbrella. We sat there for three hours, eating pizza bagels and drinking iced tea. They chain-smoked. The pace of their smoking matched the urgency of their desire that someone understand their effort to raise Larry. They had tried and tried. They were spent.

Recalling Larry's first years with them, Dawn sighed and said, "It seemed I was always driving him somewhere for some therapy or doctor or something. God only knows how many hours I spent at Easter Seals." Those early efforts led to yet more remediation and repair. But Larry did not mend easily, if at all. Language was especially slow to develop, and his speech was impossible to understand. The Kings called it "Larry Chinese."

Larry was foreign. He was not who and what the Kings had expected. Not only were his troubles hard to understand and address, but his erratic behavior seemed never to subside. Unlike Rocky, who was more compliant, Larry was unreachable: "You couldn't get through to him," Greg maintained.

Hard to contact, Larry was even harder to explain. He collected diagnoses: pervasive developmental delay, bipolar, depression, obsessive compulsive disorder, attention deficit disorder, gender identity disorder, attachment disorder. When I suggested to Dawn that some kids fall between the diagnostic cracks, she snapped, "Hell, Larry was thrown through the cracks!"

Pills, pastel and small, were prescribed: stimulants, tranquilizers, mood stabilizers, antipsychotics, antidepressants, hypnotics, neuroleptics (Ritalin, Gabapentin, Prozac, Concerta, Lithium, Abilify, Dexedrine, Elavil, Klonopin, Lexapro, Depakote, Synthroid, DDAVP, Focalin, Geodon, Seroquel). The pills pushed Larry one way and then another. They sped him up, then they slowed him down. They helped him find focus; they made him lose focus.

"Oh lord," Dawn declared, "what didn't they give him? If you ask me, they made things worse." Larry could not turn around without being prescribed a new pill, a new dose, a new time of day to take it.

Larry was ushered into the offices of seven therapists in ten years. He went from one banged-up clinic office to the next. Someone, somewhere in that revolving door, may have offered Larry some recognition, some help, some opening to express himself and find a way out of his anxiety and turmoil. But that is not how the Kings recalled his care, nor does the evidence of his life suggest that he received much, if any, truly therapeutic attention.

Greg and Dawn were bitter with the "mental health industry," especially "liberal social workers who wanted to paint [Larry] with rose-colored glasses," as Greg put it. The Kings lost what goodwill they had. They lost their child as well.

Greg would say to Larry, "Look at me in the eye; this way of behaving is not acceptable." Then, in keeping with the spirit of nineteenth-century child-rearing practices, he would have Larry repeatedly write out sentences repenting his bad behaviors. Larry would be assigned chores as penance.

But Larry was no Jane Eyre. He was not in possession of her intelligence or moral masochism. Larry ran more toward John Waters's Dawn Davenport, who, in the film *Female Trouble*, pushed over the Christmas tree when she did not get the cha-cha heels she wanted. Like Waters's heroine, Larry became a petty criminal, albeit one with limited attention and scope. He shoplifted candy. He stole some of his mother's costume jewelry. He gave away some of his loot. (He gave to one of his teachers a plastic sandwich bag full of rhinestone rings and silver bracelets.) He hid some in his room.

At the suggestion of a police officer friend, the Kings took one object from Larry's room for every new item they found there. Eventually they removed the mattress. With the aid of the same police officer, they had Larry arrested when he used a key to vandalize a tractor at a public baseball field, where he and his family spent a lot of time watching Rocky, a gifted athlete, play ball.

The cops showed up at the ball field and staged a mock arrest. They cuffed Larry and shoved him into the back of their squad car. They took him to the station, put him in a cell, and talked tough.

Larry was contrite enough. But it was home he wanted out of, as much as he wanted out of jail. Greg told me this story near the end of our outdoor lunch. The sun was in our eyes. He gathered up his cigarettes and keys, and said, as if in summation: "Larry could not learn his lesson. It made no difference."

ONE OF THE FIRST THINGS Sharon Townsend, Larry's grandmother, said to me was "Larry was always femme." The Kings were less direct. By the time I sat down with them, they had faced a lot criticism, often public, about their parenting of Larry and the ways in which they had handled his gender identity and sexuality.

When I first spoke with Greg and Dawn, I explained that I had written about gender variant boys, which was part of my interest in this story. I also told them I was gay. Dawn arched an eyebrow and replied, "Yeah, I seen your pencil case!" (looking at the small orange case next to my notebook). We both laughed. She was fast and she was funny, and, in the thick of this sad story, I was often grateful for her camp and sass.

A few weeks later, Dawn stood in front of me in line for the metal detector. She looked down at the floor and archly asked me, "Lose a nail?"

There on the floor was a fake French-tipped fingernail.

Again, we both laughed. I took these moments to be playful. They did not sting, nor did I think they were meant to. But I also wondered if she may have met her feminine son with similar playful irony, and when or if such play flipped, as it can, into shame and disdain.

Greg offered that Larry had told him he was bisexual. Greg assured Larry that there was "nothing wrong with being bisexual." Eager for me to understand that he was "not a homophobic person," Greg told me he "had no problem," he "knew gay people." He told Larry, "You're young, let's see how it goes." Greg did not like the way in which Larry had been taken up "as a cause," including the ways "gay activists took Larry up without really knowing who he was." Greg said, "He was a mixed-up young kid. He did not know himself."

Greg did, though, readily recognize that Larry was a feminine kid. Larry did not share Greg's interest in sports; Rocky did. Larry seemed more interested in costumes and had a particular fondness for a pair of powder blue athletic shorts. "They must have been meant for a girl," Greg told me, laughing. Still, Greg took Larry along to various sporting events, especially to local baseball games, as if some gendered lesson might be found there. Pictures of Larry holding a baseball mitt or a hockey stick look awkwardly staged.

Dawn was the one who named Larry's interests: craft projects, the family dog, jewelry, rock collections, and his abiding fascination with bugs. She shared many of these interests and would join Larry or teach him. She taught him to crochet.

Larry crocheted a toy for Susan Crowley's cat. "He was really good at that sort of thing," Ms. Crowley remarked. She confessed that she had "lied" to him about the toy, telling him that the cat liked it, when, in fact, the cat never went near it. "He was such a sweet soul, I couldn't tell him something like that. Besides, he really did have a good eye. He could see beauty. He would notice things I put up on the board, pictures of African art, or he would notice a lovely fabric."

Larry and Dawn made scarves for soldiers serving in Iraq. They would send off the scarves, along with toiletries Larry got local hotels to donate, and out-of-season holiday candy from local grocery stores. (Imagine a marine opening a box and finding an itchy scarf, a travel-size bottle of scented hair conditioner, and Valentine chocolates in Fallujah in July.)

There was play and identification between Larry and Dawn. One might say they were girls together: "He was a momma's boy for sure, always next to me." Along with Larry, Maeve Fox, and Dawn Boldrin, Dawn King was one of the femmes in this story. She smoked Eve Amethyst cigarettes, tapping the ash with a long, manicured fingernail. Her face was carefully applied. One imagined it took her some time to get ready. She preferred flowing tops, dolman sleeves, a hint of rhinestone.

Dawn's way of being, even her way of being a body, was theatrical. Her colored auburn hair fell around her face in ringlets, like an antebellum doll. She played "the dying girl." Mortality was visibly sinking her, weighing her down (diabetes, chronic obstructive pulmonary disease, obesity, and high blood pressure). Throughout the trial, she wore a medical boot on her right foot to protect an open wound that was failing to heal: "They tell me I might lose it, and all this is not helping!"

Dawn played "the frightened girl" when Larry would bring her a bug. He was daring and undaunted. She was phobic and hysterical: "Lord, he would come at me with them things!" she squealed.

"He always told me that he was going to grow up to become an ickyologist," Dawn proudly offered. Larry gathered the bugs in old pill jars Dawn would give him. She bought him foam-core and art supplies so he could mount his specimens. He managed to pin a couple of butterflies, but as I listened to Dawn describe Larry's bug projects, I began to think that it wasn't the collection of bugs that held Larry's interest. It was not bugs' preservation that appealed to him; it was their easy domesticity. You can catch them. They die. You can easily get more. It is hard to figure out how to keep them alive. They seem to need things you don't have.

With the aid of a kit that Dawn got for him, Larry collected black caterpillars from the passion fruit trees in the Kings' yard. He nursed them. He watched as they found a place to anchor, a place to transform into chrysalises. He witnessed their unfolding births. He watched as they paused, resting on the shells of the now-broken chrysalises.

The morning after my initial conversation with the Kings, Dawn greeted me with a hug and said, "Congratulations!" I was confused. She explained, "New York." I remained confused. She said, "Gay marriage!" (which had passed the New York legislature the day before). I said, "Oh."

"It is as it should be," she said. "It is only fair."

I began to understand that in this moment, as in many to follow, she was looking to resurrect Larry, in me. She looked not only to refind Larry but to project me as his future, his better future, the sort of future to which congratulations apply.

With her embrace came her well-guarded guilt and grief. It moved through her talk of fairness, but it also moved with her eyes. She refound Larry; she lost him. I was struck, just then, by how directly she looked at me. Dawn generally looked at me, and others, with her head canted down. It was the same gaze we saw from Larry when Ms. Fox projected his picture on the opening day of the trial. But in that moment, Dawn looked at me directly, and her gaze distinguished her mood.

It was only later that I grasped that her congratulations were also a bid for forgiveness. She missed her child. Later, she would tell me that she continued to speak to him, mostly outdoors.

———

LARRY GAVE UP WHAT HE knew to be home. He wanted out of the Kings' house. He spoke out and claimed abuse. Larry told Joy Epstein, an assistant principal at E. O. Green, and several of his teachers that Greg drank, and when he drank he got mean, at times pushing Larry to the ground. When asked, Greg vigorously denied ever hitting Larry, and pointed out that the allegations of abuse were never substantiated.

Tracy Carroll, a case manager from Casa Pacifica, a residence for neglected and abused kids, and Larry's home from November 28, 2007, until the day of his death, offered the following explanation to Marta Cunningham in her documentary film *Valentine Road*: "The county had been working to get him out. There were like twenty-two complaints about abuse and all of them went unfounded. Probation took him out of the home for some bogus vandalism and theft. It was stealing food from their refrigerator. They detained him at the juvenile justice center for one night before they went before the judge and the judge placed him with us." Ms. Carroll also suggested that county mental health workers had long been aware of "the family's issues" with Larry's gender variance.

As Greg and Dawn told this part of the story, it was Larry's nocturnal life that drove him from their home. It was not that Larry had suffered abuse, it was not that he was identifying as transgender; rather, he posed a threat. According to the Kings, Larry got up in the night and wandered the house, in search of food. He was said to have hoarded: chocolate under his bed, peanut butter in the bed. He began to use the stove at night. Sometimes he would leave a burner on. Once he put popcorn in the toaster.

They locked the door to his room, sometimes locking in the cat as well. Larry would light candles to cover the smell of the edgy, spraying cat. Then he would fall asleep.

"We would have fought tooth and nail to keep him home. But we began to fear that he was going to start a fire," Greg swore.

Dawn, speaking in the present tense, interjected, "He is going to burn down our house! He is going to kill us all!" She turned away, looked down, shook her head, and said, "That child never slept right, right from the start, never, never."

Unlike almost everyone else (teachers, social workers, Larry's friends), the Kings did not place Larry's gender transformation at the center of their story. They did not believe that he was transgender. They were vocal and adamant about not wanting him to cross-dress or speak of himself as transgender.

Greg exclaimed disparagingly, "He's calling Dawn from that place [Casa Pacifica], telling her that he's going to get a sex change, and that the state is going to pay for it!" Greg never visited "that place." For two months he did not go see his son, who was then referring to herself as Leticia.

Dawn did visit on a regular basis. But she "had no idea what them people up in there were thinking." One day she went to visit, and Larry, she told me, "came into the visiting room high, you know, manic, and flounced around in full-on regalia, flying around like a party doll!" She told him that at the very least he should match his eye shadow with his skin tone.

It struck me that Dawn was not unaware of Larry's budding desire for other boys, either as a gay boy or as a transgender girl. But she had trouble living with what she knew. Particularly how Larry's gender and sexuality related to the difficulty Larry had with life in general: "This was young, he was young, younger for fifteen, you know. And mixed up, you know. He wasn't right."

Neither Dawn nor Greg considered the possibility that Larry's gender identity might have led to some of his distress or the confrontations in which they found themselves. They dismissed the fact that Larry had been repeatedly diagnosed with gender identity disorder (now called gender incongruence or gender dysphoria). They named no moments of gender confrontation. Instead, they saw it the other way around: Larry's distressed emotional life was the source of his feminine search. By Greg's estimation, Larry's transfemininity was a way to "get girls, bad girls, to be his friends."

The Kings were unwilling to recognize that their beliefs were contradicted by their own ways of describing Larry as feminine. They were also unwilling to support anyone who related to Larry's wish to transition. And they certainly did not support his cross-gender accessorizing at school. Dawn wrote a note and went to the school to complain. She wanted it stopped, she did not believe in it, she worried that Larry would get hurt. "I knew it was going to come to no good. I knew it," she told me.

Greg and Dawn King were the targets of frequent and persistent gossip. People consistently asked me to go off the record when they expressed their uneasy feelings about the Kings. Mostly, people thought the Kings were abusive and greedy. Their motivation for taking in foster children was questioned by teachers and neighbors. Prior to the criminal case, the Kings had waged a civil suit against E. O. Green for negligence. They settled for $273,000. When I confronted them with the idea that they were seen as greedy, the Kings were incredulous. "Rumors, all rumors," Greg pushed back, declaring that the money they got from the civil suit was "put away for Rocky's education." Dawn spat, "Ain't nobody making money as a foster mom. Hell, who pays mothers, period?"

Still, the Kings spoke a language of exchange. "They didn't give us jack!," Dawn cracked, as she spoke about the lack of support that they had gotten as they tried to raise Larry. With derision, Greg spoke out against "the child abuse industry," and the ways in which he felt blamed by "experts" who were making money and not helping him.

Money interested the Kings: who had it; who didn't; who came by it dishonestly; who came by it through hard work. They were proud of their own goods and acquisitions. Sure, they wanted more. But they were hardly alone in such wanting.

Charles Dickens might have named them Mr. and Mrs. Pocket as he sought to capture the way in which money and exchange were the Kings's trade. Dickens, though, would also have captured how the Kings loved Larry and how hard they tried, limited and rough though they may have been, to make a family, to take care of Larry and to provide for him.

There would have been scenes of Christmas morning, as, in fact, King family photos attest. Larry would be smiling and toothless. He would be opening Christmas presents. They would be wrapped. Somebody had thought enough to be Santa, and had taken pleasure in the act of giving. There would be a dog wearing a Santa hat. There would be snowman paper plates, and mechanical carolers turning slowly in red velvet capes.

The Christmas decorations would still be up in February, because Larry would beg Dawn to not take them down. We would see him singing Christmas carols well beyond the date they expired. Dawn would sometimes sing along.

Still, the Pockets would bolt the front door, and clutch their purse as if to ward off accusations that their relationship with Larry brought him toward death. As if money were the sign that they were not guilty; they had done no wrong; they were owed.

Guilt was not theirs; if it came at them, it came from outside of them. They did not feel called to repent or repair. They were angry, unforgiving, and aggrieved—though not grieving. Or so it seemed.

But greed that seeks to undo guilt, oddly, leaves one if not empty-handed, at least empty. For without guilt there is no anguish, there is no internal conflict from which a resolution might come. There is no relation, because identifications are foreclosed or refused. The Pockets would be left lost and alone, because minus identifications with those we have lost, we are, well, lost.

LARRY'S FEMININITY WAS BECOMING PALPABLE, a set of gestures, a walk. This gender evolution was not simply a matter of naming himself as a girl. Larry was moving into, and embodying, "girl." Every gesture raised new questions. Every move teetered on the gap that opened in being between: boy/girl, child/teenager, black/white, home/homeless, past/present. Every move teetered on abandonment, shame, public scorn, refusal, and outright cruelty.

At least Casa provided a mirror for Larry. There were people to talk to, people who wanted to listen. There were other gay and transgender kids. There was room for fantasy, without so much anxiety about where it would lead. There was room to try on the name Leticia.

Larry was faced with a steep learning curve, and he stumbled from girlish boy to girlish girl. She ran with a host of shifting traits. The posture, carriage, the shoes were new. She stumbled because it got wiggy and giddy. She ran because girl was not going to emerge without some hustle and sting. She tripped, tangled in her unsettled and unsettling mind.

Leticia got to live only for a few weeks and in the face of tremendous anxiety about gender. In the courtroom, we never saw her at rest. She was alive only in theatrical scenes, in dramatic entrances, pageant walks, or capricious play. Even amid all that drama, she was barely recognized, and it is not at all clear how often she sought recognition. She was most always put on the defensive.

While the Leticia who made a few brief appearances through testimony in the courtroom was given to dramatic scenes, it seems that the Leticia who had briefly lived at Casa inhabited a greater range of relationships and situations. Reflecting on the changes Larry undertook in the short time he was at Casa, Larry's friend Averi Laskey said, "People like to say, 'Oh it got him more flamboyant. He started dressing up more.' No, he started dressing up more because he felt better about himself."

Richard Gonzales, one of Larry's housemates at Casa Pacifica, who spoke with Marta Cunningham in *Valentine Road*, recounted a moment of confusion as he watched Larry choose women's clothing from a bin of donated clothes. Mr. Gonzales, his neck decorated with tattooed praying hands, spoke gently, and perhaps with a hint of idealization, about the way in which "Larry showed his true self" at Casa. Mr. Gonzales held (echoing Averi) that "Larry felt comfortable where he was. So, he started coming out."

Still, even the Leticia of Casa did not wholly enter a new world. Mr. Gonzales referred to Larry as "Larry" and used the pronoun "he." At one point, he named Larry as a "brother," not a sister. In school, Larry was "Larry," and he was "he." In court, "Larry" and "he" were always spoken. No one—neither inside nor outside the court—ever spoke to me using the name Leticia or the pronoun "she."

Identities, names, and pronouns settle with time. A life unfolds, distinct from a category. In thinking about Larry's death, we are left to think that it is not simply that he will not grow up. Or that he will never arrive. Larry had only the idea of change.

The way Larry-Leticia was cut short has left us with a category problem, a naming and a pronoun problem. I mostly use "Larry" and "he" throughout this book. I cannot say that I think it is the best solution. I have chosen to primarily use "Larry" and "he" because that was the language of the courtroom, the language of the world in which I got to know Larry. "Larry" is also the language of the record, and if I change that record, we lose an important part of the story, that is, the way Leticia was not named, and her transgender identity was not granted.

History will remember Larry as Larry. Although, given what we know, we are left to ask if such remembering may not reenact the tragedy and denial of Leticia over and over again, like looping trauma. In light of that possibility, I believe I should recognize Leticia's account of herself and her plea or, one might say, her final wish. So, following Gayle Salamon, I use "Leticia" and "she" when I am writing from Leticia's perspective.

If she had lived, we would have followed her account, as one does with adolescents. We would have followed her stories and her displays of pleasure and pain, and we would have tried to understand how her history, trauma upon trauma, would undoubtedly have found its way into her gendered and sexual life. We would have followed her as she questioned, unsettled and sifted, as she practiced her signature. We would have followed her if she headed elsewhere. Leticia may have been a way station, and Larry may have grown up otherwise. That's the thing about growing up.

Leticia is perhaps best understood as a question, or the act of questioning. It seems we might do well to recognize that we do not know how to name this child. At the very least, it must be recognized that the norms about who gets to be recognized, who gets to be seen as wanted, desirable, and worthy, did not support Larry or Leticia in any life-sustaining way.

A Place They Probably
Don't Want to Go

Assistant District Attorney Maeve Fox held to Aristotle's cornerstone ethic: "The law is Reason free from Passion." Resolute in her pursuit of evidence, she marched facts before us: Here, look at this. Here, listen to what happened. Here, this is beyond a shadow of doubt. Here, here are the facts, and that, ladies and gentleman, is why we are here.

Ms. Fox's questions were precise and prepared, just like her notes, which were typed, and bound in large three-ring binders. She kept the binders in Bankers Boxes on a two-tray cart: nine boxes, five tottering on the top. Every day, in her customary three- or four-inch heels, she pushed the unwieldy cart into the courtroom. This detail might have escaped notice except for the fact that Ms. Fox, at barely one hundred pounds, weighed less than the cart.

No hint of petite fragility flitted about Ms. Fox's courtroom manner. She was direct and forceful, which some might have considered to be at odds with her appearance—those who see femininity as inconsistent with reason and assertion. She was a real blonde, with a good colorist. She was dating a hot cop. In an interview following the trial, she told me that she had "always liked clothes and dress-up," and that she "consciously decided to join Larry. Good grief, this poor kid was killed for playing with clothes and whatever he was trying to find there."

Scott Wippert, the lead defense counsel, wore off-the-rack suits, shiny from too many pressings. His appearance was as different from Mrs. Fox's tailored skirts as his emphasis on emotion was distinct from her devotion to reason. At the end of his emphatic, empathetic opening statement, he pointed to what would become a defining difference between his approach and that of the deputy district attorney: "Ladies and gentleman, this is a very emotional case. Yes!"

On the opening day of the trial, Mr. Wippert gave me his business card on which his name was framed by a pair of nineteenth-century dueling pistols. Chivalry and honor provoked and sustained the tradition of dueling, a kind of law when common law was not in place. Dueling continued as a mode of law in the American West well into the nineteenth century, even after it had fallen out of favor in eastern America in the eighteenth century. As Tom Doniphon, John Wayne's fast-draw cowboy, says to Ransom Stoddard, the citified senator played by Jimmy Stewart in the opening minutes of the film *The Man Who Shot Liberty Valance*, "I know those law books mean a lot to you, but not out here. Out here a man settles his own problems."

With his goatee and mustache, and his pale blue eyes, Mr. Wippert could have stepped out of a carriage and into a forested fog. One would have worried, though, about his aim. He was known to take to drink. His driver's license had been revoked. Robyn Bramson, his associate, drove him to court every morning.

Mr. Wippert was the Common Man lawyer who came to speak the law of the territory, not the law of the land. He read from scrawled and scrambled yellow legal pads. In the seeming haze of an overnighter, he fumbled his way to the jury box as if he were pulling Post-it notes out of his ears. Fidgeting, scratching, pacing, pausing, his drawn face agonized the room.

Mr. Wippert brought to his care for Brandon a kind of empathy born of having been a boy who knew trouble himself. He stood to represent Brandon, but he appealed to "the teenager in trouble." Mr. Wippert pointed to the fact that troubled teens these days often end up in adult courts. Brandon, who had been fourteen years old at the time of the murder, was seventeen years old at the time of the trial. In accord with California law (along with laws in thirty other states), the district attorney, Gregory Totten, had charged Brandon as an adult, and the case was heard in the California Superior Criminal Court as opposed to the Division of Juvenile Justice. The district attorney reasoned that the criminal court was the appropriate setting to address such a violent and premeditated crime.

The district attorney was granted this sentencing authority following a series of California state legislative actions taken in the 1990s. These amended sentencing guidelines were prompted in part by a pattern of gang-related violence wherein juveniles were recruited to do the gang's bidding. In an interview after the trial, Deputy DA Fox put it this way: "The gangs would get their pee-wees to do their business, including shooting rival gang members. That way, the kids were tried in the juvenile system, and then they were out in a matter of a couple of years."

Mr. Wippert, in keeping with the defense team's repeated, unsuccessful pretrial efforts to move the trial from the superior court to the Division of Juvenile Justice, emphasized that Brandon was "barely fourteen years old" at the time of the murder: "On January 24th, 2008, Brandon McInerney turned fourteen. Some nineteen days later, on the 12th of February, the shooting occurred." Again and again, Mr. Wippert conflated age and state of mind. "Brandon McInerney, his state of mind when he was fourteen at the time when this shooting occurred, that is the issue."

A bad boy standing for bad boys, Mr. Wippert did not precisely fill the role of the antihero. He got close; he possessed the alienation and the defiance. But he lacked the gravitas. His honor was tarnished by his having been disciplined by the State Bar of California for charges stemming from driving under the influence.

Still, he had guile, cleverness, and scrap, and he came prepared to project to the balcony. At the end of the opening day, he was held in contempt of the court and fined five hundred dollars for brashly asking the arresting officer if Brandon had confessed remorse. Mr. Wippert had not established the foundation for such a question, and nothing in the officer's answers afforded an opening to ask it. In defiance of established courtroom practice (the law of the land), he asked his question anyway.

MR. WIPPERT BEGAN HIS OPENING statement: "What the evidence is going to show is that what happened here should never have happened. It was an unnecessary tragedy that was because a fourteen-year-old boy was emotionally pushed to the edge, a fourteen-year-old boy who was being harassed, sexually harassed by Larry King."

Yes, Brandon had shot and killed Larry King. "We are not here to dispute that fact," Mr. Wippert said, "but this was voluntary manslaughter, committed in the heat of passion."

Mr. Wippert maintained that Larry's feminine life constituted sexual harassment sufficient to provoke Brandon to commit voluntary manslaughter. In particular, Mr. Wippert charged that it was the ways in which Larry set about to look and behave like a sexually curious and desiring girl that had brought on the crime.

"Everything that led up to this culminated in this emotional state that Brandon was in, and the evidence is going to show that he didn't shoot Larry King because he was gay, because he perceived him as gay, because of his sexual orientation or his gender identity issues. He was being targeted and harassed sexually over and over again," Mr. Wippert said.

In his version, Larry was the bully.

Larry, Mr. Wippert maintained, had gone on something of a rampage of "taunting" and "teasing" other boys: "All the boys were afraid of him. They were afraid of Larry King."

It was Larry's behavior that sparked the malice and the murder, not Brandon's inner conflicts or his budding hate. "He did not shoot this boy because he was a white supremacist. He did not shoot this boy because of his gender identity. This boy was targeting Brandon McInerney, and it resulted in everybody teasing him over and over and over again," Mr. Wippert declared.

Mr. Wippert claimed that "everybody knew about the taunting and the teasing, everybody knew about it, and nobody did anything. No matter what Brandon said to others leading up to it, nobody did anything. Nobody did anything." The "everybody" who morphed into the "nobody" to whom Mr. Wippert referred were the school administrators at E. O. Green. Through his repeated outrage, Mr. Wippert set about building the case that Brandon was abandoned and neglected by virtually everyone, from school administrators, to his parents, and ultimately the court itself.

Focusing on E. O. Green, Mr. Wippert reframed the way in which Ms. Fox had characterized Larry's gender transition, during her opening statement, as a sign of increased confidence. "That's not what the evidence is going to show. Yes, there was that period of time that he did actually start to dress like that, but this is not when his behavior regarding inappropriate sexual comments to other students began. This was a long-standing problem that Larry King had."

As opposed to gender freedom, Mr. Wippert held that what happened at E. O. Green was an "emboldened" disruption of the "entire school," one that had pitted concerned teachers against an administration that "empowered" Larry by failing to stop him from wearing women's accessories.

The administration held that Larry was not breaking any rules, the dress code specifically. Larry was wearing his school uniform and, like any other child, was free to accessorize as he wished.

According to Mr. Wippert, the conflict about Larry's manner of dress and what were called "his rights" should have been a matter of debate, not a decision that rested on district policy or civil rights. "Teachers were

emailing administrators, saying that this is the problem, and the administration said, we can't do anything. He has rights."

He cited Joy Epstein, one of the assistant principals at E. O. Green,
as having "empowered" Larry: "She told him that he has rights, that he
has gay rights. She's telling a fifteen-year-old boy this."

Moving on from the school, Mr. Wippert focused on Brandon's home
life. Mr. Wippert provided a broad outline in his opening statement.
Like Ms. Fox, he turned to the troubled childhoods of both Larry
and Brandon, but Mr. Wippert drew us closer in. He explained that
both boys were born to drug-addicted mothers, and that Brandon's
parents remained addicted to drugs throughout his childhood.

Mr. Wippert said, "You will hear that Kendra McInerney, while
she was pregnant, used drugs." He did not mention what the drugs
were, and he spoke only two more times about Kendra in his opening, each time merely identifying her as Billy McInerney's wife. In
the courtroom, no one, not just Mr. Wippert, lingered over Kendra
for long.

Instead Mr. Wippert, like every witness he brought to the stand,
turned his attention to Billy McInerney, Brandon's father, with whom
Brandon lived throughout much of his childhood. Mr. Wippert introduced Billy, a hulk of a man (six foot two, 230 pounds) as "a very
abusive, very violent, mean and cruel man." Mr. Wippert continued that
Billy was abusive not only to Brandon "but to his brothers James and
Jeremy [Brandon's half brothers; they shared the same mother]. He
would abuse and beat them for fun. He thought it was funny. He
thought it was funny to punch them in the face and punch them in
the stomach."

Billy's sadism and aggression were the stuff of small-town legend. I
would later learn, in reviewing the district attorney's investigation files,
that Billy's rap sheet included charges of domestic violence, criminal
threats, driving under the influence, child endangerment, and drug
possession. His targets were multiple, including Kendra's sons from her
previous marriage, James and Jeremy Bing, and, to a lesser extent, Brandon. He was alleged to have abused his wife, his sisters, his sons, his

friends, his neighbors, his sisters-in-law, his nephew—and those were just people who knew him.

Billy McInerney was not in court to hear how he was described or to hear the accusations of abuse. Eighteen months after the murder, he tripped at home, hit his head, and died of a brain bleed. An autopsy revealed significant amounts of oxycodone, alprazolam (Xanax), and alcohol.

"Billy, may he rest in peace, was a horrible person, and he unfortunately influenced Brandon in many ways," Mr. Wippert said, drawing us into a nest of examples of the ways in which Billy abused the boys and endangered them through mindless neglect: "Half the time Billy was so messed up on drugs, on pills, on oxy that he was just out of it. He would take Brandon to drug houses while he did drugs and got high, Brandon would just sleep on the floor."

The neglect and abuse that were constants in Brandon's childhood, Mr. Wippert asserted, were even more egregious than the neglect and abuse suffered by Larry. According to Mr. Wippert, Child Protective Services was as aware of the abuse and chaos in the McInerney home as they were in the King home, but they had not taken action, as they had with Larry.

Mr. Wippert's opening painted Brandon as a boy who grew up essentially as an orphan. "He took care of himself. He would get up and he would bathe himself, he would get ready for school, he would ride his bike in the rain, he would do all of these things himself, because there was no one."

There was barely a house at all, in Mr. Wippert's account. He explained how Billy punched holes in walls and repeatedly tore them from their beams. Brandon lived, Mr. Wippert told us, in a "house with no walls, a house with no parents."

There were no parental arms to catch him when he fell. There was no parental guidance to think alongside him. There was no adult to consider his mind, to help him speak about what he was feeling, or to reflect on those feelings. There was no one to stop Brandon from going too far. As Mr. Wippert explained, "Brandon was emotional, and this is what the evidence is going to show. He was pushed over the edge, and he didn't have anyone to stop him."

BRANDON WAS BORN ON JANUARY 24, 1994, into a blended and large family. He was also born into a tight-knit community, Silver Strand, a small, unincorporated beach town that is part of Oxnard, sixty-two miles north of Los Angeles. Many of Brandon's brethren would eventually come before us, taking their place on the witness stand to talk about their town and to speak on Brandon's behalf.

For all the telling of Brandon's life—and there was a lot of it during the trial—no one seemed able to keep track of who, exactly, was related to whom, and how. That job fell, to whatever extent it could be done at all, to James Bing, Brandon's older half brother, and Kendra's eldest son from her first marriage. With the patriarch dead and the matriarch grieving, James was the family spokesperson and the first defense witness. He came to tell Brandon's story. Darker and smaller than his younger brother, James was equally, if not more, handsome. He was a bit roughed up, a scar on his forehead, a chipped tooth, a budding gut. James could have wandered in from the set of an action bro-mance, the charming, stoned sidekick.

Mr. Wippert: "Afternoon, Mr. Bing."

"Afternoon," James replied.

Gesturing toward Brandon, Mr. Wippert asked, "Do you know this young man right here?"

"Yes, I do," said James.

"How do you know him?"

"It's my baby brother."

Following Mr. Wippert's prompt, James stood and began drawing a family tree on a large pad of paper that Mr. Wippert had placed on a tripod. It got confusing fast, as big, extended families do. James named his family, yet he could not get them into relation. Nor could he capture the timeline (who had been where when?). The fractured family split the tree beyond his capacity to draw it.

He put "Grandpa McInerney and Billy McInerney at the top."

But, catching himself, James added his father, James Bing Sr.: "I'm going to put my dad so you know where me and Jeremy came from." Jeremy was James's younger brother by two years.

He then added his mother, "Kendra McCoy." Kendra had taken the McInerney name when she married Billy, but, as James explained, "I prefer McCoy."

It was then that he mentioned Brandon: "Together they had Brandon."

There were still two other brothers: Brian McInerney, Billy's son from a previous marriage, who was a year younger than James, and Ryan McCoy, Kendra's eight-year-old son, whose father was Rory McCoy.

James wasn't quite sure where to put Brian or Ryan. He had never lived with them. Brian had lived with his mother in Torrance throughout their childhoods, and the much younger Ryan lived with Kendra, having been born several years after Kendra and Billy split up.

And when, exactly, did Billy and Kendra split up? How was James supposed to draw the split? He had stayed with Kendra, Jeremy went to live with his father (James Bing Sr.), and Brandon went with Billy.

Like an anxious student at a blackboard, James looked to Mr. Wippert, who apologized, saying, "I didn't mean to put you on the spot."

James replied by beginning to name all of his brothers' birthdays. Mr. Wippert interrupted him, saying, "Okay. You can have a seat."

As he sat down, James offered what was to become a hallmark of his testimony: "Love my brothers very much."

"Pardon me?" Mr. Wippert asked.

"I know all their birthdays. I love them very much," James said.

Love was James's campaign. He loved his friends, whom he hailed as "brother" or "uncle," "mother" or "aunt."

And love's promotion brought returns. Several of James's friends came to court as character witnesses for Brandon, speaking fondly of James as their "brother" or "son."

James wanted us to know that he called Brandon "Bear," a nickname James gave him as a child. Two weeks after the shooting, James had a life-size teddy bear tattooed across the right flank of his abdomen.

Ms. Fox asked James if he would mind showing us the tattoo. He stood unhesitatingly and pulled his shirt up over his head. Sure enough, there it was, right at the spot where a child might clutch a teddy bear to his side. A juror asked, "Can we clap?" Ms. Fox, shaking her head and laughing, said, "Excellent. Thank you very much."

While love told a good story, it wasn't as good at keeping track of time. James did explain, as best he understood, that Billy and Kendra met in the early 1990s. Kendra had come to California from Arkansas and had met Billy in Silver Strand. Kendra would later explain to me that she had hitched a ride with a trucker, as she sought to run away from her first marriage. She left James and Jeremy with a friend ("in the woods") and soon returned to fetch them. Sometime around 1991 or 1992 she moved with James and Jeremy to Silver Strand to live with Billy. James did not recall those early years with much clarity; he maintained that he was not alone, "Nobody remembers those years so well."

But everyone's memory snapped into place around an event that occurred in 1993, one year prior to Brandon's birth.

Billy and Kendra were tweaked on crystal; it likely had been days and days. How or why they began to fight, no one knew. It got physical. Billy threw Kendra to the floor. She got up, broke away, and ran for the stairs. James told us what happened next: "Um, they were arguing, and I walked out when I heard them arguing—I went out of my room just to see what was going on, and my mom started walking upstairs like, 'Fuck you, get away from me.' And he told my mom to turn around, and he had a gun. And she like turned around or—and she kept walking, and he fired and shot her in the arm, sir."

Mr. Wippert asked, "He hit her in the arm?"

James: "Yes, sir."

"Did she have to go to the hospital?"

"Yes, sir."

"And was this before she, they got married?"

"Yes, sir."

"And what happened to Billy?"

"He went to jail."

"When he got out of jail, did your mom and him get back together?"

"Yes, sir."

"And did you still live with him after that?"

"Yes, sir."

"Was that difficult?"

James began to cry. "Mm-hmm."

"During that period, had you ever seen your . . ." Mr. Wippert caught himself and asked James, "You need a minute?"

"No. I'm seeing my mom cry."

Kendra McInerney was, in fact, crying. Back then, in 1993, she had refused to press charges. She had a peace sign tattooed over the wound— a hand, with two fingers raised.

James went ahead to tell us that after Billy shot Kendra, they got married in "a drive-through in Las Vegas." James and Jeremy were in the backseat.

Brandon was born the following year. James told us that those were the good days: "Yeah. It was about like a year or two where Billy mellowed out and, you know, promised my mom he would change, you know, be different and change, and that's when they got married. So it was cool for about a year or two, and then it went back to the same way it was."

"Billy could be fun, and all," James said, as he described how they went to the beach, learned to swim, and rode dirt bikes, even as the play often got too rough, and somebody got hurt. But just about when Brandon would have started putting sentences together (around 1997, '98, or '99, James guessed), the good times faltered, the party spiked, and Billy and Kendra returned to the glitter and the grift.

Mr. Wippert asked, "How bad was the drug situation during this time?"

"It was bad," James said.

"Okay. How bad?"

"Bad. Every day. They would be up for a week and sleep for a week all the time."

"Were there a lot of people that would come over?"

"Yeah."

"And used drugs?"

"Yeah."

"It was a party house?"

"Yeah."

BILLY AND KENDRA'S DRUG ADDICTIONS were named but never detailed, or, rather, only in the most cursory of ways, during the court proceedings. Mr. Wippert alluded to them in his opening statement and questioned James Bing during his direct testimony. It seemed to me that parental drug addiction had played a role not only in the effect it had on Brandon's life but also in the disjointed way the story was told in the courtroom.

Soon after the trial ended, I sat down with Kendra McInerney and James Bing. I had introduced myself to Kendra during the second week of the trial. I asked her if I might join her as she sat outside on a bench smoking a cigarette with her friend Nancy. I told her who I was and why I was at the trial. She listened, nodding "yes," as I explained that I hoped I could learn something from the trial about boys and the dilemmas they face.

She and Nancy laughed together. Kendra said, "Well, I've got enough of them! Maybe I can help. Or maybe you can help me. What mother doesn't need that?"

Her voice surprised me. Her pitch was high, even girlish, but her voice was hoarse, ragged and raw, like a girl who had been screaming.

I told her I would be grateful for the opportunity to speak with her, and she said that she, too, would like that but thought it was probably best that we wait until after the trial.

Throughout the trial we spoke briefly, here and there. Sometimes she would ask me to help her understand something that had been confusing to her, noting that her history of drug addiction had resulted in a "few burned wires." She called me "Dr. Ken." Once, when she was crying and gasping for breath, I gave her my handkerchief.

Kendra had been seven years sober at the time of the trial and was still living at Prototypes, the rehab facility where she got clean. She worked there as an intake coordinator. "My life is a blur, until recently," she told me, referring to how her memory was faulty. Her mind did not hold: "A lot was lost. A lot is lost," she said. In this way, she was veiled and protected by what she had not seen and could not see. She was protected, but her children were not.

When we met following the trial, Kendra explained: "Yeah, I was what I think is the worst kind of meth addict. I was functional for a very long time. I had a definite routine. I worked at Vons [a local grocery store] from 1988 to 2002, about thirteen years, never got in trouble, never was ever questioned at work. So, I was functional. I worked Monday through Friday usually from three to eleven, or the graveyard shift. (I really got away with a lot then.)"

But then she would have days when she slept all day, or she would "crash for a week." Kendra said, "If I had two or three days off in a row, I would sleep all those days."

On those days, the kids were left to their own devices. Brandon became a child of the mother-beach. His care fell to others, James in particular, or "aunts" in their open-door beach neighborhood.

On the days when Kendra wasn't crashed, she would get up, do a line, and shift into mother machine. She got the kids up, fed them, got their teeth brushed, got them out the door to school. She cleaned the kitchen ("way too well"), did the laundry, put away the groceries that she had brought home the night before. She got the kids to doctor's appointments. She went to parent-teacher conferences. She went to the Corner Store for aspirin when a kid was sick. She remembered to bring home birthday cakes.

But, like the walls that Billy punched and tore down, there were gaps, holes in Kendra's story. A party swept her up, and the kids were lost in the wake. She was "gone," Kendra told me. Going was her "escape mechanism," and there was a time when she "dealt with everything by being gone."

During the trial, though, she sat soberly, daily behind her accused son, and most days wept over his fate. She had poisoned him with methamphetamine during her pregnancy. She had dropped him, reaching for the crank. She had left him to wander into a chaotic world of violent men. She had failed to protect him from his abusive father; she could not protect herself. She had left him to the care of his brothers, to the care of equally neglected children.

Yet the condemnation and damnation that might have been aimed at such a woman did not ensue. Indeed, it was just the opposite. Kendra was met by the kind of empathy that accrues to one who has failed but is not ruined. She had failed as a mother but now walked the path of recovery and restitution. She was generous with her forgiveness as she looked upon herself and as she looked upon others, perhaps most of all as she looked upon her children.

Kendra had a similarly forgiving way of speaking about her former husband. When I asked her to help me better understand Billy's addiction, she explained that he always drank, and liked barbiturates and opiates. Kendra thought that Billy's monstrousness might, at least in some instances, have been related to the times when he used methamphetamine. According to Kendra, "When he would smoke meth—some people have a chemical imbalance where you should not do amphetamines, he was one of them—he would turn into devil man, a total psychopath."

Billy's antisocial tendencies also seemed integral to the fiery bond that held him and Kendra in their protracted pattern of separation and reunion. From the time Brandon was three years old until he was eleven—from 1997 to 2005—Kendra described a life that contracted and expanded, like one of those frightening windsock men that flap at you from roadside stores, collapsing only to awkwardly and rapidly rise, flapping and waving as you speed past.

Kendra talked about the time between the late 1990s and 2005 as "party time!": "As soon as I kicked Billy out of the house, I was free. It was party time, and I went off the deep end. Billy was gone. We all went nuts."

The "monster" may have been gone, but Billy and Kendra continued to fight over Brandon's care and custody. One fight ended in Kendra's arrest, when Billy charged her with making "terrorist threats" and with domestic violence.

Kendra paused as she told me this story. "I know I was fucked up, paranoid, crazy. Who knows what happened? And you're probably thinking, 'These fucking crazy people.' And you would be right. We went nuts. And the worst part was that Brandon saw all of that. There probably was no good place for Brandon then."

But she believed, then and now, that Billy's drug use might not have been as bad at that point. "It got worse, a lot worse, after I got sober, around 2005 or so, but at that point, I don't think it was so bad."

And while Billy bully-loved, Kendra trusted his devotion to Brandon. Billy had an interest, however self-centered, in Brandon's well-being. Billy enlisted Brandon in the Young Marines, MMA (mixed marshal arts), and the Junior Lifeguard. And for many years, until the summer of 2007, Brandon seemed to "love all that stuff," Kendra said. Brandon excelled at mixed marshal arts. He spent hours at the gym and developed what everyone described as a solid mentoring bond with his coach.

MR. WIPPERT, JAMES, AND KENDRA REPEATEDLY returned to the bond between Billy and Brandon, a powerful mix of love and violence, not unlike the bond Kendra described with Billy. Brandon was the golden child, and Billy had high hopes. In particular, Billy wanted Brandon to pursue a military career. Calling Billy a "slave driver" and a "psycho-cop," James said, "We lived like the Marine lifestyle, had to make our beds a certain way, haircut a certain way, endless chores, you know, lived like a Marine Corps drill sergeant." Seeking to clarify Billy's militaristic and antisocial influence on Brandon, Ms. Fox questioned James, during cross-examination, "What did you mean when you said that your impression was that Billy wanted Brandon to be a special operative with the CIA?"

James said, "Billy obviously wanted him to be, was some type of FBI or CIA agent, something like that, and that's what I took of it, yes, ma'am."

Ms. Fox: "Special operative, though, what does that mean? Like, a trained killer?"

James: "A military . . . somebody like a Navy Seal, probably would have, yes."

Another way in which it seemed Billy carried forth his alleged "special op" wishes was the ready supply of guns in his home. Fire-arms were always at the ready. All the boys were taught how to use guns. Brandon grew up not only with guns well within reach but with a gun arm.

"There were guns all over the house," Mr. Wippert said. "It became a joke. Billy would give Kendra bullets in a stocking for Christmas."

Billy's father, William McInerney Sr., a retired locksmith with whom Billy and Brandon were living at the time of the murder, also collected guns. They were allegedly kept in a closet, secured only by an insubstantial combination lock, a curious choice for a locksmith.

Brandon grew up in keeping with Billy's fantasy. He became a quick-draw. His fists were fast. He was quick with a weapon as well. He chased his brothers with kitchen knives. He hit Jeremy on the back of the head with a shovel. Every brother has a fraternal scar or two, but the talk of Brandon's temper suggested that it spiked fast and did not quell easily.

Descriptions of Brandon's temper were almost always coupled with claims that he was emotionally stunted. Repeatedly, we were told that Brandon did not show emotion. As James said, "Brandon will never tell you that he is not happy. He will not tell you he is sad. He is just not there."

Brandon withdrew into a walled retreat of self-sufficiency: I don't need. I don't feel. I don't relate. Hit me. Your fists move through me. Besides, I can dodge and come at you when you're not looking.

Christopher Mulhardt, one of Brandon's cousins, told us from the witness stand about the time Billy armed his nephews with BB guns, loaded them into his car, and chased Brandon down the street, using him as a moving target. It seems that Brandon managed to go largely unwounded by dodging and ducking behind parked cars. The wounds he did suffer were bandaged with duct tape.

Ms. Fox vigorously pursued the veracity of such reports. And later, during her direct examination of Detective Dan Swanson, the prosecution's hate-crime expert, he would challenge the credibility of the car chase story: "Don't tell me that no one, no one, any adult who saw something like that, a guy in a car full of kids shooting at a kid running down a suburban street, that no adult would have taken action, would have called the police. I don't believe it."

Exactly how abusive had Billy McInerney been? How did he get away with it? How was it that people outside the family, particularly teachers, did not report abuse or the evidence of abuse, like bruises? And despite Mr. Wippert's claim that Child Protective Services had been engaged with the McInerney family, no evidence was presented to substantiate that assertion.

As I listened, though, I was not so quick to dismiss these stories or the charges as exaggeration. Yes, memory, cognition, and perception unravel in a house with three boys, no walls, and drug-addicted parents. The question did not seem to be one of magnitude or force per se.

The consequences of parental drug addiction alone could be enough to create a monstrous environment for a child. Abuse does not need a fist.

———

AS IF ADOLESCENCE WAS NOT going to bring enough by way of change, still more change came Brandon's way, around the time that he entered junior high. He and Billy moved, and Kendra entered rehab. For the first time in his life, Brandon did not live in the same small neighborhood he knew so well. Nor could he visit his mother, whose rehab center was for women only and did not allow boys over the age of twelve to visit their mothers.

James explained to Mr. Wippert that "around 2003" Billy and Brandon moved into Billy's father's house on Tiller Avenue in Oxnard. Like all the houses in which Brandon had lived, Grandpa McInerney's house was chaotic and overcrowded. Billy's sister, Megan Csorba—Brandon's aunt—also lived there. She helped care for the old man. William Sr. had heart and lung trouble and could not walk unaided. Another aunt, Maura McInerney, lived at the Tiller Avenue house from time to time. Maura was a rough, leathery drunk and drug abuser, with a used-up scrape of a voice.

Four adults and a teenager lived in a house with three bedrooms, one of which was given over to storage. In fact, much of the house was given over to William Senior's hoarding. Sagging boxes, stacks of papers, cartons, toppling piles of books, plastic bins, black trash bags dominated all the rooms.

Technically, Billy and Brandon shared a room. In reality, they shared a closet and some shelf space. Brandon slept on a sofa in the living room. That is, when Brandon slept. He was up most nights, playing video games until two or three in the morning, or riding his bike through the vapor-lit streets, crossing four- and six-lane roads to get to the beach. During those early morning hours, on the flat expanse of pixilated video screens, Brandon stabbed, shot, and chain-sawed thugs; he bombed soldiers, hulks, and monsters. Then he slid outdoors onto the wide, empty streets of suburban Oxnard. He dominated on his bike, pushing harder, driving into the cold, dark air. Did the occasional truck driver see the stray on the bike? Did Brandon drive by the rehab center where his mother was sequestered? Did he catch the eye of the occasional, fluo-rescent convenience store clerk? Did he happen upon anyone hanging out at the beach or sitting on the benches of the shuttered restaurant Pepe's?

Or was he ghosting, gliding on roads so familiar he did not have to think? He could fade. He could leave. A neighbor, Thea Shoemaker, described seeing Brandon, an apparition, on the street late at night. "He was really shutting down and just seemed just, just not there," Ms. Shoemaker told a reporter from the *Ventura County Star*.

During the summer of 2007, the bond between Brandon and Billy began to fray. "Brandon was finished with Billy," said James. Brandon had for many years been Billy's backup. But no more. "He was done. He shut off. He shut Billy out."

Brandon gave up on his father's pride and on the expectations of his teachers, which had been another source of pride—he was widely rec-ognized as a good student, if inconsistently motivated.

His desires led him to the Silver Strand beach, local girls, and the older friends he came to know through James and Jeremy. One of those friends was a guy named Matt Resume, a known white supremacist. Brandon and James had spent much of the weekend prior to the murder at Matt's apartment on the Strand.

Billy didn't like James and Jeremy. They amounted to nothing. They were going nowhere. Billy wanted Brandon to stay away from them. On the Sunday before the shooting, according to Kendra, Jeremy, delu-sional and cranked on crystal, ended up in jail in Kern County. Kendra had to bail him out. Two weeks prior to the murder, on a Saturday night, Billy drove to the beach to confront Brandon where he was partying with James. A fight broke out. Depending on who was telling the story, either Brandon, who had been drinking, punched Billy in the nose, or Billy, who had also been drinking, punched Brandon in the nose. In either case, it was a bloody punctuation to their deteriorating bond.

Billy started threatening to send Brandon to military school; either he got it together, or he was going. Or they were going to move to Redondo Beach, nearer to where Billy worked as a sales rep for a motorcycle dealership, and forty miles south of Silver Strand, the only world Brandon had ever known. The night before the shooting, Billy told Brandon to begin packing.

Throughout the fall and early winter, Billy made frequent visits to E. O. Green. He was agitated by the precipitate fall in Brandon's school attendance and performance. The day before the shooting, Billy showed up at the school unannounced, to talk with the science teacher, Martha Romero, and Brandon.

From the witness stand, Ms. Romero squinted and recounted the visit. She looked fed up. She brooked no nonsense and prided herself on not letting any of her "students' personal business spill into the classroom." She told Billy that Brandon's schoolwork was very poor. She said his behavior was fine, failing to mention that just that afternoon she had yelled at him and a group of boys. Brandon, along with a huddle of his friends, had been talking in "inappropriately loud" voices. They were outside her door in the walkway. She'd told them to "knock it off and get going."

Ms. Romero did not exactly fail to note any disturbance in Brandon's behavior. She failed to recognize it as anything other than what she expected; it was everyday, it was boys being boys. It was how she could notice but not heed.

Throughout the meeting between Billy and Ms. Romero, Brandon sat with his head down. Nothing was said about any personal trouble he'd been having at school. Larry King's name was not spoken. Brandon had answered "correct" or "negative," as opposed to "right" or "wrong," when asked about his schoolwork. He spoke in a way that was both formally obedient and coldly absent.

During the conference with Billy and Brandon, Ms. Romero had anxiously made one of those comments teachers make as they try to encourage a student: "You could be a leader."

Brandon, not looking up, had told her that if he were to lead, he was likely to lead people to "a place they probably don't want to go."

4

Mobbed Up

The morning of Monday, February 11, 2008, did not occasion much telling. It was the afternoon that everybody talked about. The afternoon was told and urgently retold, debated and deliberated. Witnesses and townspeople scrambled after motive as they struggled with reality's verdict.

"If you want to know what happened, you have to begin with the Monday before the murder," Detective Dan Swanson instructed. Walk backward, sort the evidence, detect, he seemed to be saying. By that, he did not mean that the story began on Monday, February 11. Rather, he was referring to the way in which Monday became a memory net, as people reached back toward that day, that day before, in their effort to gather evidence, observations, clues, and presentiments.

The search for motive is, in part, directed by judgment; the eyes frame, the ears tune as judgment directs. And judgment, in turn, relies on memory. As witnesses told their stories on the stand, their individual memories did not distinguish the sequence of the story; the basic story (this happened, then this happened) did not deviate. But the mood and the moral did vary depending on the storyteller's memories, feelings, and beliefs. Some told a story of gender hate. Some told a story of sexual harassment. But no matter the teller, no matter the story, no matter the details, the psychological condition of the protagonists remained the same: Larry was crackling. Brandon simmered.

LARRY WAS EBULLIENT, FLAMING. SNAP! He was caught in glimpses that morning and throughout the week before, whirling, popping. A dervish. Monday morning, one of Larry's classmates, Stormy, saw Larry dart down a walkway wearing a "long green prom dress." No one else reported such a sighting. Victor Vallejo, another classmate, saw Larry in a print dress (he could not recall when), it was decorated with "flowers or butterflies," and Larry wore it everywhere—"in general everywhere." Again, no one else reported this vision.

Shirley Brown, Larry's seventh-grade social studies teacher, reported that Larry ran across the schoolyard in a green "poufy" dress, though she could not recollect the day. She did not think that it was that Monday. Was it the prior Thursday? Or had it been on Tuesday? She explained to Mr. Wippert that she was so upset by what she had seen that she went to speak with the principal, Joel Lovestedt. Inexplicably (given that she had been prompted by her vision), she failed to mention the dress. When Mr. Wippert questioned her about this lapse, she responded, "Can I tell you the truth? I don't remember."

Stories such as these dressed Larry up. He wore a gossamer gown spun in the collective imagination, made with needles of rumor and play. It was as if birds rustled his crown, but not the pastel sort that find princesses. These were more like grackles.

Averi Laskey, Larry's friend and schoolmate, flew into court. A round-faced African American girl with a pinched nose, Averi didn't flinch. She had come to name names. Larry and Averi had been on-again off-again friends since the third grade, waging their friendship between their battles. Possessed by sharp tongues, they could verbally cut and wound each other and end up on the outs. Patched up, they were playful with their sharp humor.

Mostly, they were just messing around and finding their footing. Their play often consisted of little more than sparring verbally, "dishing" and "serving." They enjoyed irony coupled with theatrical exaggeration and affectation, and usually they ended up laughing.

During what were called passing periods (the time between classes), Larry, Averi, and a small group of what the teachers would call "bad girls" camped along the walkways: "Whaaaat?"—elongating and uplifting the vowel. "Werk!"—cracking the glottal *k* as they click-click-clicked their heels. "Whateva!"—tossing off a putdown as they dropped the final consonant.

But lunch hour *was* camp. It became their theater and Leticia's stage. Lunch was her moment to work her look. On the nine days when Leticia wore cross-gender accessories to school, she may have mainly worn them, the shoes, in particular, during lunch-theater. The face paint was wet and thick. The costumes were hastily arranged. This ephemeral theater consisted of quick scenes, flashes flaming.

Averi and Leticia were extravagant in their glee and their fury. Leticia was the tottering tease. Averi was at Leticia's heel. She pushed Leticia into the room before she entered. Scatter, the queen is making her entrance!

Averi would send Leticia to a table full of boys and watch them flee. Their play might have been called "Clear the Table," but they rarely got beyond the first scene, "The Entrance." Their pranking practice captured valuable lunchtime real estate. As Averi pointed out, "There's the cafeteria which mostly the losers eat in, and then most of the cool kids eat outside. So, when there was nowhere to sit down [outside], we would ask Larry to go clear a table, and he would go up to the table full of boys and ask if he could sit there, and the boys would run away and like call him names, but we all thought it was funny."

On that Monday before the murder, Larry allegedly went to a table that included Brandon. The boys quickly got up and left. Larry, Averi, and their friends swooped in, cackling over their spoils. We are the queens. You quake. Those boys had taken enough. It was time for them to move.

Averi made a point of telling Ms. Fox that she would "stand not too far from the bench just to see what happened, like to make sure that Larry wasn't like going to get hurt." ·

Ms. Fox asked, "Why, did you think that was a possibility?"

Averi quickly replied, " 'Cause boys make stupid decisions."

"Attitude-y" Averi had come to speak out for her murdered friend. Boys were trouble, white boys in particular, and people around here had been letting them get away with it for too long. She and her friends were aggrieved and suffering.

Fed up, Averi told Ms. Fox that she had once gone so far as to take things into her own hands with Brandon.

Ms. Fox asked, "Did you actually get angry at one point and do something physical to him?"

Averi: "He had called me a nigger."

"What was the context of that conversation?"

"I don't remember."

"But what did you do in response?"

"I slapped him."

Her voice rising, Ms. Fox said, "You slapped him? Where?"

"On his head," Averi said.

Averi wasn't going to back away from her indignation. If she had to make a point with a slap or the swerve of melodrama, so be it.

She was hardly alone in performing her "truth"; every witness had a personality and a point of view. Averi's just happened to be blacker and sassier than most and was arguably as close to Leticia as we were going to get.

Mr. Wippert tried to brand her as a liar.

In his first exchange with Averi, Mr. Wippert asked about her age: "Okay. And how old did you say you were?"

Averi: "Sixteen."

"I'm sorry. 'Cause I was looking at your Myspace page that says you're 18."

Ms. Fox quickly interjected, "Objection. That's improper."

Judge Campbell sustained her objection and moved to strike Mr.

Wippert's statement, saying to the jury, "Let me remind you, the statements of the attorneys are not evidence."

Ms. Fox, breaking from her usual decorum, said, "Wow."

The judge continued addressing the jury: "So anything they say is not evidence in this case. It's the witnesses who give the evidence." He then turned to Mr. Wippert and said, "Consider yourself warned."

Mr. Wippert rephrased his comment into a question, asking Averi, "Do you have a Myspace page?"

Averi said, "Yes, I have a Myspace."

"And do you have your age as 18?"

"Yes."

"Is there a reason for that?"

"Because when I made my Myspace, they didn't allow anyone younger than 18, and so everyone who was younger than 18 would just list their age as older."

"So you lied so that you could have a Myspace page?"

"Yes."

Averi's tone was flat, her gaze was direct, and they remained that way as Mr. Wippert repeatedly questioned her truthfulness. He sought to impugn her as seeking notoriety over truthfulness. He questioned her about interviews that she had given to the press. (Following the trial, Mr. Wippert would appear on the same news outlets.)

In a particularly withering exchange, Mr. Wippert returned to Averi's report that she had seen Brandon in a park near the school in the company of boys and men who "all had swastika tattoos" (some on their arms, others on their chests).

Mr. Wippert asked, "Who were you with when you saw these boys with the swastikas?"

Averi said, "A group of friends from the area. I don't remember their names."

"Okay. From the area. They were students at E. O. Green?"

"Um, I think one of them was, and most the others were older."

"When did you see, as you say, Brandon with these older boys over at the park? Was it during the eighth grade year?"

"Yes, it was during eighth grade."

"Okay. Was it after the winter break?"

"I don't remember."

"Do you remember what time of year it was? Beginning of the year? End of the year? Middle of the year?" Mr. Wippert asked, his inflection rising.

Averi said, "I'm thinking kind of like the end of the beginning of the year and kind of close to the middle of the year."

Averi stuck to her story, though she could not recall the facts, though she could not place herself with people she could name, though she could not recollect when the events took place.

Likewise, she stood by her account of observing Brandon making drawings that included Nazi and white supremacist imagery when they sat next to each other in Carole Short's honors English class (prior to Brandon getting kicked out).

After a long exchange during which Mr. Wippert questioned Averi about things that Brandon had said about Nazis and White Power, and about Brandon's drawings, Mr. Wippert pushed her to recollect Miss Short's class in greater detail, including naming the other students.

Averi: "The kids in the class? I don't know names."

Mr. Wippert: "You don't remember any of the names of any of the kids in the class?"

"I've chosen to block things out of my mind, and I don't remember a lot of kids from even the school."

"So you've blocked out a lot of the kids from Miss Short's class?"

"I know—I had several friends in class, but they were kind of bookworms, and they sat in the front."

"Okay. Why is it that you blocked out everything that happened in Miss Short's class?"

"I don't like remembering things that are negative."

"Okay. So it was a pretty negative experience being in Miss Short's class?"

"I loved Miss Short's class, but when I was sitting next to Brandon, it was mostly a negative experience."

"Okay. But as you sit here, you remember everything that Brandon ever did to you, right? You didn't block that out?"

"Excuse me?"

"You're testifying here about things that happened in Miss Short's class that Brandon said or did to you, right?"

"Yes."

"You didn't block those things out?"

"There are certain things that you can't block out."

"So the things that Brandon did or said to you, you did not block out, but everything else that was good about Miss Short's class you blocked out?"

"Negativity is sometimes more powerful than positivity."

It is easy to imagine how Leticia's flame had met Averi's flare. Just as Leticia had zipped up her brown suede boots and pounded out her walk, Averi was determined to testify. And like Leticia, Averi was refused recognition in the courtroom; Mr. Wippert painted Averi as a liar, her reality as a nonreality. Yet among the witnesses, Averi was virtually alone in her defense of Leticia's gender questioning. Others spoke about Larry as the target of teasing and taunting, but no one displayed the anger and outrage that Averi brought to the story.

Averi defied Mr. Wippert's efforts to discredit her belief that Brandon was violent and a racist. She pushed back, as if to say, "Go ahead. Call me a liar. Go ahead and turn from my truth. But consider that in so doing you are upholding murderous racism." She pushed us to deliberate on the possibility that if we were to turn away from her, we were also turning away from Leticia. One could negate her, but such an act also meant negating Leticia and the kind of defiance that was required for Leticia to embody her queenly black femininity.

At fifteen, Leticia was not only questioning her gender but finding a sexual body. And no witness stepped up to the interplay between adolescent sexuality, gender, and race, as did Averi. According to Averi, Leticia had been trying out several names, Latoya, Laquanda, and Leticia. Leticia was "the sort of girl you don't mess with," Averi laughingly pointed out in Marta Cunningham's documentary *Valentine Road*. Leticia was "flirtatious," and she and Averi enjoyed flirting with and teasing boys. Leticia was not just some drag clown. Sure, her walk needed work, but she was getting there. Sure, her makeup was a little too thick, but she was getting there, too. More to the point, as Averi declared, "She was happy."

DR. DONALD HOAGLAND, A PSYCHOLOGIST HIRED by the defense to interview Brandon, told us that Brandon had felt "squeezed and disgusted" when Larry sat down at the same lunch table on Monday, February 11. Brandon had quickly gotten up from the table and left. He left angry, or angrier. He was already pissed that his father was on his way back to school to meet with Ms. Romero.

Larry got under Brandon's skin. During the previous summer and fall, on several occasions, Brandon spoke with his friends about Larry; he had been speaking to his friends about his feelings of anger and aggression for nearly nine months. Brandon told friends repeatedly that he was thinking about jumping Larry.

Brandon's oldest friend was Kaj Wirsing. The boys grew up together, "down the block," as Kaj put it. In middle school years, they had drifted apart and had only managed to get together once that summer. Cruising around a shopping mall, Brandon mentioned his plan to attack Larry. Kaj knew Larry and also felt uncomfortable around him, especially in the gym locker room. Kaj spoke about how he just ignored Larry, and suggested that Brandon do the same: "I told him to let it go. Just look away."

Brandon also spoke about Larry with his girlfriend, Samantha Criner. Brandon told her about a gay kid at school, how he did not like the way this kid acted, and how he planned to attack him. Several times, Samantha told Brandon to drop it: "It wasn't worth it." But Brandon kept bringing it up, right up to the weekend before the murder, when he ran into Samantha at a beach bonfire. He told her that he was going to get in trouble at school that week; he was planning to attack Larry. Again, Samantha told Brandon that he was being "stupid." Samantha told

Brandon to let it go: "The person is gay and he is going to be gay, and just leave him alone."

Brandon could not leave it alone. His eye would not relent; he was tracking Larry and growing more agitated. Dr. Donald Hoagland told us that following the lunch incident, Brandon's brewing malice and disgust spiked. Dr. Hoagland held that Brandon had harbored "intense anger" for Larry, which magnified and telescoped after lunch to "a point of rage." A burning pinpoint, a bull's-eye.

After the lunch table incident, Brandon headed for the basketball court: his favorite part of the day. Brandon usually played with his friends Keith and Antwan, and sometimes with Louie and Zach. Brandon was not the most precise player, nor was he the fastest, but he was strong. Defense was his skill. In a more organized game he would have been a decent defensive guard. Basketball was the only part of the school day to which he looked forward.

The boys played on a grid of two courts, four netless hoops marooned on a blacktop landscape. Chalky residue and blistered white paint served as the court outlines. The gray glare and the white sky offered an almost lunar surface, an astral glow into which one could fold.

Jill Ekman, a seventh-grade language arts teacher, had lunch duty on Monday, February 11. She scanned the outdoor spaces where kids congregated, including the basketball courts at the edge of the flat expanse. She was not near the basketball court. But she looked on as Larry walked into the middle of the game. The game stopped. Kids "mobbed up." She made her way toward the court: "Everybody was laughing and carrying on about Larry asking someone to be their valentine." The bell rang. She told the kids to break it up and go to class.

Ms. Ekman did not recollect seeing Brandon as she broke up the rabble. Later in the day she heard from kids in her next class that Brandon was the intended valentine. Like Brandon, Ms. Ekman had also been tracking Larry. She was troubled by his transformation and his "forward" behavior. Ms. Ekman was particularly troubled by a report that Larry had chased a boy into a bathroom. Following the basketball court incident, her concern grew. She remained focused on the alleged bathroom incident and did not linger over the valentine.

But linger the valentine story did. Over and over again, it was said that Larry, wearing high-heeled boots, charged onto the court and asked Brandon to be his valentine. Remarkably, the durability of this story rested on its repetition, not its truth value. Not one kid or teacher could actually recollect hearing Larry ask Brandon to be his valentine.

MS. ROMERO'S SEVENTH-PERIOD SCIENCE CLASS FOLLOWED lunch. This part of the Monday, February 11, story was told by Stormy, a starchy African American girl, "a church girl," one of the local newscasters said. She sat ramrod in the witness seat, her hands folded in her lap, her long hair carefully straightened and curled.

Stormy told a detective that Larry got up from his seat during science class to get a drink of water. He walked past Brandon and said something. Brandon said something back to him. Or did Brandon say something first, and then Larry said something? Brandon got mad, his face turned red. Stormy could not hear what was said. But right after observing this exchange, she heard Brandon say, "I am going to kill him."

When Ms. Fox questioned her on the witness stand, Stormy told the same story with respect to sequence. But while she knew that Brandon's intentions were "violent," she could not recall hearing the threat of murder: "All I remember was him saying that he was going to do something, but I don't know exactly what he said."

Ms. Fox pressed, asking Storm what she meant by "violent."

Stormy said, "I don't know, you know, violent."

Ms. Fox reminded Stormy about what she had told the detective on the day of the shooting.

Stormy replied, "I don't recall."

But she did recall that Brandon blushed. Leticia made Brandon feel. And Brandon's feeling was visible. Brandon, who prided himself on not feeling, was left viscerally, reflexively exposed by his involuntary nervous system; he was hot with adrenaline and anxiety.

Leticia sassed her way through the encounter. With relish, she served the threats right back: "Whateva!" She perfumed her fear and laughed. Her hands fluttered, having given up on masculinity; it was meant for men.

After their seventh-period science class, Stormy, Larry, and Brandon headed to PE, their last class of the day. Brandon was walking with Keith. Leticia passed them coming from the opposite direction. Brandon moved to the other side of the walkway. But he could not stop tracking. He turned and looked over his shoulder toward Leticia.

"What's up, baby?" Leticia responded. Or "What's wrong, baby?" Or "I love you, baby." Or "Don't be a such a baby."

Everyone was left to guess. Beyond "baby," no one heard clearly. As Keith testified, Larry said something, but he could not make it out: "Just 'baby.' That's the word I heard."

Brandon turned red. Revealed again. Keith knew that Brandon was mad, because he had seen that face before: "I know what happens when he gets mad and he reacts." Although, contrary to Ms. Romero's testimony that boys grabbed Brandon's arm and talked loudly, Keith maintained that Brandon did not say anything and there was no physical altercation: "He held control and then just left."

Dr. Hoagland reported that Brandon insisted that "being hit on by a gay guy" was the "worst thing that ever happened to [him]." And that Brandon spoke of the "baby" moment as "the final straw that popped the balloon." This locution appears to be a mixed metaphor, but it is more akin to what George Orwell described when demonstrating how language comes undone as a mind comes undone.

BRANDON WENT ON TO PE. He joined in the game. Over and over again, his friends would say that he was "pretty much normal." As Victor put it, "He was just like the rest of us." Brandon "kept control" (as Keith observed). He controlled what others could see and know, even as he began to plan the shooting.

Brandon was known to be a clown or a clowning bear, following on his childhood nickname, which James had linked to Brandon's child-hood attachment to his toy stuffed bear. But Brandon's friends had long understood this nickname to mean something else. They took it to signify the fact that Brandon was a big kid who seemed always to be goofing around, and a kid who often got carried away with his strength. Kaj could not recall any stuffed bear, but he clearly remembered Bran-don as "a really big kid."

Others drew a more sinister link, including Brandon's childhood neighbor Conni Lawrence, who told a *Ventura County Star* reporter that her son knew Brandon throughout grade school. She had observed Brandon to "alternately be charming and a bully . . . Brandon picked on what was different."

Similarly, Averi was adamant about Brandon's potential for violence. Near the end of that school day, on Monday, February 11, she heard that Brandon was planning to jump Larry. She did not doubt that he had enough hate to carry out the threat. Nor did she doubt that he had the capability: "He said if he ever wanted to kill somebody, he had all the capabilities, that his father had guns."

As Averi was leaving school that Monday, she recollected that "Bran-don ran up to me and told me to say good-bye to Larry 'cause I wasn't going to see him again and then made kind of a weird smile and ran off." Disturbed, she nevertheless pushed off and chalked the threat up to bravado. She did not think things had gotten that far out of hand, or that Brandon would "act that stupid." She might have paid more atten-tion if she had actually seen Brandon and Larry interact more; prior to that afternoon, no one had actually seen Brandon and Larry interact much, if at all. None of the kids could recall any interaction between the two boys. In fact, Keith was not even aware of the alleged lunch table clearing.

However we think about the meaning of Brandon's nickname, it serves the scene well. You do not want to disturb a bear.

Brandon went on to gym. He ran around the outdoor track, a person split in two: As Dr. Hoagland explained, one half of Brandon stayed in the game, running, clowning, trying to trip a kid, while another part began to circle, cauterizing, burning the track he would loop for the next nineteen hours. Hate began to braid cognition as they became one.

Before the braid was pulled tight, he broadcast his intentions to attack Larry, once before and once after PE. Christian Garcia reported that Brandon approached a group of boys as they were getting ready for PE, saying things like "Nobody likes Larry." By Christian's account, Brandon tried to rally an ambush: "Get Larry in the middle and beat him up and shank him." A couple of the boys joined the bravado, but no one was willing or interested in carrying out the plan.

When asked by Ms. Fox if Brandon spoke of his plan in a manner that was joking or angry, Christian replied, "Just saying it. Just speaking." In a similar vein and illuminating how hate hides in the normal, Victor spoke of how Brandon "was just normal, like always, like all of us."

After PE, Brandon and this group of boys were walking to the front of the school where Brandon was to meet his father. Keith, who was at Brandon's side, did not recall the ambush plan. Instead, Keith recollected that Brandon told him he "was going to bring a gun the next day." At first Keith "didn't think anything of it, 'cause he was a clown."

Brandon then repeated his intention to bring a gun, and this time Keith responded, "You're not going to bring the gun. I don't believe that." Brandon persisted: "Yes, I am." Keith was shocked but could not bring his mind to believe what Brandon was saying: "I didn't pay it any mind." Keith heard the comment as "serious, but also in a jokey way." For Keith something was up, something serious, but Brandon's more typical clowning masked the gravity.

Brandon had been thinking about this attack for some time, as Kaj and Samantha told us in the first week of the trial. The plan, long thought about, suddenly unfolded rather quickly. Brandon ruminated little; he made decisions about Tuesday with speed and certainty.

As for Monday afternoon and evening? Brandon was as people had long known him to be: he smiled, goofed around, answered questions. Maybe he held himself back from the group a bit, especially when they did not join his plan. But he almost always stood alone. Keith, Brandon's so-called best friend at school, had never been to his house. As Kendra McInerney would later tell me, Brandon had no close friends, and that was how it had always been: "That was Brandon."

THE BOYS MADE THEIR WAY to the front of the school. They headed home on foot or boarded a bus amid the clatter and screech that flows at school day's end. Larry would eventually board the small bus bound for Casa. It was alleged that he was throwing kisses as he climbed aboard, a "pop star" (as Shirley Brown, one of Larry's former teachers, labeled him) waving to his fans. But, as with the claim that he had asked Brandon to be his valentine, no one could actually recall having seen him wave and throw kisses as he left the school grounds that day.

Prior to boarding various buses, kids milled around in front of the school. Or just hung out. Brandon, meanwhile, took a seat on an outdoor bench near the school entryway. Arthur Saenz, Brandon's American history teacher, had been called to the principal's office. He had arrived early, just as he arrived early to court on the day that he testified. He told us that he had paced and mopped his brow. Just as he did prior to being called by the clerk of the court.

Mr. Saenz explained to the defense cocounsel, Robyn Bramson, that one of his students had gotten into trouble at home, coming home after his curfew. The kid had falsely reported that Mr. Saenz had kept him late for detention. Mr. Saenz was set to address this story with the boy, his aunt, and Assistant Principal Joy Epstein. Authorities made Mr. Saenz anxious. That afternoon, as he reviewed his response to the student's accusation, adrenaline surged and his attention scattered. He took to the principal's office with speed, only to be kept waiting while Ms. Epstein oversaw the end of the school day.

As Mr. Saenz paced outside Ms. Epstein's door, he took note of Brandon sitting nearby. Mr. Saenz told the court that "Brandon appeared to be angry." It was "just the look in his eye."

Actually, come to think of it, Mr. Saenz recalled that the first thing he noticed was Larry walking in front of Brandon. Mr. Saenz had heard about Larry's transformation. A couple of students had tried to talk with him about Larry, but Mr. Saenz set aside their questions and stayed focused on his curriculum. You have to teach to "those damn tests," the clock is always ticking, and besides he wasn't sure how to even think about the tolerance they were supposed to be teaching. The whole thing confused him.

As he took in Larry, Mr. Saenz thought that Larry was also pacing. But pacing did not quite capture it. No, it was more like parading, or strutting, "cocking like a bird." "Somewhere between a cock and a parade," he said. From the witness stand, Mr. Saenz perched at the edge of his seat, cocked his head, danced his eyes, and limped his wrist to show us.

Ms. Bramson joined Mr. Saenz in showing us how Larry moved. Ms. Bramson strutted, thrusting her hips forward, or tried, but her sensible shoes were too heavy and her mince fell with a thud. She tossed her head back as though she were tossing long hair. She rolled her eyes at some figment or other, or at the ceiling. The tossing gesture, or her inability to mime, looked rather more like a tic, especially as it combined with the eye rolling. In her ill-fitting white suit and stiff shoes she seemed less "Larry" and more like a neurotic bride. (Following the trial, Gayle Salamon wryly coined this exchange a "duet of mockery.")

From the witness stand, Mr. Saenz told Ms. Bramson that he began to wonder if perhaps Larry was trying to capture Brandon's attention. It was something in Larry's eyes: flirtation? The click of the high heels also rang, bouncing off the cinder block walls and concrete walkway. A few kids were clustered around the bench. They were laughing. Mr. Saenz thought they were laughing at Brandon and making fun of him as the object of Larry's quest for attention.

Mr. Saenz did not consider that the kids could have been laughing at Leticia's floor show, hips forward, shoulders back, stomp, stomp, stomp, stomp, pose, eye, turn. Mr. Saenz did not have this way of seeing. He did not know about such things. Besides, he was drawn back to Brandon's enraged scowl.

Mr. Saenz's meeting with Ms. Epstein was delayed yet further. He paced some more, and he watched as Billy McInerney approached the school. Mr. Saenz made a point of greeting Mr. McInerney and telling him that that Brandon was a "very intelligent" young man. Mr. Saenz then used the opportunity to speak frankly with Brandon about his need to step it up in his history class: "You're just cruising around. You're doing nothing. I know you're doing well on the tests. But you gotta step up. You gotta do the work."

What happened next took Mr. Saenz aback, in what had already been an afternoon of the unexpected. Mr. McInerney threatened Brandon with military school. Mr. McInerney's face turned red, he asked Brandon what was going on: "What the heck is wrong with you?" Brandon pulled in, his posture and everything. He put his head down.

Turning toward Mr. Saenz's evident anxiety, Ms. Fox questioned him during her cross-examination about his observations. Yes, he had to admit that he was anxious and distracted as the scene between Larry and Brandon played out. He was further shaken by the encounter with Mr. McInerney. Also, he had to consider the way in which these events, as unexpected as they were, did not stay with him. Indeed, it was only after "the incident" that Mr. Saenz "put two and two together," and even then, quite a while after the shooting. Reconsidering, with the air of apology—had he been mistaken?—Mr. Saenz had to wonder if he had done "the math" to explain the shock of the murder.

That's one way trauma snags us: we are always retroactively doing the math as we try to add up and explain what we failed to see in time. In a way, we might think of memory as addition. Memories are built retroactively and then rebuilt and rebuilt. A witness to a murder, even someone like Mr. Saenz, who was not an eyewitness, is not faced with the simple matter of noting empirical facts and adding them up, but the urgent and ethical call to recount what happened in order to fight reality, the reality of Leticia's death, the reality that Brandon had become a murderer.

Mr. Saenz had to admit, as he spoke with Ms. Fox, that he had reconstructed or reinterpreted these events in an act of afterwordness in order to make sense of what he could not understand. He knew Brandon to be "good" and "respectful." Had he somehow been misled? Mr. Saenz had no motive to lie about what he saw. But he did have reason to try to assemble a story that would account for that which he could not account. He did have motive to gather his perceptions of that Monday afternoon and attempt to line them up with the shattering events of the day that was to follow. Looking into the middle distance, Mr. Saenz said, "This thing, this thing was hard to shake."

LATER THAT DAY—OR, AT LEAST, sometime between the Casa school bus departing E. O. Green and the next morning, Leticia deflated. We do not know if she popped like a cartoon balloon, or if she waffled and flattened like one of those new Mylar disks. But we do know that the float that carried her away from school that Monday did not return her the following morning.

Dawn Boldrin, Larry's homeroom teacher, conjectured, during an interview with me, that Larry had gotten "popped" sometime Monday evening "in a fight with another kid at Casa." The following morning, she noted that his right eye looked red, and there was a bruise on one of his wrists. Larry had, by Ms. Boldrin's account, "pushed it" that Monday afternoon. If he kept it up at Casa, she proposed that maybe some kid counterpunched. She also noted that on Tuesday morning "Larry wasn't himself, not happy, like he could be." Not falsely adapting to a world that repeatedly abused him. Not smiling as he was shunned, told that he did not belong, and cast as unthinkable.

Leticia may have been brought down by some encounter with abuse that evening, or she might have come down in the free fall of depression. Or did she intuit cruelty's approach? For surely someone as experienced as she would have known the signs. That Monday afternoon, Leticia had tried to tell Ms. Epstein that she was sick, and that she wanted to go back to Casa. (Mrs. Epstein had refused the request.)

By all accounts, Casa had been Leticia's longed-for shelter. But had the events of the school day followed her, caught her in an updraft, and thrown her out of time? The abused lose time, they lose track. (Was abuse coming? Or had it just left?) Leticia was moved along by the schedule time of residential life: groups, study hall, yard. There was dinner. There was "lights out."

Maybe Leticia slept (some). Her room overlooked a common yard and a staff parking lot. Given her long-standing habit of waking in the night, did she hover in a half state as she folded into the blue, vapor-lit curtains? Perhaps she arranged the many pillows and animals that lived with her in her plump bed. Might she have noticed how they were drained of their colorful life and turned ghostly by the blue-white light?

Brandon came home to find his Aunts Megan and Maura, and his cousin Brittney. They were busy trying to sort out Grandpa's overrun house. He sought refuge in the yard and began washing his father's old truck. He sang "I Hate Children" ("smack, smack, smack"), a song by the Nardcore band Aggression. He drank a soda, he laughed with Brittney. He teased her about the truck, telling her that someday it would be his.

Eventually, Maura and Brittney left. Megan helped the old man, who lived in a separate room at the back of the house. Dinner may or may not have been made. Billy may or may not have crashed there. The house returned to the kind of neglect that Brandon knew to be home: no one to see him.

Brandon has not described that evening. Yet we do know that at some point, he went in search of the .22-caliber handgun. He may have gone into his grandfather's gun closet as the old man slept. (The door may have been open, or Brandon may have known the combination.) The gun may have already been out somewhere in the house. He found the appropriate bullets and loaded the gun, or the gun may have already been loaded. Did he practice putting it in his pocket? Did he draw? Did he telescope and aim? He wrapped it in a white hand towel and put it somewhere for safekeeping; he has not said where.

Like Leticia, Brandon rarely slept. He played video games well into the night. The games move forward through acts of killing: that guy, then that guy, then that guy around the corner. He pulled the game-stick trigger over and over again. Limbs, chests, heads exploded. Blood pixilated. Did it stain his eyes? Or did it bleed into the dull pulse of rumination, as murder's plan looped?

5

Yeah, Leticia

The story of the murder was told within the first four days of the trial. Then it was gone. Not to return until the end of the trial, across two more days of testimony from Dr. Hoagland, a clinical psychologist for the defense.

Murder was not in the courtroom for long. But it lingered with me.

I kept waking up. One night, during the second week of the trial, I got up and wandered around my room at the Extended Stay. The dark room was surprisingly light. I was convinced that it hummed. I turned on the lights and stood in the bleaching fluorescence. I sat down to take some notes, but I could not think.

I put on some clothes, and I walked outside with my tape recorder. There, I found myself in the parking lot, where it was oddly dark for a place that was floodlit. There were nine cars and three vans. Most of them were silver.

I paced the lot's grid. Eventually, I began to talk into the recorder. I talked for forty-seven minutes, according to the time mark on the recorder. I remember talking about what it was like to bring murder into one's mind; the speed of the act: a matter of seconds; how quickly we turn from the dead; the force of murderous finality; the burden to think fairly about an act so cruel; the fear of the dark; the haunting push of anxiety that you can only feel, not name. Mostly, I recall trying to say something about the resounding trauma, as the murder returned to those whom it had inhabited, and how they were returned to the murder against their will, against their mind.

The next morning, I got up and pushed the PLAY button. I heard the sound of distant traffic, the hum of air conditioners, a high-pitched squeal (floodlights, crickets?), and the sounds of walking, rustling. This went on for a few minutes; a far-off siren pierced briefly, more sounds of walking. Then silence.

The following week, I woke in a muted scream, and before I knew what I was doing, I was standing, struggling to free myself from a sheet. 3:24 (the red digits burned). I recognized this night terror; it has snared me for years. I was swimming in murky gray-green water, I could not hear, but still knew that I heard a child, a child whom I knew to be a patient of mine. I pushed into the gray-green, struggling to see, struggling to hear. I turned one way and then the other. My chest tightened, but I kept pushing, until I woke tearing at the sheet, gasping for air.

I sat on the corner of the bed and caught my breath. I took a sip of water and choked, struggling again to breathe. Eventually, I got up, ate some stale crackers, and began to take some notes. I wondered, "What does it mean to awaken?" This was not, originally, my question. It was a question asked by Freud and later by the French psychoanalyst Jacques Lacan, as they both considered what it might mean to awaken from a traumatic dream. Freud, who famously spoke of dreams as "the guardian of sleep," spoke of such awakening as a failure of the dream to keep us asleep. We dream in order to stay asleep, perhaps especially in the face of trauma, in order to suspend that which we do not wish to know or bring into consciousness. Lacan, working alongside Freud's ideas, went a step farther and suggested that awakening brings us toward the traumatic impossibility of facing the death of another. Awakening, then, is not just occasioned by the repeated failure (swimming toward the lost child); we also wake into the repeated trauma of survival (leaving the child in the dream so as to breathe and awaken in a different place).

Three weeks later, and five weeks into the trial, I was swimming in an outdoor pool. The water was fast. The day was sunny and clear. I took a break and rested my head on the tiled edge of the pool, or rather pressed the base of my skull into the edge. Through my clouded goggles I squinted into the sun. I stayed that way for a while. It wasn't until I began swimming again and was into my fourth lap that I realized that I had been imagining being shot in the head.

The following weekend, I began to watch classic westerns: *Stagecoach*, *The Man Who Shot Liberty Valance*, *Shane*, *Red River*, *The Searchers*. A surprising number of westerns involve courtroom scenes, fathers or fathering figures teaching boys to use guns, a brown "other" (often a woman), and, as I already noted, the battle between the law of the land and the law of the territory.

I became obsessed with a scene from *Stagecoach*. I made a video of it with the camera on my phone and watched it over and over again: three men on horseback charge into a town; we see them from behind; they are filmed at a low angle; they ride away from us into the distance; they pull up in front of a saloon, the only light on the horizon; they jump off their horses; they run into the bar and shoot it up. People are screaming, women especially, and four of them, barmaids, burst out of the swinging doors, screaming, stumbling.

Slowly, during these moments of loss (the blank tape, the child I cannot find in the dream, the imagined gunshot, the barmaids screaming), I began to understand that trauma can only be written of when we are within its grip. Murder and the testimony about murder resist simple representation or comprehension. As the noted trauma theorist Cathy Caruth writes, psychic trauma is indirect. Our minds cannot collect and structure trauma in any coherent way. Consciousness lags while trauma lurks, nestled in our minds, fragmenting, undoing, and resisting cohesion.

Trauma happens so fast, it can almost be said that we know it only when it is too late. Testimony is our desperate and ethical effort to catch up, to set things right. Testimony is not the simple reiteration of facts, even if empirical facts are seen and known, as they were in this case.

Rather, testimony is an urgent story that continues to escape witnesses, even as the court report constructs the transcript.

ON THE MORNING OF FEBRUARY 12, 2008, Dawn Boldrin, Larry's and Brandon's homeroom teacher, was "running," she wrote to me in an e-mail. She had nursed the baby at five. She showered and then found a blouse that would button. She cursed those Hollywood mothers who retouched their postpregnancy photographs. She cursed the snaps of her black slacks as she put on the slacks, again. At least they fit. She grabbed her favorite cardigan.

At 7:50 with her Starbucks vanilla latte in hand, she dashed from the parking lot to Room 22, for her first-period eighth-grade English composition class. This was her second week back from maternity leave. Kids, including Larry and Brandon, squabbled in and took their assigned seats. Just about everyone was half-awake. Most of the kids had not eaten breakfast. Others bounced on a Monster or a Jolt or Doritos. Ms. Boldrin called roll. She told the kids to settle down. She told them again, this time a little louder.

Today was the day their research papers were due. They were behind. They were supposed to have read a book or studied a song that in some way reflected on tolerance. In the summer of 2011, over drinks at a local sports bar in Camarillo, Ms. Boldrin explained that "the whole unit was based on civil disobedience. Civil rights essentially is what it was. You had Anne Frank with Martin Luther King. It was a wide variety, and basically it was just focusing on differences and accepting differences. And, yes, the irony is not lost on me." The entire class had read sections from *The Diary of Anne Frank*, and that meant, according to Ms. Boldrin, that the girls were writing about Anne. The boys, again according to Ms. Boldrin, were mostly writing about Hitler: "He was popular, as well as techniques for killing, like mustard gas, different things like that. They're boys; the boys love the weaponry stuff." Larry was writing about songs from the civil rights movement of the 1960s and 1970s.

Ms. Boldrin could not believe that Larry "was still writing." Actually, he had barely begun. He could not build on anything. His work was start and start. His mind jumped around ideas; it jumped around moods and perceptions.

Brandon had made even less progress. His motivation was gone. All he had managed to do was check out a library book on the life of Hitler. Academic success was not much on his mind or the minds of many of his mates. One half of these kids would not walk across a high school stage to collect a diploma. Several would not make it to high school at all. "Girls get pregnant. Boys go to juvy. They are dropped. They are the dropped" was how Ms. Boldrin summed it up.

Ms. Boldrin will tell you that she is "strict," and that she "runs a tight ship," as she said from the witness stand. She will make a point of it, telling you more than once. But her desire to relate overrode her aspiration to be exacting with her students. She liked to talk. She enjoyed relating to the kids and wasn't put off by how they expressed themselves. Kids liked Ms. Boldrin. She was popular. She was a pretty, brown-eyed California girl with a broad smile. She wore a silver ring on her right thumb. Pop songs are written about girls like her.

Plus, Ms. Boldrin was impulsive, a quality that runs counter to the rigidity of strictness. She paused over ordering a third strawberry Cosmopolitan during our interview: "I shouldn't, but what the hell." In class, she could "pop" and yell, but that is not the same thing as being strict; indeed it may be just the opposite. That morning, she "gave it to them" for not working harder.

Larry struggled to listen. He was a cascade of tiny distractions: the fluorescent lights, their bleached blue light, the chipped edge of his nail polish, the sounds of other kids moving about, crackling like candy wrappers.

"Pay attention!" "Go to sleep!" "Stay asleep!" Larry could never get it right. He woke in the night. He never slept well, "Maybe three hours most nights," Dawn King reported. He didn't get that circadian rhythm thing. The morning was a startle. The night was a full stop. How could you get the day started when the night had never really taken hold?

Today, he was wearing no accessories, no makeup, just the standard-issue uniform: white polo shirt, blue pants, black sneakers. Well, almost no accessories. He wore a pink belt, a trace. On his way into the school that morning, he had told Ms. Epstein that he was going to have a "good day." He told her what she wanted to hear. Once inside the schoolyard, Larry told one of his classmates, Rayven Griffith, that he was "bummed out" and tired. It is not hard to imagine that Leticia was tired of being shoved against the walkway walls, tired of being called a fag, and tired of the shame.

Later, Brandon would tell Dr. Hoagland how, on that same morning, he had forgotten the gun when he left home. Billy was waiting in the car to give Brandon a ride to school, and it wasn't until Brandon came out the door of their house that he realized that he had forgotten the gun. Brandon signaled Billy to wait a minute, so that he could run back in and get it. During homeroom, prior to going to the computer lab, Brandon had unzipped his backpack, reached in, got his hand around the cool metal, shook it gently, and freed the gun from the towel. He palmed the gun and slowly put that hand in his right sweatshirt pocket.

Ms. Boldrin reiterated that they were behind, and that they were to collect their things and follow her to Room 42, the computer lab. The kids filed out. They walked along one of the outdoor sidewalks that were sheltered by an overhang, jostling and talking along the way. Ms. Boldrin walked from Room 22 to the computer lab with Larry. She described Larry as "quiet, smaller, just your typical quiet, small reserved boy" when she first met him at the beginning of the year and prior to her maternity leave. She explained that even during the two-week period of her return, when Larry "got in people's faces," that he was "actually very kind to me, always."

Ms. Boldrin thought of Larry as "sweet and simpleminded, and slow; boy, was he slow." She felt him to be less mature than his classmates, a child playing while his peers turned toward disaffection, guarded secrets, and the confused pursuit of their bodies. Ms. Boldrin placed Larry at a sixth-grade level in terms of his social maturity (an eleven-year-old, not a fifteen-year-old). She worried that he might get hurt, and in fact he had already been hurt, maybe even the day before, not to mention the countless other times.

As they walked together, Ms. Boldrin thought that Larry looked "like he was trying to be happy. He wasn't actually super happy, but he was trying." In that crevice, she tried to guide him. She knew that some of Larry's troubles stemmed from his relations with his peers. She was concerned about how his classmates were reacting to the way he was dressing, to the makeup, and to his newly polished sass.

Ms. Boldrin and her fellow teachers were not working with the idea of Larry as transgender. Lacking ways to think about or distinguish gender identity from sexuality, the teachers collapsed Larry's "obvious femininity," as Ms. Boldrin put it, with what they presumed to be a gay identity. As they walked, Ms. Boldrin let Larry know that she understood the sweep of impulse and the giddy pleasures of being girly. She knew it. She knew it in relation to her three daughters. She also told Larry that she had observed similar behavior in some gay men, including someone in her own family.

But she needed him to check the "full swing of his coming-out." She needed him to take note of his classmates, who were young and did not understand. As they walked together, Ms. Boldrin explained, "This is hard on them, and you need to maybe not be so pushy with it." She told him that he had a right to be different. But he did not have the right to demand: "You cannot make everybody believe the way you want them to believe, and it's not your right to try."

As we sat at the bar, a baseball game was on the large-screen television, which nobody seemed to be watching, I could see that Ms. Boldrin had been sincere in her wish to support Larry. But at the same time, I watched as she wrestled with her own impulsiveness; she called it "going off the cuff." She punctuated her self-descriptions with "Bam!" "Boom!" "And Bam Again!" On the Friday before the murder, Ms. Boldrin had given Larry the gift of a green dress. Previously, she had given him a small set of brightly colored nail polishes.

By the time of trial, this information about the dress had been widely circulated, had been mentioned in the local paper, and was part of what little national news coverage the story garnered. She told me that most everyone had angrily questioned her judgment in giving Larry the dress. Her fellow teachers had denounced her action. Her best friend at E. O. Green, seventh-grade language arts teacher Jill Ekman, had sharply criticized her. Dawn Boldrin defended herself: "That kid was happy!" The dress was not for school, and the gift was not from her but from her daughter. Ms. Boldrin gave the dress to Larry after class, not in front of other children.

Ms. Boldrin was harshly judged for acknowledging Larry as a girl—or, as she would have it, a gay boy. People later went so far as to say that she was responsible for Larry's death. The gift of the dress was too much. She went too far and encouraged Larry to go too far as well. Later, Ms. Boldrin would have regrets. Still, she would not back away from her wish, or his. If the clock were turned back, she would still give him the dress.

Ms. Boldrin understood people in the swing of impulse. So did Larry. He liked a party dress. So did Ms. Boldrin. "I still want the cops to give me back that dress," she said.

They got to Room 42, and Ms. Boldrin pointed to a seat for Larry at a table at the back of the class. Other kids filed in. She assigned them seats. She told them to get busy.

Brandon was one of the last to enter. He had been walking at the back of the group with his buddies Antwan and Rafael. His light brown hair was buzzed. He wore a blue hoodie that hung loosely over his school uniform, and his brown backpack was slung over his shoulder. In keeping with teenage custom, Brandon had detailed the bag. He had drawn an *X* through the second *O* on the bag's brand label: Volcom. In the four spaces created by the *X*, he had written the letters *N, A, R, D*, short for "Nardcore," the name of the punk/surf/skateboard music scene that took root in the early 1980s in Oxnard. The music scene was by now largely gone, but vestiges of surfer territorialism and beach localism held on. ("Locals Only" had been a popular song by the Nardcore band Aggression.) Along with "NARD," Brandon had penned "SSL," the tag for "Silver Strand Locals" on his bag. The two *S*'s were drawn like lightning bolts.

As Brandon entered Room 42, Ms. Boldrin pointed to a set of three chairs at the very back of the room and told Brandon to take one.

Ms. Gomez, the eighth-grade guidance counselor, immediately summoned Larry to the "fishbowl." Head down, he made his way to the small glassed-in cubicle that joined the computer lab. On their way to the lab, Ms. Boldrin, as part of her talk with Larry, had explained to him that he would have to meet with Ms. Gomez. He had not been doing his homework or completing any of his assignments. At this rate he would not graduate from eighth grade. As Gayle Salamon pointed out, he would not "walk," a phrase that rang with new meaning and consequence as Leticia was beginning to master the heels upon which eighth-grade girls teeter toward their diplomas.

Yet again, Larry was at risk of missing a childhood milestone. Yet again, he was failing. Yet again, he was the object of public scrutiny and criticism. Yet again, he was left to weather the dejection and exclusion as he made his way among his peers: lacking, defective, problematic.

Dr. Hoagland would later tell us that Brandon spoke of Larry as "a problem for everybody." Killing Larry was purifying the flock: "I thought it was a good thing to do. Everyone hated him. He was causing a problem for everybody."

The problem returned to the classroom and took his seat. Larry reached for his backpack and pulled out a handful of disorganized papers. He pushed the crumpled papers around his desk. He wrote "Leticia" at the top of a paper but didn't get any farther than that. The room was overcrowded, overlit, and overloud. Craning around their computer cubicles, kids talked to one another.

Leticia was surrounded. Perpendicular and to her left, Abiam and Jesus were sitting at a table without cubicle dividers or computers. Jesus was ribbing a girl named Jackie, who sat a few feet to his right and behind Leticia. Jackie sat next to Yuliana and Brandon in a row of three chairs that pushed up against the back of the room. Abiam and

Jackie were laughing. Yuliana was the new girl. This was her third day at E. O. Green.

Brandon sat directly behind Leticia. Quietly he pretended to read his book on Hitler. We do not know precisely what was on his mind; he has not told anyone. But we do know that he had access to the video *Tactical Readiness: Shooting in Realistic Environments*, which would have instructed him to scan the room, zoom in on the target, telescope, watch how the target moves, judge the distance, judge the angle. The video would have also coached Brandon, a seasoned marksman, to do what he already knew: rehearse the grip (finger pad, not the joint, on the trigger), use the left hand to steady the gun, point both thumbs at the target, stand with your hips and shoulders square, lean in to absorb the kickback, bend your knees slightly, sight with your left eye closed, line your right eye up with the front and rear sight, but softly, don't overfocus.

The .22 rested in Brandon's pocket, the journeyman killer's gun, the Saturday night special. The gun had been well used. Brandon had shot it lots of times when Billy took him and Brian, Brandon's half brother, Billy's oldest son, to a ragged stand of woods, where they would target practice. Brian lived with his mother but shared Billy's interest in the military and marksmanship. At the time of the murder, Brian was serving in Iraq. But on those hot childhood afternoons in the past, they had retreated to the wooded shade, where they had shot at cans, bottles, trees, rocks, bits of trash, and the occasional bird. Brandon was a good, practiced shot. He had fired hundreds of rounds using the .22 and a variety of other guns. He had studied marksmanship; he had read manuals and watched instructional videos (some of them easily found online).

Brandon sat quietly for about five minutes as the other kids talked or worked on their papers.

Then Jackie, taunting Larry, asked, "Are you changing your name?"

Larry answered, "Yeah. Leticia."

Jesus laughed.

Two to three minutes passed.

Brandon stood up, reached into his pocket, pulled out the gun, raised it straight up, fully extended his arms, got his sight aligned, and pulled the trigger. His heart was thrumming with determination. He took a quick breath to quiet the noise, the recoil. He stood, squared with his target (now slumped), corrected his sighting, and fired a second round. Two or three seconds had passed.

The problem was solved.

The shots hit Leticia at the base of her skull. Dr. Ronald O'Halloran, the Ventura County chief medical examiner, explained that it was not clear which shot hit first. Gunshot number one, as Dr. Halloran nevertheless called it, "fragmented as it pierced the skull just above the base and traveled left to right through the occipital region." Fragments, microrazors, tore through other parts of the right side of Leticia's brain. This shot, Dr. Halloran explained, "caused extensive trauma to the brain and was the major source of trauma to the body." The shot tagged as number two hit the top of Leticia's neck at the base of her skull on the left side. That bullet did not enter the skull; rather, it grazed it, pierced Leticia's cheek, and ended up just behind her left cheekbone.

Vision, the primary function of the occipital lobe, was likely the first brain function to go. How did it go? Did it explode? Did it pinpoint? How did hearing fade? Was "Leticia" still practicing her ear? Was it Jesus laughing? Or was it the explosion of the gun? Did Leticia know, if only in the quiver of a millisecond, the tripping of the hair trigger that the traumatized know too well?

The time was just shy of 8:30. It was sixty-seven degrees and clear.

Dr. O'Halloran and the paramedics believed that Larry immediately lost consciousness. Others were less sure. Joy Epstein, who ran from the central office to the classroom, breathlessly calling 911, believed that Larry struggled to find her voice as Ms. Epstein spoke his name. She also believed he was in pain. Similarly, a police officer thought Larry responded to his name as he spoke to him later in the emergency room, even after Larry had been sedated.

In the immediate aftermath, though, the eyewitnesses struggled even to find Larry in the room. Did he fall? Was he on the floor? Yuliana thought so. Abiam thought so. Mariah wasn't sure. Nor was Jesus.

Horror had fractured surrounding time, space, even personhood. As Yuliana put it, "I was just shock. Everybody was just shock."

Even as there was no space between shock and self, as the shots rang—one, beat, beat, two—everyone reflexively searched for the source of the noise. Many of the kids in the class and in neighboring classes thought balloons were popping.

Ms. Boldrin, who was at the front of the class, turned, thinking the noise was "an explosion." From the witness stand, she explained, "When I turned, I saw the smoke, and then I definitely thought it was a computer exploding or a firecracker."

Looking across the room and over the computer cubicles, she could see that Brandon was standing. She screamed, "What the hell are you doing?" She could not say how, but somehow she understood that he was the source of the noise. She wondered if she knew because Brandon "was the most still person in the room." Then again, she said, "The truth is, I just didn't know what I was seeing at that point."

Ms. Boldrin's scream was punctuated by the second shot. She still could not see the gun and continued to think that Brandon was exploding firecrackers. She watched as he appeared to drop something, pulled up the hood of his sweatshirt, and walked out the door to his immediate left at the back of the room.

She found it hard to reconstruct what she did next. She knows that she was screaming. She knows that she yelled at the kids, instructing them to exit through a door at the front of the class: "But I don't recall the steps that I took to do it." During our interview, she recalled seeing blood on Yuliana's shoes, and said, "It was like her second day. She didn't even know Larry's name." Ms. Boldrin noticed that her own blouse was wet, but did not understand how that could have happened. While recalling these chaotic moments for me, Ms. Boldrin suddenly realized something had happened to another of her students: "Jackie just disappeared. Her mom had overdosed a few years before the shooting. I'm not sure anyone knows where she is."

Perception, memory, history, time lost hold. Every witness was left to narrate and reconstruct from inside shock. Mere feet away from Brandon, Abiam turned with the first shot. He heard Ms. Boldrin scream. He froze: "I look at Brandon again, I'm staring at him, and then the second one goes off, and then—I know what happened, but I—I blanked like." Abiam could not recall seeing the gun. It was the sound that stayed with him.

As Brandon opened the door to leave the room, Abiam's eyes followed him. He watched as Brandon folded into the sun and a populated residential street. It was not until the day after, as he explained to his brother what had happened, that Abiam realized that he "saw something that wasn't there." As his brother helped him to recognize, there are no houses or people outside that door. There is a drab huddle of three portable classrooms.

With the kind of gravity that we associate with the elderly whose minds have been rearranged with grief, Abiam looked down, lost in recollection on the witness stand. He shook his head. He did not look up as he continued, "And then I looked to my left, and I see Larry on the ground. He was looking at the sky."

E. O. Green became pandemonium, a palace in the middle of hell. Sentries got word to the central office. Guards were called, the police, paramedics. Warnings were broadcast: "Lockdown. Lockdown. This is not a drill. Lockdown." Doors were locked and barricaded, windows shuttered. Frantic children took cover under their desks. Frantic teachers put their hands over their mouths to signal the need for silence. Noises ran along the outdoor walkways. Sirens approached.

Dawn Boldrin had "pushed" her kids into the adjoining room at the front of the computer lab. She yelled to Ms. Gomez, "He has a gun, he has a gun, he's shooting!" Speaking in the present tense even after Brandon had walked out the door, even though she had never seen the gun. Ms. Boldrin could not exactly recall how she knew that Brandon had a gun. Ms. Boldrin explained to Ms. Fox, "I don't know. Again, I don't know how I knew that's what happened after that had happened." Decisive sequence and definitive knowing were not up for the offing.

Then "it clicked that Larry was in there and that he had shot Larry. I don't know how I knew, but I did," Ms. Boldrin explained, continuing to tell us that she never saw Larry as he lay on the black-and-white tile floor, bleeding out, thrashing, and vomiting. That job fell to Catherine Womack, a speech and language therapist, and David Rodriguez, a school psychologist, who worked in the portable buildings opposite the computer lab. They came running when they heard popping sounds and Ms. Boldrin screaming. Mr. Rodriguez had correctly and "regrettably" understood the sounds to be gunshots.

Ms. Womack saw a body, flailing, and "blood, a lot of blood." Disoriented, she eventually grasped that it was Larry. She called his name, but he did not respond. It was then that she saw the gun lying near his body. She kicked it across the room thinking that he had attempted suicide, and as if he could reach for it again.

Mr. Rodriguez, who was on Ms. Womack's heel, went immediately to Larry, took out a handkerchief, and attempted to stanch the blood flowing from the back of Larry's head. The small white square quickly reddened. His hands dripping with blood, Mr. Rodriguez shouted for paper towels, anything that he could use to stop the "rhythmic spurting blood." Gray, avuncular Mr. Rodriguez raised his palms up as he sat in the witness stand as if to show the blood and the helplessness as it continued to flow.

The paramedics arrived and began their methodical six-handed blur: Direct pressure and occlusive dressings were applied to the external hemorrhaging, Leticia's clothes were cut away as she was quickly assessed for other wounds, her airway was checked—breath sounds were shallow—her neck was braced, she was strapped to a body board and hoisted onto a gurney, then they ran, ran down the hallway, ran out the door and into the ambulance. They ran with Leticia, who was dying but not yet dead.

WHEN BRANDON LEFT THE BUILDING, he walked into the gray-white concrete glare that led from the school. He skirted the mentholated edge of McCarty Park and its stand of towering eucalyptus trees. He crossed a dry concrete ravine and walked into the grid of bleached boxy houses that bordered the school and led to his house. His hood was up. His ears rang.

He took out his cell phone and called his father. He told him he was going to be arrested. It was 8:36 AM. Billy would later tell Detective Mike Young at the Oxnard Police Department, "He said he was getting arrested. I didn't want to get any more into it." Kendra, however, reported that Billy called her to say that Brandon had been arrested and that there had been a shooting. Confused and frightened, she cried, "Did Brandon shoot somebody?" Billy told her, "I haven't talked to him."

Brandon was arrested ten minutes after the murder. He was about a half mile from the school, still a long way from home. Officers in an unmarked car spotted him walking fast and talking on his cell phone. The cops slowed down, turned around, pulled alongside him, and asked if they could speak with him.

Brandon offered no resistance, saying, "I did it. I'm the one who shot him."

When Mr. Wippert asked the arresting officer, Peter Freidberg, if Brandon had expressed remorse upon arrest (the question for which Wippert was held in contempt), the officer replied, "No. He just seemed confused."

Footage taken at the Oxnard police station a half hour following Brandon's arrest showed him sitting in a small room with a table and two plastic chairs. He put his forehead directly on the table. Limp, he did not move. Brandon sat up when Detective Mike Young entered the room. Detective Young spoke directly and with the resonance of a father's grief. He asked Brandon where he lived. Detective Young mentioned skateboarding and martial arts. Brandon answered the questions with a crisp programmed "Yes, sir" or "No, sir." He did not make eye contact. He did not move. Nothing was said about the shooting.

Detective Young left, and Brandon sat alone for a long time, his head once again on the table, not moving. The detective returned, took some photos, and removed the handcuffs. Brandon silently complied. His fingers were tested for gunpowder residue. He offered his hands without comment. He was then alone again and slumped forward across the table. Out of sight of the camera, the detective or someone else tossed Brandon a bag of chips and slid a bottle of water across the table. Brandon opened the bag, ate two chips, took a drink of water, then stopped and placed his head back on the table.

Detective Young returned. Brandon was asked to undress. He did so silently while the detective took a series of pictures. Brandon's clothes, now evidence, were put in brown paper bags, the crinkling of which made the most noise during these scenes. He was given a large white paper jumpsuit. He put it on, the proper costume for a ghost. The end of this day would never end.

Billy and Kendra were interviewed in a separate room. As details of the morning unfolded, Billy cried out as if to refute or push back the words of the detective: "Was there a fight? Inside a classroom? No, no, no, no, no, no!"

Kendra screamed. She steadied herself with a hand on the edge of a chair. She mumbled over and over again: "Oh my God. Oh my God. Oh my God." She interjected, as much as asked, "How?" How could this happen? Then, "This is not happening."

She asked about "the boy": "Is he in the hospital? Will he live?" The officer told her that they did not know. She looked down and repeated his words twice: "We don't know if he is going to live. We don't know if he is going to live."

Later footage of Kendra and Billy during what was called a "visitation" showed them clutching and caressing Brandon. Billy, as if blinded, cried and called into the room, to the gods, "What has happened? What happened to Brandon? I don't understand. How did this happen?"

Brandon's answer, as though he were deaf, was to stand among them, oversized, silent, stiff, whited-out.

The small room was made yet smaller by the abundance of chairs that lined its walls. They stood like mismatched sentries, surrounding Brandon and his parents.

"I shot him," Brandon said.

Kendra and Billy wept and embraced him. Kendra said, "I love you more than anything. We will do everything. Pray, Brandon! Pray to God! We will get through this. Whatever happens, it will not be forever. We will get through this."

Billy continued to wail, yelling, "What am I going to do?"

Kendra maneuvered them into three of the chairs, saying, again, "No matter what, Mommy and Daddy are here." She looked at Billy, who sat on the other side of Brandon, and said, "Billy! You have to be strong for Brandon."

Billy spoke inaudibly.

Brandon said, "Does James know?"

Kendra said, "Thank God, no."

Brandon said, "Tell him no one will fall."

Billy told Brandon, "You can't talk to anybody," as Kendra spoke over him: "We will be praying for you. We are here for you. Pray that he is alive."

Interrupting, a police officer stuck his head in the doorway and told them that they had to wrap up their visit. Brandon was about to be transported to the Ventura County Juvenile Center, where, as it turned out, he would live for the next three years.

Billy stood and said, "We need to talk to a lawyer and figure out what happened."

Kendra attempted to stand but crumbled to the floor; prostrate, she grabbed Brandon's shins and wept uncontrollably. Brandon gently helped her to a chair.

Kendra struggled to her feet, then she and Billy held Brandon as if to buoy him.

As Brandon left the room with the police officer, Kendra said, "You are the love of my life." And then she called after the officer, saying, "I am so sorry. Is there any way that we can keep track of how the boy is doing, who the boy is?"

The officer did not answer.

LETICIA WAS A LESS-DEAD GHOST, still on the border. She was, by that time, in the emergency room of St. John's Regional Medical Center. Her heart rate was stable. She could not open her eyes, but her pupils were reactive, indicating some brain function. She continued to thrash and seize. She was administered morphine and Dilantin, a seizure medication. She was restrained. She was intubated because she was struggling to breathe.

Dawn King had been running some errands and happened to be near E. O. Green when she noticed "an army" of police cars speeding toward the school. Dawn turned toward the school, parked her car, and got out. Officers were busy marking off the area with yellow tape. A small neighborhood crowd had started to gather. Sirens continued to approach. It seemed from every direction, perhaps even the sky.

People were talking about a shooting. She pushed her way forward until she could get the attention of a police officer. She told him that her sons were inside. He replied that such was the case for many of the people who were beginning to gather. She told him that her boys were Larry and Rocky King. He told her to wait.

"It's a wonder I could stay on my feet," Dawn recalled. Then with the rattle of her characteristic smoker's laugh, she continued, "Hell, I didn't. Good thing there was a cop car there to catch me." She leaned against the car. The noise closed in. Why did they tell her to wait?

A short way off she heard, "the victim's mother." She held on to the car; she struggled to catch her breath. Quickly, quietly (what were they saying?), two officers explained that Larry had been shot and that he was on his way to St. John's Hospital. They explained that they would take her in a squad car. She asked about Rocky. They told her that the school was in lockdown. She demanded they get him. She was not leaving without him.

And suddenly, she and Rocky were sirened into an emergency room. Clutching Rocky, she struggled to see Larry amid the nurses, doctors, tubes, lights, cops, and curtains. On the way in the car, this was not what she had imagined. She "saw Larry talking," and she was talking to him. But why was there a tube down his throat? Why was half his face bandaged? Why was he not moving? Why was he not talking? He never stopped talking.

Was it a doctor? Or was it a cop? Maybe it was a nurse who kept saying "shots to the head," as Dawn's mind spun in a violent revolt. She stepped forward and reached for Larry's hand, restrained at the wrist. She said, "It's okay, Mama is here, Mama is here." Tears (when had she begun to cry?) streamed down her face. She searched the room for order (this was a school day), identity (she was a mother), or rules (children are not shot in the head).

Dawn had tried to reach Greg at work, but there was no cell reception where he worked. The police found a way to contact Greg's boss, who told him that he needed to go to the hospital. Something had happened to Larry. The police had been vague with details, but they had offered to come and drive him. Greg decided that it would be faster to drive his own car. On his way to the hospital, he listened to a talk radio program, where it was reported that a boy had been shot and killed at E. O. Green; the boy's name was being withheld until the family had been notified.

When he arrived at the hospital, Greg was met by the same confusion that had overtaken Dawn, made even more unthinkable by the fact that he thought Larry was dead. But, unlike Dawn, Greg made order; he threatened it into place even when the odds were stacked against him. A former military man, he believed in authority and the chain of command. He focused on the surgeon's assessment. The worry was swelling and infection. The solution was an induced coma. There was talk of transferring Larry to UCLA for surgery once he stabilized.

Larry was taken to the hushed world of the ICU. Dawn sat with him. Mortality seeped into her. Greg shook off the shock and paced. He set about to collect details from the outside world.

Earlier, he had spoken with the cops: "The first time I heard Brandon McInerney's name was in the ER," Greg would later tell me. At that point, though, Brandon was a vague actor. Greg did not spend a lot of time thinking about him. No, in this hell, Greg raged at "the system" and the misguided authorities that had already come between him and his son. Greg lived in a world inhabited by a vengeful god. Brandon would pay his price, but so, too, would the "child abuse industry" and the "school who had decided parents didn't matter anymore." They would pay for not listening to him.

Greg, Dawn, and Rocky eventually found their way home. It was dark when they left the hospital. The cool California evening released them from the hospital's dead air. Larry's shooting was at the top of the local TV news. A report was recorded in front of E. O. Green, where a shrine was beginning to collect around a tree: a Mylar balloon, a stuffed bear, notes, cards. *Veladoras* huddled/clustered on the sidewalk; many of the candles commemorating a particular saint—St. Jude, Miraculous Mother, the Sacred Heart. To Dawn's ear, the news was delivered by a woman too eager to be speaking about death.

She watched as Rocky let the dog out the back door. She began to cry as she thought about how Larry "had loved that silly little dog," a simple bond, a trust of which Larry knew so little. Dawn would later tell me that she often walks out the door and into the yard. She softly beseeches, "Larry?"

Dawn Boldrin saw the same news footage. It marked the beginning of her habit of watching television crime shows well into the night, night upon night: "You know, those *Unsolved Myster[ies]*–type things." She is not sure she slept. She recalled nursing the baby. And it was then that she thought back to her wet blouse: "I had leaked breast milk. It is some kind of fear/flight thing," she told me. She worried that her inability to stop weeping would harm the baby.

Just past midnight, Leticia suffered a stroke. Lightning and oblivion passed, brain function stopped, and veiled infinity opened. Larry was pronounced brain dead at 2:00 AM on February 13.

The Kings reported getting a phone call early Wednesday morning from the attending physician at the hospital, informing them that Larry had suffered a stroke. They did not debate ending life support. But then came the question of organ donation. Dawn didn't like the gruesome thought of knives cutting her child. Generosity was not much on her mind. But Greg convinced her; someone could be helped. It was the right thing to do.

And so it was around that idea of help that the Kings undertook the day. Larry's death quickly became his organ donation, a story that just as quickly became a romance that sought to fend off the story of Leticia's life. Multiple organs and lung tissue were harvested.

Leticia's organs took off by helicopter. Her cadaver was zipped into a blue body bag and wheeled to the morgue. The body bore two identification bracelets. On the right ankle: LAURENCE [*SIC*] KING. On the left ankle: JOHN DOE (a placeholder for a party whose true identity is unknown).

Greg reportedly heard and proudly maintained that Larry "saved seven people's lives," including the romantic detail that on the following day, February 14, Valentine's Day, Larry's "heart and lung tissue went to a ten-year-old girl."

PART TWO

———

HATE

6

Sad, Real Hate

Detective Swanson: The big question here is not so much that the crime happened, there's no question about that.

Mr. Wippert: It's why.

Detective Swanson: The question is why.

Mr. Wippert: That's the hardest question to answer, right?

Detective Swanson: It wasn't hard for me.

Foursquare detective Dan Swanson was the prosecution's hate crime expert. Even as he crested forty years of age, he remained astronaut handsome. A twenty-year veteran of the Simi Valley Police Department, Detective Swanson had spent much of his career working on gang-related crime. For ten years, beginning in 2000, he had focused on the rise of white supremacist organizations in Southern California.

On July 18, 2011, the tenth day of the trial, Detective Swanson took the stand, testifying as the prosecution's key and final witness. The defense finished cross-examining him twenty-four days later, on August 11. Detective Swanson was not on the stand all that time, though it sometimes seemed as if he were. His testimony on behalf of the prosecution took three days, but his cross-examination was then delayed by two weeks, after the judge ruled in favor of a defense petition that allowed them additional time to prepare: the defense claimed that Detective Swanson's presentation for the prosecution included materials—charts, graphs, photographs, videos—that the defense should have seen prior to his testimony.

Allegations about hate and arguments about violence rarely left the stand after Detective Swanson's first day of testimony, whether or not he was in the witness chair. His testimony set the terms for the deliberation that would come to define the trial.

The prosecution held: that Brandon was a murderer; that he was a member of a criminal street gang, enflamed by white supremacist ideology; that he hated in keeping with his clan; that he was a self-declared vigilante homophobe; and that he had hunted and executed a gender-variant kid.

The defense countered: that Brandon was a well-liked kid from a close-knit beach town; that there was no gang and no white supremacist influence, but rather the presence of an oppressive police force; that Brandon had seen hard times, including abuse and neglect; that he had run afoul of the law, as had many in his community, but that he was a good kid, a "normal boy," who had been pushed by sexual harassment into the ruin of manslaughter.

ONE AFTERNOON NEAR THE END of the trial, I met Detective Swanson for lunch at Rich & Richer, a Thai restaurant in a strip mall. Double Windsor, square jaw, he was the kind of guy who sat facing the door.

We ordered lunch and began talking. Eventually, we ordered dinner. He ordered five iced coffees. After ordering his fifth, the waiter tried to cut him off: "Too many ice coffee, too many." Then the waiter turned to me and pleaded, with good humor, "Tell him, too many, no good."

I laughed. I was, after sitting through six days of his testimony, familiar with the will behind Detective Swanson's order.

AT ONE POINT DURING OUR lunch, Detective Swanson said, "I'm like a dog with a car."

From the witness stand, he repeatedly made a case for the chase, for the expansiveness of going after more evidence and yet more: "It's all about the totality of everything involved, not a single item or belief."

He followed a kind of additive reasoning, adding on and adding on in order to construct an irrefutable argument. He would not confine his testimony. He spoke in paragraphs, fast paragraphs, packed with detail. As Kathleen De La O, the court reporter, put it to me in an e-mail, "Swanson was one of the two hardest witnesses I have taken in my career. The density, speed, and syntax were crazy-makers!"

During Ms. Fox's direct examination, Detective Swanson turned the court into his reluctant classroom. He traced the roots of modern-day white supremacy, tracking it from the Ku Klux Klan and Nazism to modern-day white supremacist organizations (in particular, the Confederation of Racialist Working Class Skinheads) to Brandon McInerney's front door.

Detective Swanson itemized racist organizations, big and small. He cataloged their symbols. Named their leaders, national and local. Described their crimes and vigilante brutality. He used charts, lists, photographs, and videos to illustrate their carnage.

"It's all part of the puzzle," he would say over and over, as he launched into elaborate explanations that often created more of a puzzle than they solved. When Ms. Fox asked about the role of violence in the white supremacist movement, Detective Swanson answered, "Not everybody who is identified as a white supremacist is going to go commit an act of violence. No. It's always an individual. You have to evaluate each individual case on its specific merits, which is why when you're talking about the subject in general as I was doing from an historical standpoint, that's to give a perspective and understanding of what it means. Remember, I talked about from the very beginning, it's an umbrella.

"When those same people live in the same geographic area, they typically form what we call a white supremacy gang, even though the turf aspect of a gang is really not an aspect of what connects them. It's their ideology and common belief.

"Yet, I have never run across a group that solely said . . . 'We promote separatism. . . .' What I have come across is a variety of organizations that will mention 'We do not condone unprovoked acts of violence or acts of violence that are not promotional for the cause,' but then they always put the caveat, 'We do condone acts of violence against—to defend ourselves or to defend some member of the race.'

"They leave that little caveat in there because they recognize the reality of how they're [going to] run across some situation where there's going to be violence. That's the nature of how they operate."

As Detective Swanson spoke, one idea seemed to trip the wire of the next idea and the one after that. He would chase each idea with steely determination and reiteration. His speech pushed into the courtroom with a kind of polite pugnacity. His wish to be right drove him to the "the next . . ." and "the next . . ." as he sought to school us with dates, names, symbols, signs, maps, and timelines. In his quest to summarize history's slow march, he elaborated and complicated, and he did so with obsessive speed.

Dawn King fell asleep. A juror's head nodded forward, and she jerked herself back to attention. Brandon's aunt audibly yawned. Those who had probably been better students when they were in school shifted in their seats.

On the first day that Detective Swanson testified, I passed Mr. Wippert in the hall during a break. He looked at me, arched his eyebrows, and said, "Riveting, eh?" After Detective Swanson's second day of testimony, Mr. Wippert shouted to me across the shimmering, ninety-seven-degree parking lot, "Had enough school?"

Mr. Wippert rarely spontaneously spoke to me, much less shouted, but when he did, it was usually to joke, as if we were a couple of smart-ass high school boys laughing at unearned authority. Much of the time, I think Mr. Wippert perceived me with fair accuracy, and that included these joking occasions. I knew much of what Detective Swanson was teaching, or I knew enough. And yes, I was impatient, as I had been with overprepared teachers who turned over every detail in such a way as to muddle rather than clarify.

Near the end of Detective Swanson's direct testimony, Ms. Fox made an effort to get him to summarize his opinion as to why "the defendant killed Larry King." She beckoned with her hands, spinning them one over the other, as if to say, "speed it up."

Detective Swanson said, "Bias against Larry King's perceived gender and sexuality pushed Brandon McInerney to murder. White supremacy and gang affiliation supported that bias, period." Such punctuation had not been our experience of Detective Swanson until then.

In the cascade of Detective Swanson's rapid-fire history lesson, ideas about hate, and, in particular, ideas about the nature of bias and hate that are directed toward gay and transgender people, got left behind in World War II. We learned about how homosexuals were targeted and killed by the Nazis. But there was no attempt to account for how the bias Brandon allegedly harbored might have been triggered by something personal, or even social, in the form of ordinary homophobia or transphobia. Instead, the prosecution focused exclusively on the bias of white supremacist and Nazi ideologies.

At one point, Detective Swanson did link the seeds of white supremacist bias with the ways in which it fosters racial and homophobic violence. "White supremacists see themselves as having been robbed of white privilege, as other races are breeding faster, and taking valuable resources and space. To win back their white power, they advocate the preservation of a pure and superior white heterosexual race. Such preservation calls for the elimination of homosexuality ('a crime against Nature')."

But as Detective Swanson's testimony wore on, the network of ideology, symbolism, criminality, and hate that he so earnestly and exhaustively sought to make *specific* paradoxically became *abstract*.

The hate and violence he detailed seemed far removed from the boy sitting in front of him, wearing a pink shirt and a gray sweater vest with white piping. Brandon became an abstract hater, an ideologue. Larry became a theoretical homosexual, tied to vague implications about reproduction.

FROM THE START OF THE trial, weekends left me pacing in Room 230 at the Extended Stay. I tried to write, to read, to cull my notes, but I was too restless. Laundry took up an hour or so. I could eat only so many Cheetos from the vending machine. I went outside and paced the empty industrial neighborhood that surrounded the hotel. The July heat beat up and down, from the gray-white streets and the white-hot sky. In the manner of a mirage, it seemed as if the shimmering heat was constructing the unpopulated, uncertain buildings as I passed them by. I welcomed the clarifying rattle and reality of a nearby freight train.

On my second weekend, I drove around Brandon's and Larry's neighborhoods. I drove to E. O. Green and got out of the car with my camera in hand. Opened in 1960, the unadorned, one-story pale, green-and-white cinder block building is situated on a broad expanse of grass and asphalt playing fields. The building's form follows function. Classrooms line up at ninety-degree angles, forming grids that are joined by outdoor walkways, a structure at once barren and airy.

I walked around, taking pictures. I aimed my camera between a fence and a gate to get a photograph of Classroom 42. But like a school closed for the summer, the place felt forbidden and forlorn. The only sounds were the noise from the traffic speeding by on busy South C Street.

I walked the path I surmised Brandon would have taken after the shooting. It was all concrete glare, sidewalks that abutted two-lane streets, houses that seemed as much driveway as house. I stood on the corner where Brandon was arrested. A car came one way and then another car the other way. Whatever story that corner had to tell seemed long gone.

The neighborhood was as eerily empty as the school. I had seen a few kids playing in the park near the school and a couple of men working on a motorcycle in a garage. The bleached bungalows showed few signs of life. Blinds were drawn to the white, Southern California mid-day sun. Here and there, something green: a ragged palm, an orange tree, a willful bougainvillea vine. Here and there, evidence of children: an overturned dirt bike, a toy truck, a faded plastic basketball hoop, the orange rim gone to soft cherry.

Brandon's house announced McINERNEY with a carved wooden plaque in the front window. The greeting and the house, a one-story ranch that looked more like a cabin, stood apart from its prefabricated neighbors. The McInerney house looked like a weathered sailor in the wrong part of town. Human hands had been involved. The house was paneled in cedar, which had become worn and dry, and was pulling away. A hose coiled on the sidewalk; a scrawny rose of Sharon stood near the door; a wooden starfish held up by nautical rope hung on the door that someone had begun to paint white, but had given up, halfway up, a long time ago.

Following Larry's death, his family moved away from the house in which he had grown up. Their new two-story white house stood marooned and unadorned on a corner of scorched grass. The front door had been repaired with plywood and did not look usable. A decorative fan-shaped window peeked over the plywood, a withheld greeting. It was as if the house had no face. I sensed that the door mattered little, because the Kings most likely came and went through the garage. The driveway took up much of the front yard. The Kings' white van was parked there, a yellow SUPPORT OUR TROOPS decal plastered on the hatchback door.

ON MY THIRD WEEKEND, I drove seventy-six miles up the coast from Chatsworth to a hotel in Santa Barbara with a saline lap pool. From that point on, I left the court every Friday afternoon, drove to Santa Barbara, and returned to Chatsworth on Sunday evenings. I spent those weekends swimming until my shoulders gave out, and it was a struggle to hoist my small suitcase into the car to head back. In between swims, I sat outside, taking notes.

On my first weekend in Santa Barbara—which, as it turned out, followed on Detective Swanson's direct testimony—I befriended eighteen-year-old Alex Ramirez, a pool attendant. He was a big kid, with big feet. His round face was made yet more so by a halo of buzzed, coarse black hair.

"What are you doing?" he asked. He was not looking at me but at my chair, covered with books and stacks of notes. I looked around and granted that I did look like a librarian at a pool party. It was a clear blue day, and most everyone else was listening to music, napping, or reading paperback mysteries.

I laughed, as if to say that the chair was not me. Then I explained that I was working on a book, that I was attending a trial in order to write about it. Alex asked about the trial, and as I began to give him the basics, he excitedly interrupted me, saying, "Yeah! Do you think he's a Nazi?"

"No, I don't think he's a Nazi," I said.

Alex had been reading about the trial in the *Ventura County Star*. "But I knew about it, like when it happened," he said. "You know, I knew about it from the news, the TV, like the day it happened. I was in eighth grade, too."

With barely a pause, he began to speak of another murder, the murder of a boy in his Santa Barbara neighborhood, who was shot and killed in July of 2008, five months after Larry died.

"I came home, and it was on the news. It was like, I couldn't believe it. I knew him. Unreal. There were helicopters. My mom made me stay inside, for like a week."

He smiled, and that is when I noticed his stern metal braces. Over time, I would note that on any given day the mismatched bands that joined the upper and lower braces were green, red, or yellow, one day, pink.

Alex was the same age as Larry, and he was also the same color. Here was a brown boy following the murder of another brown boy in the local paper. I asked if he could remember what he thought when he first learned about Larry's murder.

He looked down and softly said, "Sad, real hate."

Over Alex's shoulder stood the stucco clubhouse. Two miniature orange trees bracketed the entryway. The box hedges were perfectly manicured, and a vine crept up the side of the building, from which saffron trumpet flowers drooped in the afternoon sun.

This was the other California. Water was served with cucumber slices.

Alex began to speak about how parts of Oxnard were "rough." His mom would not let him go there. He said that there were "a lot [of] gangs, and a lot of kids get killed."

I knew he was speaking almost exclusively about brown kids, the majority of the kids at E. O. Green. He was talking about brown kids like himself and Larry.

One of Alex's fellow workers called to him from across the pool. We were interrupted.

Swimming laps that afternoon, I pondered the way in which anti-black racism was being denied and stripped of meaning in the court. Because race had been deemed inadmissible as evidence in relation to the hate crime, it entered the trial only through the defense team's cross-examination and in reference to the charge of Brandon's budding white supremacy. Witnesses were routinely asked if Brandon had black or brown friends, to which they all said yes. Over and over, we were presented with the friend defense. Brandon played basketball with a couple of black kids, and that association was held up as evidence to refute racism.

Antiblack racism could only be denied, not examined. The court instructions left us to see Larry as black, but we were not invited to think of him as black. We could see but not recognize, which is precisely one of the ways in which racism functions. Not long after the trial, in the wake of the deaths of Eric Garner and Mike Brown, discussions about black invisibility would once again erupt in the United States.

But in 2011, in the Superior Court of California, Larry's brown life barely registered.

"IF YOU WANT TO UNDERSTAND the person, you got to go through their stuff," Detective Swanson explained to Mr. Wippert as they spoke about the search of the McInerney home on the afternoon of the shooting.

On the third day of his testimony, Detective Swanson set aside history and ideology (to the extent he was able) and commented specifically on a set of Brandon's drawings, some found in his home and some found at the murder scene, in his backpack.

In answer to Ms. Fox's questions about the drawings, Detective Swanson brought them into evidence as data points that illustrated Brandon's engagement with white supremacy and the Silver Strand Locals (SSL). The SSL was a gang that had yet to be "stepped up"; in other words, law enforcement, including Detective Swanson, believed there was a street gang that operated in Silver Strand, but as of the time of the trial, no one who was an alleged member of the SSL had been charged with a "gang enhancement." California law, through the STEP Act, charges and punishes convicted gang members more harshly (sentences are enhanced).

Brandon had not been charged as a gang member, a point to which Mr. Wippert returned repeatedly, but Detective Swanson saw the drawings as evidence of Brandon's allegiance to the SSL and white supremacist ideology. Two hundred and four of Brandon's hand-drawn symbols were tagged. Fifty-six referenced the SSL; others referenced Nazism and white supremacy. Particular images, such as swastikas, the SSL tag, deadheads, lightning bolts, were, indeed, pervasive. Detective Swanson emphasized to Ms. Fox that "the difference here is context, the quantity, to the exclusion of other things." He reiterated to Mr. Wippert, "It's the repetition that becomes significant because it shows influence and it shows adherence."

Along with the pervasive and repeated images, which Detective

Swanson traced to their Nazi, neo-Nazi, white supremacist, racist, and gang sources, a number of "unique drawings," he noted, combined or blended symbols from the Nazi era with skinhead and white supremacist symbols. Detective Swanson held that these drawings signaled the bond between Brandon and Matt Reaume, James Bing's roommate at the time of the murder, and a well-known member of the Silver Strand community. Detective Swanson said of one of the drawings, "I have never seen this anywhere else except in Matt Reaume's home and Mr. McInerney's drawing."

Routinely and adamantly, Mr. Wippert questioned the meaning of the drawings and the meaning of the very act of drawing; how much did the drawings tell about Brandon and his beliefs? What was their truth value? Drawing did not make one a white supremacist, Mr. Wippert asserted. And Detective Swanson reasserted that it was the contextual link to white supremacist symbols, the quantity of the drawings, their repetition, and the accumulated knowledge found within them that made them significant.

Detective Swanson rarely attributed emotion to the drawings, focusing instead on the symbols and on how far Brandon had traveled down white supremacy's path. His caution regarding how to look upon drawings as expressive, or as routine ways that people emote and make meaning, was shared, if not magnified, by the teachers from E. O. Green, who either claimed no knowledge of the drawings or scoffed at them, dismissing them as doodles.

Just prior to Detective Swanson's return to court for his cross-examination, English teacher Dawn Boldrin said, "One of the things I have noticed is that boys love to doodle, and they doodle like crazy and they're very attracted to shapes, and the swastika is a shape. The swastikas, lightning bolts, all those things are very cool."

Ms. Boldrin thought of doodling as boy fun. Still, she had sometimes sent students for counseling based on their doodling. Symbol and color were her guides.

Ms. Boldrin told us that the doodling she reported was "Brown Pride doodling," referring to the tag used by various Mexican American gangs, including Locos, Sureños, and Raza. She went on to say, "I have also reported doodles that depicted murder and death and blood and guts and guns and explosions and just pure violence."

Ms. Bramson asked, "Would you report a doodle of a swastika?"

"No," Ms. Boldrin said.

"Why?" asked Ms. Bramson

Ms. Boldrin said, "Because I doodled swastikas when I was young. They're cool little symbols, and I just, they're all over the place. They're even in my house at this point, with some of the motocross where we have . . . so it's just one of those things. I didn't take it as like a significant symbol."

On the third day of his testimony, Detective Swanson, using Power-Point, projected an image onto the screen situated over his shoulder, a drawing that he believed was made by Brandon (see figure 1a) and likely inspired by/copied from a photograph called "Guard Duty" (see figure 1b). Detective Swanson went on to show us two other guard drawings (see figures 2 and 3), and suggested that the models for these drawings could have come from *The 12th SS: The History of the Hitler Youth Panzer Division*. Another source for these drawings could have been a drawing in Matt Reaume's home. Detective Swanson deduced this link based on the way the helmets were drawn in accord with the unusual way that Mr. Reaume drew helmets: "Look at the seemingly innocuous small little detail, the two rivets which are common to helmets, but are not a common detail in drawings, especially when someone is simply sketching" (see figure 4).

Detective Swanson explained that the first drawing (figure 1a) was "merely a connecting item," showing the link between the books found in the McInerney home and the drawing. The other guard drawings were presented as examples of Brandon's interest in the guards that served in Hitler's youth division.

Aside from mentioning something about the "tone of the officers' faces," Detective Swanson did not elaborate on what he thought the

FIGURE 1A

drawings might express. He limited his interpretation to deduction or additive reasoning.

Brandon sat among us, silent and still. Emotion, when it did appear (a handful of times), was more like intimation, a tight-lipped smile, a quick darkening of his eyes. Arguably, through these drawings, Brandon *spoke* for the first and only time during the trial. The series of drawings brought us face-to-face with resonant emanations that led us to feel rather than simply to see. Drawings or paintings often lead you to feel before you begin to narrate, or to make a story out of what you are seeing.

Guard duty.

FIGURE 1B

I have come to think of Brandon's drawings as a portfolio with a memory of its own, and that this memory can tell us something about him in the days and months leading up to the murder. Many of the drawings come to life through superimposition: the local is overlaid by the global; the personal is overlaid by the cultural. The drawings gave us representations of a boy's blended inner and outer worlds.

But what the portfolio had to tell had limits. I could not look at Brandon's drawings with a mind uncontaminated by the murder that brought them to my eyes. Reading the past backward, through retrospective knowledge, is a compromised undertaking, and whatever is to be gleaned surely cannot be read as causal. The pencil was not the gun.

FIGURE 2

FIGURE 3

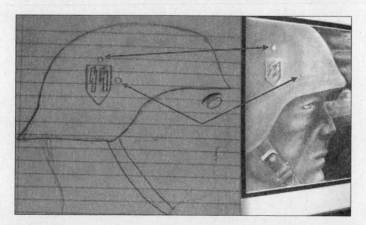

FIGURE 4

If we look at the drawings of the SS guards alongside two other drawings that carefully render symbols of allegiance (see figures 5 and 6), we are offered a pattern, similar images that not only tell a story of practice at drawing Nazi and white supremacist symbols, but also convey an emotional tone and raise a number of questions.

Detective Swanson was keen to show the jurors the ways in which Brandon combined Nazi, white supremacist, and Silver Strand Local (SSL) symbols. Detective Swanson said that he had never seen images quite like these; "They combine various aspects of white supremacy, like the White Pride World Wide symbol [the iron cross surrounded by the phrase "White Pride World Wide"], or the swastika surrounded by a diamond [the signature of the American white supremacist movement], along with Nazi symbols, like the runic SS."

In figure 6, by Detective Swanson's account, Brandon "connected influences from both white supremacy via Nazism and influences from the Silver Strand Locals. The specific connection here is the Nardcore sign, not only in the general design of the swastika [surrounded by a diamond and overlaid by a circle], but actually in how the paper was also cut to simulate a diamond. This is very unique. I've never seen this combination of Silver Strand Locals related items and Nazism anywhere else except in Matt Reaume's home and these drawings from Brandon McInerney."

As I looked at the drawings of guards and badges, both in the courtroom and over time, my eye was drawn to the focus, and the control of the hand that had rendered them. The drawings were not dashed-off doodles. There was effort, there was thought. They were methodical. They were the result of practiced determination.

One way to look at adolescence is as a time of practice. Identities are practiced, haircuts become experiments, and nascent political beliefs are flexed. Social life is practiced, friendships steady and veer, groups form. As well, older kids are sometimes sought out. You can get out of the house with them. You can discover new worldviews.

Brandon was unhappy at home, deeply so, and it is not hard to

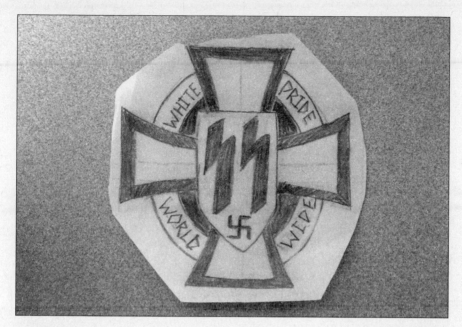

FIGURE 5

FIGURE 6

imagine that he turned to his older brother and his older brother's friends as a way out. It is not hard to imagine that he would have sought to match the beliefs of their social world in order to belong, to forge a new identity, to grow up.

I came to think of Brandon's drawings of the badges (figures 5 and 6) as the practice of multiple pledges of allegiance. They can be seen as the wish to join a club and to be identified with the beliefs and the social place that clubs provide.

Many adolescents set about to draw their way into the future. They are rightly known as social artists. When I studied Brandon's pictures of the guards, I kept searching their faces. In figure 1a, the face flattens out and loses the careful reach toward realism that characterizes the rest of the drawing. Still, the face has the impassive cast found in all the guard drawings. Did Brandon draw the guards in an act of mirroring—or as an act of wishing? "Guard Duty"—there's a kind of redundancy in that title—is how others, even Brandon's own mother, generally described Brandon: guarded, impassive, inflexible. Did he see himself in these guard images, or did he search these faces, their blankness, looking for a way to look? Looking out, not in, the guards shuttered their imperfect emotions and internal states. There was barely a ripple on the surface.

Figures 2, 3, and 4, which Brandon drew freehand, are more expressive. They are also surprising in their fidelity to perception rather than verisimilitude. An art teacher might have looked upon these drawings and commented on the skill of "the line."

Yet in their freeness, they are arguably more guarded than Brandon's other drawings. It does not appear that these men speak. Their mouths are either missing, or barely etched. Theirs is a paranoid duty, a stance that renders them mute. Their eyes look straight ahead. As we face each guard, he refuses our gaze. Detective Swanson offered the drawings as evidence of the ways in which Brandon was practicing a set of beliefs, a set of ethics, a way of being a boy. Detective Swanson argued for the work of the symbols, the belief that could be found in their rendering. But evidence of what Brandon was practicing can also be found in the ways that the guards are shielded and armored. They repudiate the "other," giving little evidence of their psyches, maybe even seeking to eliminate it, except as they are enjoined to think of violence as a kind of duty.

VIOLENCE APPEARS, IN MANY FORMS, throughout the drawings, but in three drawings violence is part of the *drawn experience*. These drawings don't hide or mask their intentions; they radiate their drive to eradicate and expunge, to murder.

Figure 7 serves as a good example of cultural memory, as the local meets the national meets the global. Brandon paired the local Nardcore tag with the National Socialist swastika. Later, Detective Swanson would tell me that he had only seen this combination of the Nardcore tag with the swastika in drawings made by Brandon and by Matt Reaume. Above the NARD/swastika and just to the left, there is another coupled symbol, a swastika overlaid on a diamond, the signature of American white supremacist organizations.

In this drawing, "the Jew" is reiterated threefold: "JEW," the Star of David, the Star of David overwritten by the circle-backlash, or the universal "No!" This reiteration results in a kind of "Jew" cascade, culminating in renunciation. I came to think of this drawing as an electrified killing field; the two principal "characters," the deadhead and "JEW," are struck by lightning bolts that emanate from electrically charged swastikas (another common white supremacist logo).

Eva Hoffman, the Polish American writer and academic who has written extensively about the intergenerational transfer of trauma, might call the "Jew" repetition found in this drawing a "broken refrain," a refrain that speaks to how hate can be transmitted through emotional force devoid of thought. The unconscious is free to malice, and the malice and murder are thereby neither felt ("No!") nor grieved. The loss is reframed as purification.

FIGURE 7

The animation and spontaneity of this drawing are matched by a similar visual landscape in figure 8.

Once again, we can see the kinetics of practice and combination, called a "mess of different images" by Detective Swanson. Nazi, neo-Nazi, white supremacist, and local tagging symbols and signs rain down on the page. Nine swastikas roam the page. A large swastika houses the SSL tag and the Nardcore tag. Again, a deadhead is a focal point, this one decorated with a swastika, the SS lightning bolts, and the White Pride World Wide symbol. SS and SSL occur repeatedly and in a variety of styles. Again, lightning bolts infuse swastikas.

Detective Swanson did not linger over the doodles. He was quick to move on. But I found that the animation and spontaneity of these drawings made them the most convincing documents in his cache of evidence;

FIGURE 8

they seemed dynamic proofs of an ideology shaping the mind of a young person.

The third violent drawing (figure 9) drew reflexive, audible gasps when it was projected in the courtroom.

Detective Swanson focused on the way in which this drawing was "very stylized," stylized in such a way that he presumed it was a copy. His research, however, did not lead to an original: "Reaching out to organiza-

FIGURE 9

tions including the ADL, Southern Poverty Law Center, and the U.S. Holocaust Museum, I could not find any reference to this exact image."

This drawing operates with blunt force and crushing intention. One recoils from this image in response to the threat it projects, as it seeks to dominate and menace. Presumably intended to symbolize the Nazis' determined extermination of the Jews, the drawing is nationalist in that respect. Yet I found myself thinking about the hand drawn by a free hand, as opposed to the ruled line of the swastika and star, and how that drawn hand must hurt, even though it shows no signs of damage. It is the Star of David that bleeds, not the conquering, plundering hand, backed up by the symbol and ideology of National Socialism. Once again, I was reminded of how Brandon was repeatedly described as unflinching and how the other kids spoke of him as being carried along and away by his own strength.

Detective Swanson projected another drawing (figure 10) and focused on the originality of the image. "There is no original Nazi imagery of this bird, this eagle that has a shield with the SS on it. This is a creation of an original image."

I did wonder, though, in league with Detective Swanson, whether Brandon had copied the drawing of the hand crushing the Star of David, presumably from a drawing he found, perhaps the drawing of a friend, and if this drawing of the eagle might not also have been a copy.

Yet Detective Swanson's phrase "creation of an original" seemed apt to me in thinking about how adolescents often copy and modify in their quest to become original and independent. They also often seek

FIGURE 10

independence through a kind of triumphalism, a kind of complete domination/conquest that means, for the winner, there is no wound, there is no chaos, there is no vulnerability, no loss, no awkward body, no uncertain desire.

Was this Brandon's effort to turn away from ordinary life and to powerfully seek another life? Such are the wishes of many teenagers; such are the drawings that fill their notebooks.

Yet even as we grant Brandon this common feature of adolescent life, we are left to contend with the ideology with which his raptor took flight and the beliefs it sought to preserve, clutching a swastika in its talons.

7

Save Brandon

"Unlike the Prosecution, we have nothing to hide," Mr. Wippert told us on the morning of July 22, the morning after Detective Swanson had finished his testimony for the prosecution, and the morning the defense began to present its case. Mr. Wippert exclaimed that the defense planned to bring "the good, the bad, and the ugly to the stand."

From July 22 to August 9, as the defense prepared to cross-examine Detective Swanson, the defense attorneys used their time in court to bring before us a parade of disparate witnesses, including Brandon's relatives, neighbors, friends, teachers, and his correction officers from the juvenile center where he had been living for the past three years. These witnesses were brought to the stand to refute the prosecution's allegations that Brandon was a racist, a white supremacist, a kid who had been absorbed into a neighborhood gang.

These witnesses were not brought to the stand in any particular order. The hallway outside the courtroom was a scramble, and on several occasions we were left to wait until Sheriff Anton, the bailiff, could find the next witness, or until he gave up, and we went on to whoever happened to be there. The prosecution repeatedly objected to not knowing who was coming to the stand on any given day, and to the consistent way in which the defense had not provided them with any background information on the witnesses.

I NOTICED THEM BEFORE I knew what I was seeing. Samantha Criner wore several on her thin tan arms: four baby blue rubber bracelets on her left arm, five on her right. They moved up and down as she gestured from the witness stand on July 12, during the second week of the trial.

It wasn't until two weeks later, when I was talking to Kyle Benavidez, a tattoo artist who had a studio in Silver Strand, after his testimony on July 27, that I saw that he, too, was wearing one. "It says SAVE BRANDON. Kendra had a bunch made up, you know, to show support," Mr. Benavidez volunteered as he held out his wrist.

When I asked Kendra about the bracelets the next morning, she smiled, pleased, it seemed, by the show of support. But as to the origins of the bracelets, she shrugged and said, "I don't know. I think they are selling them at the Corner Store," by which she meant a dusty, old-fashioned convenience store in Silver Strand, of the sort that used to be around before franchises pushed them out. A week later, when I went to the Corner Store to inquire about the bracelets, the clerk either did not know about them or acted as if he did not know.

When the defense began to present its case, many witnesses came before us wearing the bracelets: neighbors, teachers, friends, and relatives. Even defense cocounsel Robyn Bramson wore one. Following the trial, Ms. Bramson had SAVE BRANDON tattooed on the underside of her right wrist by Mr. Benavidez. At a dinner with me following the trial, she extended her arm, fist closed, and offered SAVE BRANDON as symbolic of her tongue-tied affection: "I just don't know, I don't know, I don't know what it is. I just love that kid, and *this* makes me happy when I look at it."

In keeping with Ms. Bramson's declaration of love, the defense gathered Brandon's Silver Strand neighbors to serve as character witnesses. These witnesses, like Samantha Criner, Kyle Benavidez, David Wentworth (a retired Silver Strand restaurateur), and Tyler Treves (a musician who lived on the Strand), came to court to speak on behalf of Brandon and their small stretch of beach, "one mile long, one block wide."

Brandon had spent much of his childhood on the Strand, prior to moving in 2002, when he was eight years old, to his grandfather's house on Tiller Avenue, in Oxnard proper. Even then, Brandon returned to the Strand almost every day. Silver Strand is an unincorporated beach neighborhood at the southern tip of Oxnard, something of an outlaw cousin, reluctantly governed by the county of Ventura. The McInerneys were Silver Strand locals; Brandon still thought of Silver Strand as his home.

A smudge of coastline, the Strand consists of two main roads and a handful of lanes that run from the main road (Island View Avenue) down to the beach. Locals describe the beach as the windiest stretch of the California coastline. Old men use leaf blowers to clear their driveways of sand; the young just plow through.

Small houses and apartment buildings tumble, one atop another, down the lanes to the sea. Similarly humble bungalows once lined the beach, but by 2008, Angelinos, locally known as "Southers," had begun buying up the beachfront, tearing down the cottages, and constructing "million-dollar" weekend homes.

Beginning in the early 2000s, rebuilt "tear-down" houses had also started cropping up on the small streets that run down to the beach. Stark, face-lifted modern houses abutted the more modest ranch houses owned by working-class locals, many of which had been passed down from one generation to the next. The ranch homes had the lived-in, paint-peeling, wear-and-tear quality of beach houses, roughed up by weather and renters. Cement donkeys pulled carts filled with sun-bleached plastic chrysanthemums, and wooden pelicans guarded driveways.

"There is one way in and one way out," James Bing said with a laugh, as he described the isolation of Silver Strand, a place reachable by only one road; a place almost completely surrounded by the Channel Islands Harbor to the north and a naval port (Port Hueneme) to the south. The port is a naval construction battalion, and its rusty industrial hulk brings the beach to an abrupt end. The barbed wire that marks the battalion's perimeter runs right into the sea.

The Silver Strand witnesses were eager to refute claims that their town was host to a criminally based gang, the SSL. And to clear up any charges that their localism was founded on racism. Turf-based localism was a thing of the past, they told us, a relic of the ways surfers jealously guard a good surf break.

Yes, a sign used to be posted on a lifeguard station that read, IF YOU THINK YOU CAN JUST PULL UP AND PADDLE OUT, YOU'RE WRONG. OUR LOCALISM IS STILL IN FULL FORCE. But that sign, and what it broadcast, were long gone, according to the locals. A storm had carried the sign out to sea.

"Those are old days," Kyle Benavidez contended, even as he told us that a photo of the old sign was now posted on many of his neighbors' Facebook pages.

The locals wanted the jury to see and understand the dignity and fraternity of their community. They felt that the ways in which their working-class community came together to support one another in the face of economic and cultural changes were being overlooked and misunderstood in the courtroom.

Ms. Criner, in response to a question posed by Ms. Fox about the meaning of "SSL," replied, "Is it a gang? No. It is a beach." When questioned by Ms. Bramson about any racial tension in Silver Strand, Ms. Criner said, "No. There's just a beach. Everyone goes to the beach, yeah everyone, and it is nice to everyone and gets along." The personified beach, we would learn, was a "family," "a giant family," a "mother," indeed, "many mothers."

David Wentworth, a round fellow who wore a Panama straw cowboy hat, and red suspenders to anchor his jeans below his jolly gut, thundered through his testimony, pounded on the ledge of the witness stand, and bellowed over Ms. Fox's objections to assert that his town

was being "besmirched by this accusation that we got a white supremacist gang somewhere hiding."

Mr. Wentworth and his neighbors spoke as hardworking people whose
town was under threat, *not* by gangs or racism, but by market values that
were pushing them off their beloved beach, and by an increasingly intru-
sive police state, which hassled local folks who were setting out to enjoy
the pleasures of their beach. The Man was breathing down their necks.

The townsfolk held to their view of Silver Strand as a "family," seemingly unaware of the evidence that contradicted their assertions—even
of the contradictory evidence that they would in due course offer
themselves.

Samantha Criner was, one might even say, blissfully unaware. On
the witness stand she repeatedly responded to the attorneys, Ms. Fox in
particular, with "I don't know" or "I don't remember." At one point, sum-
ming up for Ms. Bramson, Samantha said, "I don't care to know what
I don't know."

The Silver Strand witnesses denied knowledge of any history of criminal activity that would suggest gang activity. Mr. Benavidez, tattooed
teardrops dripping from his eyes, FUCK YOU—CALL THE COPS! perma-
nently etched above his right eye ("It refers to his baby mama who kept
calling the cops on him," James Bing explained after the trial), told us
that he moved to Silver Strand when he was seventeen years old. Prior
to that, he had "grown up around gang violence and gang-related
crime," and Silver Strand was nothing like that. "You know," he told
Mr. Wippert, "it's never been like that. Just never."

Mr. Benavidez defined a street gang as "a group of people that are
out to make a name for themselves causing trouble. You know, they're
on drugs causing a ruckus, you know what I mean, going in other neighborhoods, tagging it up, causing problems, you know, yelling at—yelling
at other gangs, stuff like that."

Mr. Wippert followed up, asking, "You said that you identified as a
Silver Strand local. And at any point in time, you know, again prior to
the shooting, did you ever—was Silver Strand, in your opinion, Silver
Strand Locals ever a gang—"

"No," Mr. Benavidez interrupted.

"—a criminal street gang, as you just defined for us?" Mr. Wippert continued.

"No."

"And, had you ever known of any people who identified themselves as Silver Strand Locals to have identified themselves as white supremacists?" Mr. Wippert said.

"No," Mr. Benavidez said. The people of Silver Strand policed their own, Mr. Benavidez told us, and they were doing just fine.

During her cross-examination, Ms. Fox returned to Mr. Benavidez's assertion that gangs brought crime to neighborhoods, and that Silver Strand was not the site of such crime. She ticked off the names of twelve people and, with each name, asked Mr. Benavidez if he knew these people. He indicated that he knew all of them, and identified them as residents of the Strand.

Ms. Fox then detailed the criminal convictions of five of the twelve people, naming crimes that included: assault with a deadly weapon, possession of methamphetamine with intent to sell, making criminal threats, grand theft—the same crimes Mr. Benavidez had linked to gang activity.

Mr. Benavidez answered "yes" each time Ms. Fox asked him if he was aware that the man she'd just named had been convicted of that crime. He noted that many of them had been in and out of jail for much of their adult lives. Voicing what could be heard as his devotion to his beach family, he wanted Ms. Fox to understand that one of the men was out of jail, and that he was "doing good right now."

Questions asked about Matt Reaume produced a tempest of evasive energy. All the townspeople, save for Mr. Wentworth, indicated that they knew Mr. Reaume. They all denied any knowledge of his connection to white supremacy, an avowal that seemed unshaken by evidence of Mr. Reaume's documented public commitment to White Pride World Wide and the Confederation of Racialist Working Class Skinheads.

Ms. Fox projected a photograph of Matt Reaume wearing a White

Pride World Wide T-shirt and raising his arm in a Sieg Heil salute. She asked Mr. Benavidez if he was surprised by this image. He replied, "A little bit." Later, he explained his tempered response to Mr. Wippert: "If that's what [Matt] did when he was in prison, yeah, he might have still had a little bit of those ideas in his head, but they were never forced upon anybody or his friends or anything like that in his neighborhood."

As for the White Power flag that decorated Mr. Reaume's apartment, Mr. Benavidez called it "silly." Mr. Treves, a frequent visitor at Mr. Reaume's home, also made little of the Nazi-era drawings or the White Power stickers on the refrigerator: "They were in German, and I can't read German. I figured it was some kind of beer." When Ms. Fox asked Mr. Benavidez if he had seen Mr. Reaume wear a White Power World Wide T-shirt, he replied, "I might have. I don't recall, you know what I mean. It's nothing significant that would stand out."

BRANDON STARTED TALKING ABOUT WHITE supremacy in the summer of 2007 around the same time he started talking about Larry. Brandon's friends Kaj Wirsing and Samantha Criner reluctantly spoke about Brandon's interest in white supremacy and his concerns with Larry, from the stand on July 12, during the second week of the trial. When Brandon had mentioned his interest in white supremacy to Kaj, Kaj had pushed back, calling it "stupid." At least that was what Kaj reported to Mr. Wippert. When asked about this moment by Ms. Fox, Kaj said, "I don't recall." He also told Mr. Wippert that Brandon had shown him a drawing of a seascape with a swastika drawn on the horizon, and again, Kaj called it "stupid." Kaj responded to almost every inquiry made by Ms. Fox by saying, "I don't recall." But he did tell her that Brandon had mentioned how Larry troubled him. Kaj had a similar kind of uneasiness "especially in the locker room." He added, "But I told Brandon to just ignore him."

At first, on July 12, when Ms. Fox questioned Coppertone-pretty Samantha, she denied that Brandon had ever said anything about white supremacy. Samantha was also reluctant to talk about her relationship with Brandon.

Ms. Fox asked, "Did your relationship with the defendant change into something other than just friends?"

"I guess boyfriend/girlfriend, if you could put a title to it. Do you want to title it?" Samantha said.

"And how long do you think you were boyfriend and girlfriend?"

"I don't know. Only a couple of weeks before it happened."

Samantha grew skittish, as well, when Ms. Fox asked about Brandon's alleged interest in white supremacy: "Did the defendant ever talk to you about skinhead stuff?"

Samantha said, "Mmm, no. He talked to me about—'cause when we watched TV he'd want to watch the History Channel, and I never wanted to watch the History Channel 'cause I thought it was boring. So, I mean, if the skinhead stuff was on TV or something, but I don't really like talking—I don't like talking about that stuff."

Yet it was Samantha who told police officers on the day of the shooting that Brandon had starting talking about white supremacy right around the same time that he started talking about Larry. Brandon had told Samantha about a "gay kid, who was, like, girlie," and about how this kid "bugged him."

Ms. Fox asked Samantha, "Were you surprised when Brandon McInerney told you that he was going to beat this kid up because he was gay?"

Samantha said, "He didn't say he was going to beat him up."

"Didn't you question him and tell him, 'Don't beat this kid up, that would be stupid'?"

"No. I said, 'If you do, don't get in trouble.' I just knew . . ."

"But you thought he should go beat him up?"

"Well, I'm not going to stop him from what he's going to do."

"So he did tell you he was going to go beat him up?"

"No. I told him—'cause I know he's capable of doing it. I said, 'If you do, don't get in trouble.'"

"Do you remember responding to Brandon that he should just leave this person alone because the person's going to be gay and there's nothing he can do about it?"

"Yeah. I said, 'It's not worth it.'"

Samantha ("You can call me Sam") appeared to be more comfortable during her cross-examination with Ms. Bramson. She mostly told Ms. Bramson how much she had wanted Brandon to grow his hair long, and reiterated that Brandon liked to watch the History Channel, whereas she liked "MTV, you know the reality one, and the like fake ones, you know movies and stuff." She liked to watch "funny things," and while Brandon may have talked about skinhead stuff, she thought it was "boring, very boring." She said, "He'd talk about that stuff that I don't have no idea who or what he was talking about."

The one person who took direct action with Brandon upon learning of his interest in white supremacy was his brother James Bing, who spoke at length with Mr. Wippert on August 3, after Detective Swanson's direct testimony. Like Kaj and Samantha, James took note of Brandon's interest in white supremacy in the summer and fall of 2007. Thinking that Brandon was "going through a little kid phase," James told Mr. Wippert he thought that Brandon could do with some education on these matters. So James asked Matt Reaume, with whom James was living at the time, to speak with Brandon.

Mr. Wippert asked James, "During the weekend before the incident, did you ask Matt to have a discussion with Brandon about white supremacy or white separatism?"

"Yes, I did, sir," James said.

"And why did you do that?"

"Brandon just brought it up one time, and I'm not a fan of that, so I wanted him, you know, to hear it from an educated person who's been educated on it before he talked to some knucklehead about it."

Pacing in front of James, Mr. Wippert said, "Okay. Now, tell me about this, when did this discussion about white separatism even start?"

James said, "Well, Brandon told me about it, you know, about, 'Hey, I just got these ideas about it and stuff.' And, well, one day we were walking in the mall and he brought it up, and so I asked Matt, you know, to tell him about it, to tell him what you know about what a white separatist is, you know."

Mr. Wippert voiced his surprise that James would trust a known white supremacist like Matt Reaume to teach Brandon. But James maintained it was Matt's knowledge that qualified him: "He was in prison. He read books on it. He was educated on his beliefs. Matt's a very good man. He provides for his family, has a job. He's a great member of society who has that white separatist belief."

Racism and white supremacist beliefs did not run against the good of society; they ran, by James's account, alongside society. Similarly, race hate seemingly did not counter that which could reasonably be understood as a "good man," a family man, a man who could be trusted to guide a fourteen-year-old on matters of social justice.

During the trial, we often heard about Mr. Reaume—from Detective Swanson, Ms. Fox, Detective Jeff Kay, James Bing, and others. In her opening statement, Ms. Fox mentioned that a summons had been issued for Mr. Reaume to appear in court. But he was in the wind. Only rumor kept him on the witness list. Still, as *testimony*, he showed up often, and often contradictorily.

Using the overhead projector that sat on his table, Mr. Wippert projected a photo of Mr. Reaume wearing a White Pride World Wide T-shirt onto a screen just to the right of the witness stand, and asked James Bing if he had ever seen Mr. Reaume wearing the shirt that he was wearing in the photo.

"Did you go into public with Mr. Reaume when he was wearing that shirt?" Mr. Wippert asked James.

"Yeah. Yes, actually I have," said James.

"Okay," Mr. Wippert said, scratching his head. "And do you—did you recognize what that symbol is or do you recognize what that symbol is [a red circular logo denoting the Confederation of Working Class Skinheads]?"

"No, I have no idea what it means," James said.

"Okay. Did you have any clues that that might have anything to with white separatism or white supremacy?"

"I figured, but most wouldn't have probably have an idea what that is."

The townsfolk, in speaking with Mr. Wippert, repeatedly asserted that signs and symbols did not frame, shape, or influence their neighborhood; they were simply background. Friendships, relationships, and family were what mattered. Hard times, lean times, and struggle in the face of a world that favored those who had more and who struggled less were what kept the Strand going.

Mr. Wentworth, the paterfamilias of the townsfolk, told us that he did not know Mr. Reaume, but Ms. Fox produced a photo that depicted Mr. Wentworth's two grandsons, along with Brandon McInerney, in a group with Mr. Reaume. It looked as if Mr. Reaume was holding a beer in one hand and making a Sieg Heil salute with his other hand.

Ms. Fox pointed to Mr. Reaume in the projected photograph and asked Mr. Wentworth, "You see what that guy's doing in that picture?"

Mr. Wentworth replied, "No, I don't. That's pretty fuzzy."

Rephrasing, Ms. Fox said, "That guy is doing what is commonly referred to as a Sieg Heil and he's sitting right there in the midst of that group with your grandsons."

Mr. Wentworth interrupted, "You mean he's holding his arm out?"

Members of the gallery and the jury laughed, as Mr. Wentworth squinted at the photograph and shrugged.

Ms. Fox, grinning herself, asked, "Would that surprise you?"

"He's holding his arm out like this," Mr. Wentworth said, raising his arm straight up and out.

Ms. Fox, her tone becoming more firm, said, "I want you to assume, for the purpose of the question, that this is what he's doing," as she made the Sieg Heil gesture.

Mr. Wentworth said, "Uh, yeah."

"Would that surprise you?" Ms. Fox said.

"I don't know if it's a Sieg Heil or a Hi," Mr. Wentworth said, laughing, as did many people in the courtroom.

In his cowboy hat and red suspenders, Mr. Wentworth could have been a rodeo clown, dodging reality's force while he made the audience laugh. Look away; ignore the threat. Many people in the room seemed to be enjoying his comic performance. But I kept looking back and forth between Mr. Wentworth and the figure of Lady Justice as she was depicted in a large bronze plaque above the judge's desk (the only decoration in the room). There she stood, blindfolded, holding a scale in one hand and a sword in her other hand, the personification of justice and the embodiment of divine order. Where, I wondered, was the order in the repeated claims made by Mr. Wentworth and his neighbors that what we were seeing we were not seeing; rather, what we were seeing was what we had decided we were seeing?

Ms. Fox, grasping, it seemed, that Mr. Wentworth was not going to recognize what it was that she saw, and wanted him to see, shifted tack, saying, "Okay. Are you aware that your grandsons are friends with a guy named Matt Reaume?"

Mr. Wentworth said, "No. I don't think they brought him to the house."

"Okay. And you have stated when speaking with Mr. Wippert that there are no white supremacists in Silver Strand, right?"

"No, I didn't say that. I said I don't know any."

"Oh, okay. But, I do believe that you said there are not white supremacists in Silver Strand."

"If I did, I misspoke. I never met him. I'm not aware of any."

"Fair enough. Okay. That is fair enough."

Mr. Wentworth would prove to be the only witness to recognize the possibility of white supremacy in Silver Strand, but even his admission was tempered by his position that someone like him, a well-known member of the Silver Strand community, could not know about the presence of white supremacy in this small town.

No one had brought a white supremacist home.

And the home, the family, the territory were positioned as the opposite of hate. Yet the casual racism with which some of the Silver Strand townsfolk told the story, the sort of racism that might go unnoticed around a supper table with like-minded kin ("In closed doors," as James Bing put it, when speaking about Billy McInerney's racism), suggested that hate might have played a bigger role than the locals were able either to see or to conceal.

Once again, Samantha Criner summed up the evasion rather well.

Ms. Fox asked Samantha, "Have you ever observed any racism in Silver Strand?"

"I wouldn't title anyone as racist," Samantha replied.

Her brand of unthinking could be heard over and over again through the claim that one was not a racist if they had an ethnically diverse friend. Every townsperson was asked if they knew people of other races. Everyone knew a black guy. Everyone touted the Strand's diversity. In doing so, Samantha said, "Obviously white, and then there's—we have a couple like Mexicans, and then there's blacks, and I don't know. What other races are there? I don't know."

Ms. Fox raised the possibility that the Strand's diversity was not without division. Specifically, she drew our attention to the term "kook," a local epithet used to call out difference, to name outsiders.

Ms. Fox asked Samantha, "Kooks. Do you know what kooks are?"

Adjusting one of her large gold-hooped earrings that had gotten caught in her hair, Samantha said, "What? Oh yeah, I know what kooks are."

"Yeah. What are kooks?" Ms. Fox said.

Samantha, still adjusting her earring, said, "People that don't live on your beach."

"And they're not welcome, are they?" Ms. Fox said.

Samantha, pushing her hands against the ledge of the witness stand, said, "I just don't think we'd acknowledge them as, well—"

Ms. Fox also questioned Mr. Wentworth about the meaning of "kook," asking him, "Do you know what the term 'split kooks' means?"

"Split tooth?" Mr. Wentworth asked. He got his biggest laugh of the day and began to laugh in return.

Ms. Fox projected a photo. It depicted a wall on the outside of a public restroom in Silver Strand that had been spray-painted. She said, "See on the right-hand side there where it says, 'split kooks'?"

"Split kooks? Split tooth?" Mr. Wentworth said, topping his last laugh.

Ms. Fox approached the witness stand shouting (wearying perhaps of her role as the straight man), "K-o-o-k-s."

"I don't know what that means," Mr. Wentworth said.

"And have you never seen that?"

"The split kooks, nope."

Mr. Wentworth's claim unraveled, though, when he volunteered a report of racial bias and vandalism that had occurred on his block: "There was this thing that happened about ten years ago down at the end of my street, some Koreans lived there, house on the beach, and there was all this excitement one day, and I walked down there to see what was going on. Somebody sprayed some stuff on the garage door, and they put ssl on there, and people were real upset about this." Ms. Fox later presented a photo of the very incident and pointed out another phrase on the door: GO HOME KOOKS.

Pressed again by Ms. Fox, Mr. Wentworth had to admit that he knew the phrase to be a derogatory name, often aimed at Asians, and at people from Los Angeles who had bought beachfront property. Still, he remained adamant that the incident did not mean anything more than the foolishness of a "couple of kids with a spray can."

Similarly, Samantha Criner did her unwitting best to deny the presence of hate. Despite her "I don't know" refrain, she consistently found her way to the hate that surrounded her.

Ms. Fox brought to Samantha's attention a letter that she had written to Brandon while he was in juvenile detention.

Quoting from the letter, Ms. Fox said, "You wrote, 'I'm thinking about taking boxing, self-defense classes, ha, ha. All this crazy shit happening, black president, ha, ha. I need to know how to fight for myself.' What did you mean by that?"

Samantha stared at Ms. Fox, for perhaps the first time in their exchanges, and told her, "I think it's good to have self-defense."

"I'm sorry?" Ms. Fox said.

Again, looking directly at Ms. Fox, Samantha stated, "I want to take boxing classes to learn self-defense."

Ms. Fox said, "I guess the part I'm not getting is what does self-defense and knowing how to fight for yourself have to do with having a black president?"

Samantha, shrugging her shoulders, replied, "I don't know. I don't know either. I guess my thoughts are kind of all over the place."

Later, when Ms. Bramson asked her, "Would you consider yourself a racist?" Samantha answered, "Me? No. No." She then added, "I just meet a lot of people, and a lot of them aren't white. I feel like whites are the minority now."

Samantha elaborated on this sentiment during an interview with Marta Cunningham in the documentary *Valentine Road*. We see Samantha looking through a stack of letters from Brandon that she had carefully kept in a carved wooden box. She held one up and whispered, "This is the first one where he put 'Samantha McInerney' and I was like—oh, my gosh! When I think about a guy being one to marry, like for the rest of my life, he's definitely probably my number one pick. 'Cause he's like the one that's ever cared. I just love him—way too much."

We don't hear the interviewer's question, only Samantha's answer: "You think a beach, you think like white surfers or something. White is a minority now. You don't see a lot of white people, like, fully white people, like me, white. Or like Brandon. We are white-white."

DETECTIVE SWANSON'S TESTIMONY FOR THE prosecution was in effect countered by the character witnesses who came to court to claim Brandon as kin. But what was the reality of the witnesses' experience with Brandon? His bonds were few, and the townspeople's efforts to speak up for him often led them to speak up for their town instead. It was as if they were in court on behalf of a son whom they did not exactly know, but knew they were supposed to love. As Kyle Benavidez put it, "Nobody wants to see their kid get into trouble, and like I've said, I've known him since he was in diapers, and the last thing we want to see is a kid we're watching grow up get in trouble."

Mr. Benavidez moved to the Strand while Brandon was living with his father in Oxnard proper. Brandon would have been at least eight years old when Mr. Benavidez met him. It was not clear that Mr. Benavidez spent much time with Brandon. Yet he was in court to offer his testimony about Brandon's character.

Mr. Wippert asked Mr. Benavidez, "Based on your experience and growing up in that community and knowing Brandon McInerney, do you have an opinion on whether he's a violent person?"

Mr. Benavidez said, "No, he's not."

By then, a debate was under way with regard to what was called Brandon's "character for violence." Along with the Silver Strand townsfolk, the defense brought to the stand correction officers from the Ventura County Juvenile Hall. Interspersed with the townspeople, the correction officers, who had been living with Brandon for the past three years, were also in court as character witnesses.

Scott Aveson, a supervising correction officer, spoke of Brandon as working on his GED and "gaining many honors," both for his academic work and for following the rules and protocol of incarceration. Brandon, said Officer Aveson, got on well with the staff of the hall. He was polite and respectful. With an amused nod, Officer Aveson explained that Brandon had once gotten into trouble for having a pet lizard: "We released the lizard and kept Brandon."

When Ms. Fox began her cross-examination, she explained to Officer Aveson that she was going to show him a video and ask him to comment on what he saw. The bailiff dimmed the lights. Ms. Fox played the video on a large screen.

In silent grainy black-and-white slow motion, two men played Ping-Pong, while another sat at a nearby table. The game stopped, and the two men joined the third man at the table. One man suddenly jumped up and started hitting the smaller man sitting next to him, pummeling him to the floor. The bigger guy continued to throw roundhouse punches, right, left, right, left. A man in a uniform entered the scene and struggled to pull the big guy off the smaller guy on the floor, who was, at this point, curled in a fetal position.

We were disoriented and disquieted. The lights came back up, but their fluorescence did not help. The big figure in the footage was more corporeal than a ghost but in a blurry, oversized white T-shirt, and distorted by slow motion (even as he threw punch after punch), he seemed to be of another world. We struggled to refind our own world in the courtroom.

Ms. Fox asked, "Mr. Aveson, can you identify the attacker in this film?"

Officer Aveson said, "Yes, Brandon McInerney."

Almost every person in the courtroom, including members of the jury, looked toward the person who was seated next to them, seeking direction. An elderly man in the front row of the gallery exclaimed, "Wait a minute!" voicing our need for more time to gather our perceptions.

But Ms. Fox was already reading from Officer Aveson's Incident Report and asking him if he "had characterized this incident as an assault." Officer Aveson said, "Yes."

Ms. Fox asked him if he thought that "Brandon McInerney had a character of violence."

Officer Aveson said, "No."

This line of questioning would be repeated with several other correction officers and would produce the same result. Travis Prater told us that Brandon was "respectful" and "not provocative." Officer Prater said, "He does not talk trash, he does not do that." When queried by Mr. Wippert about the fight we had just witnessed, Officer Prater reported that he did not know about it. Mr. Wippert then asked about character and violence. Officer Prater told him, "[I am] not going to answer. I am not going to answer about character. They fight for a lot of reasons."

When Ms. Fox began her cross-examination, she asked Officer

Prater if it would surprise him "to learn the defendant had received letters from known white supremacists while he was in the Juvenile Hall?"

Officer Prater replied, "Yes, it would."

Ms. Fox followed up, saying, "That would seem out of character for
you, right?"

Again, Officer Prater answered, "Yes."

Office Prater was, it seemed, willing to speak about character at that
moment.

Ms. Fox asked Officer Prater if he knew that the defendant had been
involved in six to ten fights.

Officer Prater said, "No."

"Even when the correction officer struggled to stop the fight?"

"No."

"Does that change your opinion regarding his violent character?"

"I think fighting is violent."

Ms. Fox once again instructed the bailiff to dim the lights and showed
another clip of a fight. We watched as the same figure, now made clear
to us as Brandon, charged across a room toward another inmate and
began punching him, driving him to the ground, roundhouse punching
the boy until a guard entered and pulled them apart.

The lights came up, and again, we struggled to orient. Jurors who
had been leaning forward, straining to see, adjusted themselves in their
seats. Kendra McInerney, dry-eyed, looked straight ahead.

Ms. Fox asked Officer Prater, "Does viewing that video change your
opinion in any way?"

"No," Officer Prater said.

"Would you call what you saw an assault?"

"On the video, I would say it was an assault."

"Does that change your opinion in any way that McInerney has a
character for violence?"

"No."

Ms. Fox took a step back, as if pushed by his response. She threw
her hands into the air, saying, "What do you mean by that?"

Officer Prater, unmoved, said, "We have multiple fights, but I don't know what the reasons are. Minors seem to work their problems out by fighting. I don't know if it is a character trait."

The next person the defense called to the stand was Mario Perez, a tall young man, who was wearing a dark suit that looked new and uncomfortable. He told Mr. Wippert that he knew Brandon for the entire time that Brandon had lived in the juvenile center. He smiled at Brandon as he said, "He was always friendly to me." Brandon and Officer Perez shared an interest in sports. They played fantasy football and talked "a lot about basketball, mostly sports, a lot about sports."

The room brightened. We shifted from the lock that had frozen us. Officer Perez was handsome and personable, and we welcomed his friendlier tone. Following Mr. Wippert's questions, Officer Perez explained that "minors worry to show fear. They worry that they could be seen as weaker and they could be picked on." As he saw it, a lot of fighting was offensive, a bid to hold dominance. He implied, with a hint of pride, that Brandon was effective at doing just that. In keeping with his coworkers, Officer Perez did not believe that Brandon was a violent character.

Ms. Fox began her cross-examination by asking Officer Perez if he would be surprised to learn that the defendant was found to have had SSL and white supremacist materials in his cell. Officer Perez answered that he would be surprised.

Turning toward his account of offensive efforts to maintain dominance, Ms. Fox asked if Officer Perez could distinguish between fighting that was a matter of self-defense and fighting that was offensive.

Officer Perez said, "Words alone cannot justify a physical attack. But if somebody believes they are under imminent attack, it might be defensive, offensive."

Ms. Fox asked, "What then is assault?

Officer Perez replied, "If one person is fighting and the other person is not fighting, that is an assault. When they are kicked when they are down."

"Dim the lights." Another video.

We saw a group of young men seated at a table. Many other people stood around or sat at tables. Two guards were seated behind an elevated desk. Quickly, even in slow motion, one young man, who we now understood to be Brandon, jumped up and began punching another inmate.

The inmate who had been attacked ran toward the guards. Brandon followed and shoved the young man into the desk, knocking him to the floor, pummeling him over and over again. The guards made their way from behind the desk and struggled to pull Brandon off the other guy. It took several attempts by two large men to pull Brandon off the boy, who was lying on the floor with his hands covering his head.

Watching Brandon fend off the guards, I was struck by his size and power. When the lights came back up, I looked over at him. He wore a light blue sweater vest. He sat at the defense table playing with his water bottle. He could have been waiting for a college admission interview.

Ms. Fox, continuing to question Officer Perez, asked, "Would you say Mr. McInerney has a general character of violence?"

Officer Perez said, "Yes, he has been involved in violence."

"How would you classify what you saw?"

"An assault."

Ms. Fox, abruptly, not savoring the admission of assault, asked, "You like Mr. McInerney. He is a friendly person, yes?"

"Yes."

"Certainly not so always, not so always to the other residents." With that, Ms. Fox sat down.

Mr. Wippert was quick to his feet, as if to break up a fight. He went back to Ms. Fox's earlier assertion regarding white supremacist materials found in Brandon's room.

Mr. Wippert asked Officer Perez, "Based on the Brandon that you know, were you surprised to learn this?"

Officer Perez said, "Yes."

"And he gained honors, yes? Extra points for chores, yes? He was in good graces with the hall staff, yes?" Mr. Wippert reiterated what had now been asserted several times.

"Yes."

Mr. Wippert was doing what he did so well: turning us from Brandon, the roundhouse thug, to the "Brandon that you know."

But something about Mr. Wippert's effort, his pace, the pitch of his voice, was different this time. There was urgency. Some hint of anxiety had crept in.

In that anxious crevice, I found myself thinking about the idea of surprise. Hadn't we heard, over and over, that Brandon was considered by adults to be a respectful, if distant and unemotional, kid? Had he not been known throughout his life to be a "good kid" with adults, but a kid who often got in trouble with other kids? Why did the trouble continue to surprise everyone? Wasn't Brandon shooting Leticia enough to signify Brandon's violence and antisocial tendencies? Or was it still such a surprise as to be blinding? (I thought about Yuliana, the girl who had been seated next to Brandon when he shot Leticia, as she said, "Everybody was just shock.")

Was it possible that the surprise *was* the point of the story that was unfolding before us? Brandon blended in. He got along. Until he didn't.

"ALL THAT LOOKING AT LARRY, and we missed the bigger problem," Susan Crowley, Larry's seventh-grade special resource teacher, intoned regretfully, as we sat together at her dining room table after the trial. Ms. Crowley was pointing to the way in which Brandon's normal-boy masculinity shielded him from sight. Boys will be boys. And one of the ways that they get to be boys is that they get to be invisible. Lost in the glare of Larry's "problem" femininity was Brandon's presumed and invisible masculinity.

A hallmark of the boys-will-be-boys psychology is the idea that boys are aggressive, rambunctious, and given to roughhousing. They are seen to be more physical and decidedly less psychological. Brandon looked like such a boy, and people were eager to see him in that light. He was handsome, strong, blond, and athletic. He could have been cast in an advertisement for "Boy."

During cross-examination, Ms. Fox drew Mr. Benavidez out on this point. She asked him, "Would it surprise you that as far back as December of 2002 that Brandon McInerney was suspended from school for physically fighting on school grounds? Did you know that?"

Mr. Benavidez said, "No."

Ms. Fox repeated his response, in the intonation of a question undoing his assertion, "No? Yet, in 2004, he was disciplined when he tackled another kid at school? Did you know that?"

"No."

"In 2005, November, he was suspended from school for engaging in inappropriate name calling, hitting other students and other bullying behaviors after already receiving warnings. Did you know that?"

"No."

"In 2007, he and another kid were disciplined when they were roughhousing around and Brandon McInerney hit the kid and busted his lip. Did you know that?"

"No." A hint of pique entered this assertion.

"Do any of those things change your opinion in any regard?"

"No. If I may say something, it's like my son gets in fights at school, but it doesn't make him a gang member—"

"No, we're not talking about being a gang member. We are talking about his character for violence."

"Yeah, but still a good kid, though, you know what I mean."

Walking from her desk to Mr. Benavidez on the witness stand, Ms. Fox said, "That's actually two separate things, though, Mr. Benavidez, the question was whether you considered him to be—"

"No."

"—violent. And your opinion is still no, correct?"

"Nope."

Ms. Fox stepped closer to the witness stand, then asked, "Do you consider shooting a violent act?"

Mr. Benavidez said, "Yeah."

Yeah, Brandon was violent; everyone had to begrudgingly admit. "Yeah, but still a good kid." Looking at the evidence, witnesses like

Mr. Benavidez were forced to see the violence, but they still refused to know it. They refused to know what they knew, and translate that knowledge into "character," which is a way that we commonly talk about how we know someone; how we know who they are.

When asked by Mr. Wippert if Brandon had a "violent character," Tyler Treves laughed and replied, "No. Brandon was just a fun-loving boy hanging out with everybody." Continuing to laugh, Mr. Treves recalled how he once "saw Brandon chase a cat on a Big Wheel!"

Boys will chase cats. This is true of some boys, maybe many. I preferred chasing the dog. In my lame defense, I took him to be smarter than the cat and in on the game; the dog chased me back. Boys routinely struggle to get a grip on their aggression and their concentration (as do girls, though it often emerges in different ways). Boys often run amok. Such observations are commonplace.

In recent years, though, child psychologists who study boys, myself included, have tried to distinguish between the standard-issue energetic disorganized boy and those boys who, as a consequence of neglect and abuse, spiral into more antisocial kinds of aggression; put simply, boys who grow up neglected don't learn to live in relation with others. They are sometimes described as lacking a psychological self and live instead through a physical self. They *think* with their bodies before they call on their minds. They can, and sometimes do, break their toys and injure their pets, their siblings, and their parents. They often live as isolates and are given to paranoia, which in turn fosters violence. They fight to fend off the neglect that has shaped them and continues to haunt them.

Their status as fighters is often seen as boys being boys.

Still, most boys don't chase cats. And almost no boys murder another boy, even boys who suffer neglect and abuse. Ask any seven-year-old boy, never mind a fourteen-year-old, if it is okay to shoot someone in the head (never mind twice). He will look at you with concern and say, "No."

Many days, I sat in court angry and despairing on behalf of children, boys in particular. The court proceeding offered such a low opinion of them, a view that did not hold up in the face of the variety of the boys who came before us: starched, grieving Abiam, who made us look along with him as he "looked at Larry looking up at the sky"; frightened, barely audible, baby-faced George, who wore a Metal Militia T-shirt (a reference to a song by Metallica on the album *Kill 'Em All*); gooney Jesus, who leaned back in the witness-stand chair, put his hands behind his head, and laughed anxiously; just and forceful Keith, who conveyed our collective ethical obligation to preserve life, especially lives that are vulnerable and precarious. In Keith's darkening eyes was his disgust for the way in which Brandon had stepped out, way out, of what is considered to be a normal boy.

Still, the story that made Brandon out to be a normal boy was told. Reiterated by teachers, townsfolk, correction officers, and the laughing tenor of the courtroom. Boys, it was said, are bullies. They fight. They use guns. They are cruel and intimidate others. They have limited empathy and cannot be trusted to tell you what is on their minds, because they don't know to begin with. They defy commonly held ethics; they violate the basic rights of others. If they were adults, we would call them antisocial; we would call them criminal.

Psychologists speak of such boys as having what is called a conduct disorder. Indeed, that is precisely how Dr. Kris Mohandie, the expert psychologist who testified on behalf of the prosecution, diagnosed Brandon. But by the time Dr. Mohandie took the stand near the end of the trial, he was left to swim up the *normal boy* stream.

ON AUGUST 10, THE TWENTY-SEVENTH DAY of the trial, Detective Swanson returned. It could be said that he returned as a changed man.

Under direct examination by Ms. Fox, Detective Swanson offered summations and opinions. But they did not breathe with the same precision as they did in his cross-examination with Mr. Wippert. Detective Swanson ("I love the hunt") was alive and focused when faced with an opponent like Mr. Wippert.

"Brandon McInerney is a member of Silver Strand Locals, that's your opinion, right?" Mr. Wippert asked Detective Swanson.

Detective Swanson: "Yes."

"And you believe that Silver Strand Locals is a gang, correct?"

"Correct."

"And that Brandon McInerney was Influenced by white supremacist ideologies, right?"

"Yes."

"And specifically by Matt Reaume and CRW [Confederation of Racialist Working Class Skinheads], right?"

"Most . . . I believe that he was influenced by Matt Reaume specifically—and Matt Reaume is a member of CRW, so it's a logical conclusion."

"And in your opinion, all those influences created a bias in Brandon McInerney such that he shot Larry King because of that bias. Is that right?"

Detective Swanson, leaning forward in the witness seat, and looking forcefully at Mr. Wippert, said, "No. In fact, I was very specific about separating that on several occasions on direct. My actual opinion is that Brandon McInerney had a preestablished bias, one that he had from some unknown time—expressed to Samantha Criner—as well as a statement specific to Larry King about Larry King's sexuality a week before the murder. He also went out of his way to express his intent to kill Larry King, including the specific manner and time he was going to do that."

"Okay," Mr. Wippert said, trying, it seemed, to stem the tide.

But Detective Swanson did not stop. "White supremacy and the Silver Strand Locals provided influence and support for that thought process, something that would tell him it was okay to shoot and kill Larry King because of his sexuality."

Mr. Wippert and Detective Swanson exchanged fire for three days. In a twist of casting, handsome, well-built Detective Swanson was Jimmy Stewart metaphorically pounding the witness stand, while red-eyed Mr. Wippert was a reedy, reeling John Wayne, determined to face down the law of the land as he made his stand for the territory.

Mr. Wippert said, "Well—wait a minute." He crossed the room, wiped his nose, took a drink from a Diet Coke can, and looked at his legal pad. "That's your . . . that's what you're here for . . . right? . . . you're here." His speech was slurred and slowed. "You're here to give the opinion as to why . . . that . . . this was done and it was your ultimate opinion that Brandon committed this offense because he was motivated in part or in whole by his white supremist ideology?"

Detective Swanson interjected, "No. You're skipping a most important step there."

"You say. Okay," Mr. Wippert said, not asking a question.

But that did not stop Detective Swanson, who pounced, summarizing his opinion about what had happened and why: "White supremacy and the ideology and the violence it espouses, specifically to how it addresses dealing with homosexuals, was support for the murder. Everything about that ideology says it's okay to shoot Larry King if you think he's homosexual. It's okay to shoot a homosexual. They're an abomination.

"But to say that because white supremacy says okay, that's why he did it, that is not what I'm saying.

"I'm saying, as I said very clearly, he had an expressed bias against Larry King because of his expressed belief, again, true or not, that Larry King was a homosexual.

"The day before the crime, he expresses to a total of five people, five, at varying times, his desire to either commit an act of violence or his specific intent to come to school the next day with a gun and shoot Larry. Not only is he talking about committing an act of violence, he's saying how he's going to do it, and he's saying who he's going to do it to. All of that shows a bias against Larry King specifically because of Brandon's belief that he's a homosexual, and that fits part and parcel directly in the definition of what a hate crime is."

Mr. Wippert turned away from Detective Swanson, walked back to his desk, once again wiping his nose, and said haltingly, "Again, that's your opinion. Again, that's your opinion. And I'm going to go over some of those statements because you're picking and choosing many of these statements."

Detective Swanson shot back, "Yes, the ones that are relevant."

Searching through the papers on his desk, Mr. Wippert asserted that there were "personal issues" between Larry and Brandon, issues that were not about Larry's gender, but rather, issues that constituted "sexual harassment."

Detective Swanson retorted, "There's nothing—not one thing—that directly attributed any conflict between them—that it was not connected in some way to either how Larry conducted himself or Brandon's belief that Larry was homosexual."

Detective Swanson, rivaled only by Larry's friend Averi Laskey, became the deceased's most outspoken defender. During our lunch near the end of the trial he said to me, "I don't care if Larry came to school every day, every single day, in a dress. I don't care if Larry asked Brandon to be his valentine. Such behaviors do not lead reasonable people, even teenagers, to shoot someone in the head. What happened is extreme, and honestly, any effort to explain how it happened is bound to fail. What happened moved beyond what we can understand. But what happened had nothing to do with Larry's behavior. That just doesn't add up."

Pushing against Detective Swanson's overriding will, Mr. Wippert tried to corner him and catch him out, yet Mr. Wippert was the one who was pacing like a trapped man. Numerous times on the first day of the cross-examination, and many times during the following two days, he lost his train of thought, at one point muttering, "I'm losing it." Twice, he complained that he could not see: "Sorry. My eyes are going bad."

That afternoon, Mr. Wippert challenged Detective Swanson's interpretation of a drawing made by Brandon (see figure 11).

During direct examination, Detective Swanson had linked a drawing of an eyeball with a swastika superimposed over the pupil to a "lone wolf theory." Detective Swanson held that it was "common knowledge among white supremacists" that this image, which originated with Tom Metzger, the founder of CRW (The Confederation of Racialist Working Class Skinheads), was part of Mr. Metzger's call to incite violence against

FIGURE 11

minorities. Detective Swanson linked the drawing to Tom Metzger, to Matt Reaume, and to several photographs of wolves found in Brandon's cell at the juvenile center.

Mr. Wippert referred to Detective Swanson's earlier testimony, regathering Swanson's claim about the eyeball and the lone wolf theory. Mr. Wippert then moved to his overhead projector.

He said, "Let me ask you this, what if you had found a picture of a duck in Brandon's cell, would that make any difference to you?"

Detective Swanson asked, "Are you serious?"

Mr. Wippert, grinning, replied, "Yes."

Detective Swanson, his tone rising, said, "I mean that most professionally, sir, but that sounds like a joke."

Mr. Wippert, making a backhand gesture, as though to dismiss the detective's tone, asserted, "I am serious."

Detective Swanson said, "Of course not. It's a duck. It would be meaningless in this case."

Mr. Wippert, turning on the overhead projector, asked, "Well, could you turn around and look at this exhibit? You wouldn't think it was a lone duck theory? There's swastikas in the duck's eyes, right?"

Mr. Wippert had projected an image of Donald Duck with swastikas in his eyes, although his projector and his image were so poor it was difficult to see. At first, I thought they were a pair of gray bedroom slippers.

Detective Swanson, searching the image, concluded, "I have no idea what that is."

Mr. Wippert, laughing, said, "Never seen that one before, huh? Let me bring it to you. Have you heard of the lone duck theory?"

Detective Swanson repeated, "I just want to clarify that you're being serious. I have not testified to anything that I thought was a joke about this case or white supremacy, sir."

Moving quickly, returning to the projector, having never handed Detective Swanson the image of the duck, telling Detective Swanson that he, Mr. Wippert, "was asking the questions," Mr. Wippert put a second image on the projector.

He continued, "Just so you know, sir, a photo of President Obama with swastikas in his eyes. Have you ever seen that?"

Detective Swanson, looking around the room, as if to locate himself, answered, "Never seen that before, and I wonder where the inspiration for that photo came from, though."

Mr. Wippert: "You don't know what the inspiration for that photo was, but it's swastikas in the eyes of our president."

Detective Swanson: "I've never seen that photo. I have no idea where it came from, who created it, or when it was created."

Pacing, brandishing a stack of papers, Mr. Wippert put another image on the projector, this one of Queen Elizabeth with swastikas in her eyes.

"What in the hell is he doing?" an elderly man in the front row asked loudly.

"Going crazy," his friend said.

Mr. Wippert put yet another image on the projector and said, "All right. This one actually might be more appropriate. This is President Bush with some swastikas in his eyes. You ever see this photo?"

Detective Swanson, again searching the room, looking at the judge as if he might act to restore some order, asked, "How is that appropriate?"

"Answer the question. Have you ever seen it?" Mr. Wippert said emphatically.

"No," Detective Swanson said.

Mr. Wippert asked, "Never seen any other photos with swastikas in his eyes?"

Detective Swanson: "No. And I'm still not sure if you're doing this as a joke or not."

Suddenly, Mr. Wippert returned to his desk. He appeared to be looking for something. Taking hold of a piece of paper, he reviewed the way in which Detective Swanson had linked the drawing of the eyeball with the swastika-eyeball from Tom Metzger ("You found it on his Web site. Right?") to Matt Reaume ("You found a similar image in his house. Right?") to Brandon ("You found the image you showed us in some papers in a notebook. Right?"). Mr. Wippert was not looking at Detective Swanson, and he did not appear to be addressing the detective. It was as if he were summarizing the sequence for himself.

Mr. Wippert said, "Those are the steps that led up to your opinion. You saw a drawing of an eyeball and put all of this together, right?"

Detective Swanson, responding forcefully, angrily, said, "No, that is completely wrong, and I've said on several occasions including today that white supremacy is an influence and the aspects of what it teaches and what it promotes and supports—"

Mr. Wippert interrupted, "Your Honor, I'm going to object as nonresponsive. I'd ask that it be stricken."

The judge, looking wearily upon the scene, concurred with the objection. He said, "Everything after 'no, that is completely wrong,'" was to be stricken.

With that, Mr. Wippert abruptly sat down, saying, "I'm done. Thank you very much, sir."

I half imagined that Mr. Wippert was going to say, "Ha! You've been punked!" But no one was laughing.

The mood in the court was actually one of fear. A woman sitting behind me said, "This is getting frightening." I took her to mean that the bullying dimension, coupled with the disorganization and paranoid aggression, had left her unmoored, as it had left me.

My own anxiety and heightened attention led me to wonder if what we were witnessing did not mimic Brandon's life: disorganization, chaos, paranoia, hyperactivity, loss of coordination and perception, menacing. Men fighting.

Brandon sat still, as always. My mind turned back to the drawings, and I began to think about the demands of guard duty: pull away, pull in, arm. Watch the horizon. Learn to see fast. Mute feeling, mute pain. Take orders. Seethe. Snap.

8

A Green Dress

It was the afternoon of July 28, the eighteenth day of the trial. We had all just returned from lunch and the noonday glare. Madame Clerk handed two brown paper bags to the defense cocounsel Robyn Bramson, who set about to open the smaller of the two bags from which she pulled out an even smaller bag. The little bag, the sort that was made for gifts, had seen some wear. Black and magenta leopard print with a hot pink interior, it had once been trimmed with black marabou; a couple of sad tufts held on. Ms. Bramson looked inside the crumpled little bag and pulled out yet another even smaller bag, a clear plastic cosmetics clutch. She fingered assorted cosmetics (mascara, Day-Glo green and yellow nail polishes, a pink lip liner) before she put them back in the clutch, which she returned to the gift bag and set it aside.

Wearing a stiff gray suit, the sort that is called women's business attire and sits on a woman's body as opposed to fitting her, Ms. Bramson returned to the smaller of the two brown paper bags and took out a pair of shoes, black matronly wedges. She struggled to balance the shoes on the ledge of the judicial assistant's desk.

Then Ms. Bramson turned to the larger industrial-grade bag, made with adhered layers of thick brown paper, and sealed with broad bands of cellophane tape. She pulled at the tape; it would not give. The judicial assistant offered a pair of scissors. Ms. Bramson cut through the tape, and still the bag would not yield. Persisting, she pried it open, as the bag crinkled and clacked (a herald!). She pulled out a dress.

She asked with more formality than was her custom, "May I approach the witness, Your Honor?"

"Yes," the judge replied.

Ms. Bramson draped the dress over her forearms and walked across the courtroom, holding the dress as a lady's maid might. Everyone leaned forward, carefully, quietly, so as not to disturb. It looked as though she were carrying the body of a dead girl. The gauzy, lifeless dress was yellowgreen, shrill, fleshly, small, so very small.

Kendra McInerney began to weep as Ms. Bramson turned to the witness, Dawn Boldrin, Larry's homeroom teacher, who was making her second appearance in the court.

Haltingly, Ms. Bramson asked, "I'm handing you—well, I'm holding up in front of you—a green dress. Do you recognize it?"

Ms. Boldrin said, "I do." She began to weep. "Sorry. I do, yes. That was my daughter's tenth-grade homecoming dress."

"You okay?" Ms. Bramson asked.

"Yeah, I'm okay. I'm sorry. You know—girls," Ms. Boldrin said with a weak smile.

The room welcomed Ms. Boldrin's girly charm, her large brown eyes magnified by tears, even as we could see that she was not "okay." Just as we were assembled to contemplate the murder of a girl whose existence, while she lived, had not been acknowledged as a life.

The dress had been mentioned so often it had lit up in our minds like a costume and had taken on a kind of drag grandeur. It had been called "puffy," "poufy," "glittering," and "flowing." In my mind it was an old bridesmaid's gown, Kelly green satin that would engulf anyone who put it on.

Ms. Bramson walked back across the room and folded the dress, the way a mother might attend to her daughter's carelessly discarded clothing. As she did so, we saw clearly that this dress that had become a symbol of sexual harassment and gender gone wild was simply a little girl's party dress. It looked stiff and itchy. Ms. Bramson carefully put the dress back in the large brown bag.

Ms. Bramson crossed to the defense table and picked up a piece of paper. She explained that it was a photocopied photograph. We could not see the image from the gallery. She asked Ms. Boldrin if she recognized it.

Ms. Boldrin said, "I sure do," and started to cry. It was a photograph she had taken with her cell phone upon Larry's request, she explained. He wanted Ms. Boldrin to send the picture to her daughter by way of a thank-you. Ms. Boldrin looked toward the back of the room, where her daughter was sitting. Ms. Boldrin put her hands to her eyes and wept.

Ms. Bramson turned away, tearfully, saying, "Now you've got me going."

She then put the photocopied picture on an overhead projector and asked the bailiff to dim the lights. We saw Leticia blurred by the black-and-white photocopy, blurred even more by the projection. Apparitional, she hovered. Despite the blurry image, we could see that she was holding a dress up to her chin. The photograph was a close-up, and we could only see the bodice of the dress; it bisected the photo. Leticia was also wearing gloves. They glowed in the blown-out photocopy like her wide illuminated smile that dominated and hung in the projected air.

Kendra, Brandon's mother, was sobbing, her head bent forward, rasping as she struggled to breathe. Ms. Boldrin struggled as well, and spoke to the room as if she were talking to a friend, "Sorry. Man. Phew."

Ms. Bramson asked Ms. Boldrin if she had, in fact, sent the photo to her daughter. Ms. Boldrin explained that she had: "I sent it to my daughter because my daughters—I don't know. I think as a mother I tried to raise my daughters to be good people, and I had noted to them why Larry was in foster care because he was being beat for being—"

Ms. Boldrin was cut off by Ms. Fox, who objected to these comments as hearsay. The judge instructed the jury that they should disregard what Ms. Boldrin had just said.

But the judge's order was overtaken by a ricocheting clatter. Greg and Dawn King had abruptly stood up. Their auditorium-style seats sprang back and hit the seats' backrests. The noise of their chairs met the clatter of the door as they shouldered their way out of the room.

Dawn King, stepping through the door, hissed "Assholes!" without turning around.

The following day, the defense alleged that Dawn King had aimed her comment at Ms. Boldrin's daughter, who was sitting in the back row of the gallery. Dawn King did not defend herself and (like James Bing) was ejected from the courtroom. She would not be allowed to return until the verdict and sentencing.

At the moment Leticia entered the room, arguably for the first time, bringing with her the impact of her gendered life, the Kings left. Up to this point in the courtroom, Leticia had been quiet among the small dead. We rarely heard from her in court; her words were rarely quoted. Her wishes were consistently edited, sometimes denuded, but more often exaggerated. Her desires had not been *seen* until now: some makeup, a girl's party dress, high-heeled shoes.

In the wake of the Kings' abrupt departure, I looked around, "What just happened?" people in the room seemed to be saying through looks of fear and confusion. Minds skip a beat in the midst of such heightened emotion and confusion. I wondered if we might have found our way into the kind of upheaval in which Leticia so often found herself.

Moments such as these, no matter their dramatic trill, passed quickly in the courtroom. The business of the court moved along, and Ms. Bramson made her way back across the room. She returned to the smaller of the two brown bags and pulled out a pair of brown suede boots. With them in hand, she walked back to Ms. Boldrin on the witness stand.

Ms. Bramson said, "Miss Boldrin, I'm approaching you with a pair of boots. Do you recognize these?"

Ms. Boldrin, with a faint smile, answered, "Yes."

"And how do you recognize them?"

"I'd watch Larry walk down the hallways in those things."

"And how—how high would you estimate the heel is on these boots?"

"Is that an inch and a half to two inches? They were too high, put it that way, for him."

Ms. Bramson brought out another pair of boots and the black wedges, and Ms. Boldrin, following Ms. Bramson's questions, described the boots as "black patent leather . . . ankle length boots." Yet by Ms. Boldrin's lights, distinguishing between the pairs of shoes did not matter. What mattered was Larry's effort to walk in them: "The problem being he walked—they were difficult for him to walk in." At the same time, she could see that he enjoyed "clip-clopping around": "Larry liked to hear the noise when he walked in those."

Like the green dress, the boots were sad. They were at once limp, matronly, and worn out. Their heels were much lower than other teachers had described them. (Shirley Brown, for example, spoke of Larry wearing "four inch heels.") The noise they made, the practice they had survived, the femininity that they had helped to accomplish were over. Ms. Bramson returned to the judicial assistant's desk and put the boots back in the brown paper bag.

THE DENIAL THAT LETICIA MET with in life was mirrored in the court. Those who sat in the courtroom never learned that she had explained that she was a "transwoman" when speaking to her PE teacher, Kenneth Davis. I learned this a year after the trial while reviewing the deputy district attorney's investigation files. At the time Leticia appeared in court and at the time the Kings left the room, the word "transgender" had been mentioned once by a parent/witness who had observed Leticia while dropping her son off at school. This mother remarked that she was "surprised that E. O. Green had such a tolerant policy toward transgender children."

Leticia was granted permission to use a private bathroom, as opposed to the boys' locker room. This negotiation, this recognition of Leticia came and went during the trial, provoking little curiosity. The wish for privacy was named as "gay," despite the way in which the request came after Leticia's explanation to Mr. Davis that she no longer stood to pee. Leticia was not speaking as an anxious gay boy; she was speaking as a transgirl.

Even more telling is the intimacy expressed in Leticia's complaint to Mr. Davis that boys forgot to put the toilet seat up. This raw detail, skin to clammy seat, brings us closer to Leticia's fleshly body and genital experience. What body was she seeking to find through this daily experience? What did she imagine as she began to shape her body by shaving her pubic hair (yet more fleshly, yet more naked) as I learned she had when I read the coroner's report? We don't know how these fantasies and embodiments may have evolved.

Just as Leticia's transfemininity struggled to find a name and a body in the courtroom, the idea that a boy could wish to be a girl was spurned at E. O. Green. Even though changing gender is a common fantasy, one that most everyone has entertained at some point, it is nevertheless an idea that is met with regular resistance. Most of us live with and settle into our natal bodies and the social conventions of gender with little thought. Seamless social norms shape us; we are mostly unaware, and rarely question. We might wish to weigh less or swagger more, but for the most part, we make our compromises and move along.

Taking action, making a claim, and accounting for one's self as a transgender person is rare. And transgender life was not as well recognized or documented in 2008 as it is today. Laverne Cox, the statuesque transgender actress, had yet to appear on the cover of *Time* magazine, as she did in June 2014, heralding "The Transgender Tipping Point: America's Next Civil Rights Frontier." The president of the United States had yet to utter the word transgender, as Barack Obama did in January 2015 during his State of the Union address. Yet to make national headlines was seventeen-year-old Leelah Alcorn's suicide, linked in a note she posted on Tumblr to her feelings of despair around ever transitioning successfully and the oppression she faced as a transadolescent. Caitlyn Jenner, the heroically former boy/man (Bruce), had yet to go on national television and tell Diane Sawyer that he was a woman, as he did in April 2015 to an audience of 17 million. The US secretary of defense, Ashton Carter, had yet to announce that the Pentagon would lift its ban on open service by transgender troops, as he did in July 2015.

Still, there were likely about seven hundred thousand transgender people living in the United States in 2008. Like Leticia, they were showing up at schools, at the hardware store, on the bus, at PTA meetings. The oppression they faced was widely documented (if not nationally reported), including homelessness, unemployment, incarceration, assault, and murder.

Leticia was rare, to be sure. But she was hardly the only transgender adolescent to show up at an American school in the winter of 2008. Yet her gender questioning alone was enough to upset the social order at E. O. Green, or, more to the point, the order that the teachers sought to enforce. Her gender questioning was only weeks old, although her girlishness and her sexual curiosity were not new. As Averi observed from the witness stand in the first week of the trial, "Even back in third, fourth, fifth grade, it was fairly obvious that he was—he had a lot of feminine qualities to him. In the way he acted. He didn't look very feminine, but the way he acted."

Teacher Shirley Brown, speaking from the witness stand on August 1, a little over two weeks after Averi had testified, also described Larry as "always having been, you know, feminine." Ms. Brown, wearing a boxy white blouse, brown slacks, and heavy black crepe soled shoes, went on to tell Mr. Wippert that Larry had begun to question his sexuality at least a year before the murder, when he was in seventh grade. Larry had told her that he thought he might be gay, and asked Ms. Brown what she thought he should do. Ms. Brown had responded, "Nothing, nothing is what you should do." With an expression of sour satisfaction, she told Mr. Wippert that she had "cautioned Larry to hold back on any decision-making and to wait till his junior year in high school." Ms. Brown had directed Larry to the closet.

Similarly, Susan Crowley, Larry's seventh-grade special resource teacher, who spoke in heartfelt ways about her affection for Larry, both from the witness stand and when I met her at her home two weeks after the trial, also indicated that she did not believe junior high was the proper time and place for sexuality. Ms. Crowley's sentiment surprised me. Unlike Ms. Brown, Ms. Crowley did not radiate propriety. She wore six earrings in each ear. She had traveled with the Peace Corps prior to "settling down" and teaching. Her home was decorated with African and Polynesian art. She reminded me of the hippie girls who were older than I was when I was in junior high school: the girls I looked up to.

On my visit to Ms. Crowley's home, after we had been talking for a while, I told her that I was surprised by her opinion. It struck me that such thinking was out of touch with modern kids, and with a school population where kids like Larry, at age fifteen, were still in junior high.

I thought that Ms. Crowley and her fellow teachers had confused Larry's sexuality and gender. Everything about Larry had been gathered under the umbrella term "gay," and the term was both overbroad and imprecise. I explained that while some gay boys are feminine in their bearing and being, boyhood femininity does not automatically add up to homosexuality. Gender intertwines with sexuality, but it does not define sexual preferences in the way that the teachers were presuming. The teachers had presumed that Larry's femininity signaled a gay identity. I added that Larry may have used the word "gay" to try to say something about his sexual wishes, but that this term felt off the mark, especially in relation to his life just prior to his death.

This point seemed important because during the last weeks of his life, Larry, by everyone's account, had been energetically engaged in questioning his gender identity. Not his sexual identity per se. I wondered if Larry had been reaching for a transgendered identity, as was, in fact, his claim. If that was the case (no matter where that identity was leading), it meant that his sexuality at the time of his death would then have to be understood as "homo-erratic," a play on "homoerotic" coined by Gayle Salamon. In other words, Leticia was a transgirl who desired boys.

Ms. Crowley looked down at her hands, then out toward a set of tattered Tibetan prayer flags draped over a pond in her garden. (She strings new flags every year on the anniversary of her mother's death.) She said, "Yes, yes, I think you are right. Yes. How did I not know? That is terrible."

But Ms. Crowley did not waver regarding the place for frank sexuality in junior high. At first she spoke specifically about "Larry's immaturity, despite his actual age," and her belief that he was "spinning" in ways that caused her to worry: "He needed a firmer hand. He did not have it. You have to understand that he was very dear, but not very steady."

Ms. Crowley then shifted to speaking pessimistically about E. O. Green as a poor broken-down school in a poor neighborhood. A worn-out mother, E. O. Green had originally been designed for six hundred children; at the time of the shooting there were over one thousand students. The cupboard was bare. Pencils were hard to come by. Many teachers brought in their own supplies, which they took home with them every night lest they get stolen. The school was failing at the basics, and by Ms. Crowley's estimation it could not take on one more thing: "I tell the girls to button up their blouses and open their book."

Gender, sexuality, and race were matters of discipline, not education.

On July 31, when Jill Ekman, a seventh-grade language arts teacher, took the stand, she spoke directly to the need for discipline. With the bearing of an athlete and her light brown hair pulled back in a tight ponytail, she told Mr. Wippert that she had been cataloging claims about Larry during the last month of his life. He blew kisses. He chased boys. He flirted. He proposed. He taunted. But her primary concern, as she told Mr. Wippert, was that Larry was chasing boys into the boys' bathroom: "He followed a child into the bathroom, according to my knowledge, and that is sexual harassment in my mind, or bullying. It was taking away the rights of the child to go to the restroom. I mean, it wasn't right."

Ms. Ekman had to recast her tale of harassment when Ms. Fox cross-examined her right after she spoke with Mr. Wippert. No, she had not witnessed Larry chasing any boys into bathrooms. And, yes, she had to admit that four, no seven, no two boys, Victor and Jesus, no it was one boy, Victor, who had complained to her about the alleged bathroom incident.

Ms. Ekman held that the boys wanted to beat Larry up for "what he was doing to them." They were being called gay—everybody was being called gay—and "they didn't like that stigma." The week before Brandon shot Larry, Ms. Ekman had counseled the boys in her homeroom class to "stay away" from Larry.

And she had confronted Larry about his appearance on several occasions in late January of 2008, a couple of weeks before he was killed. She had spoken to him when she came upon him in the outdoor walkways. The first time, he had been wearing makeup. She told him to wash it off, and so he did. A few days later, she found him wearing makeup again, and again she told him to wash it off. He told her that it was within his "rights" to wear makeup; she grew angry. A few days later, she confronted him once more. This time she had chastised him for chasing boys. He had told her that he liked chasing boys and making them squirm.

The squirming boys did not tell quite the same story. Victor had to admit, when questioned by Ms. Fox during the first week of the trial, on July 7, that he had told Ms. Ekman the chasing story after the shooting. And he told Ms. Ekman the story after he had heard it first from George; it was a story George would later deny. Jesus, despite George's denial, told Ms. Fox that he had seen Larry chase George, but not into a bathroom. And only after Jesus had put his finger in the air and said, "I smell queer!" George had joined in the teasing, and Larry had chased both boys across the playground.

Jesus, seventeen years old when he got to the witness stand, still could not stop laughing when he thought back to the time Larry chased him. In fact, Ms. Fox, uncertain as to how to interpret Jesus's behavior, spoke with him about the serious nature of the proceedings. Somewhat chastened, he nevertheless kept laughing, because the boys were just playing with Larry. It was a nip, not a bite. That's how Jesus saw it. Plus Larry served it back: "Larry could *run* in those heels. It was sick!"

Ms. Ekman saw it otherwise. She told Mr. Wippert that about a month before the shooting, Larry "started getting a little more forward. He was very cocky, and he was never cocky and disrespectful in seventh grade." And Ms. Ekman had pushed back against Larry's gender questioning and transgender practice. To Ms. Ekman, Larry's appearance looked foolish. It looked manic. It looked dangerous. "Wearing makeup as a boy in junior high could cause potential problems with other kids teasing him and causing disruption in the classroom," she declared. Larry had gone too far. To Ms. Ekman, the rule of order superseded Larry's individual rights.

THROUGHOUT THE TRIAL, BEGINNING WITH Mr. Wippert's opening statement on the first day of the proceedings, "rights" were spoken of as "rights that had gone too far." There was rarely any defense of Larry's legal or constitutional rights within the court, nor had there been any at E. O. Green. In the court, as had been the case at E. O. Green, the task of naming and defending Larry's rights fell to Assistant Principal Joy Epstein.

On July 11, during the second week of the trial, Ms. Epstein, a curvy blonde in a dark blue summer dress, explained to Ms. Fox that near the end of January 2008 (she could not remember the exact date), a substitute teacher had sent Larry to her office. The teacher had refused Larry entrance into class. Ms. Epstein recalled that Larry was "wearing feminine purple eye shadow and earrings along with high-heeled boots, but he was in his uniform with the blue pants and the white shirt which was our designated school uniform." That morning, Ms. Epstein consulted her superior at the district office, who instructed her that in accord with California Law SB 777, the district policy did not allow for discrimination based on gender presentation.

From the witness stand, Ms. Epstein recounted for Ms. Fox how she had told Larry, in late January of 2008, that "he was within his rights with what he had on," and she had walked him back to his class and informed the substitute teacher of the district policy. Then or

thereabouts, she had also told Larry that "junior high is the most difficult time for all students and that by dressing the way that he was
dressing it would bring—it could possibly be very difficult for him,
and it was his choice." She went on: "I remember my exact words. I said,
'More power to you, if you can get through it.'"

Ms. Epstein had further consultations with the district office, a
meeting with Joel Lovestedt, E. O. Green's principal, and meetings
with her fellow assistant principals. These meetings and consultations
had resulted in an e-mail that was sent to the faculty on or around February 4, 2008. The e-mail instructed teachers and staff that in accord
with the district's gender nondiscrimination policy, Larry was within
his rights to wear feminine accessories so long as he was in his school
uniform. The e-mail also suggested that Larry's gender variance was
an opportunity to "teach tolerance."

Despite the guidance offered by the e-mail and despite an eighth-
grade core curriculum that included a unit focused on tolerance, not one
teacher, with the exception of Dawn Boldrin, took the opportunity to
inquire about the meaning of rights, the freedom to name oneself, or
the struggle to claim a minority identity. No effort was made to talk
about or teach gender as an *idea*, one that may have offered the kids
more room to consider Leticia and to reflect on their own gendered
lives.

Nor was there any effort among the teachers or the administration
to help the kids develop the empathy that one extends to a child who
is known to be fragile. Larry had always received special education support services. He was possibly one of the children at E. O. Green most
in need of care and understanding.

Yet the treatment of Leticia at E. O. Green was one of steady and
angry opposition to helping her or even to thinking about her; the chief
objective at E. O. Green was to stop her. As Jill Ekman put it, "Teaching tolerance was not the answer for what was going on." Discipline was
called for. Ms. Ekman's signal anxiety—her fear that trouble soon
would be upon them—was on high. Specifically, she feared that the
boys would get in trouble for attacking Larry. She listened to the

boys, and to her mind the stories of Larry's provocations were true, no matter rumor's embellishments. The stories carried aggression. She could feel it.

On the Friday before what Ms. Ekman referred to as "the incident," she had filed a grievance with the administration. She had questioned the administration's judgment. In particular, she believed that Ms. Epstein was not acting with due care; her mistrust was shared by several other teachers. They believed that as a lesbian, Joy Epstein could not see the situation clearly. The teachers felt that Ms. Epstein was using Larry to push her own "gay agenda." The administration turned away Jill Ekman and her grievance, stating that the school was simply following district policy.

Shirley Brown, who had been one of Larry's seventh-grade teachers, shared Jill Ekman's view of Ms. Epstein from the witness stand in answering a question posed by Mr. Wippert: "I think she had her own agenda. I think she wasn't forthcoming with that." Ms. Brown confided, "I stayed away from her." Ms. Epstein's candid manner troubled Ms. Brown: "Her own personal issues with being gay—I never really have heard in education somebody announce it so forthrightly."

Again, the closet was the solution. Not dialogue. Not tolerance. Not community. When I raised this idea of "the closet as solution" with Dawn Boldrin during an interview on July 31, she laughed, and said, "No shit, Sherlock!"

Still laughing, she asked, "What planet do you live on?"

"A different one," I replied.

During the first month of the trial, while booked into Extended Stay on summer break from teaching and on leave from most of my private practice, I had been doing evening phone sessions with several patients, including a young transboy who was preparing for "top surgery" to construct a more masculine chest. I had known and worked with this boy and his family for five years. My work with him and other gender-expansive and transpeople was complex, as befits idiomatic and intricate human psyches. I had worked with his school to help them introduce and educate their student body about gender and transgender experience.

In the middle of New York City, a world distinct from the one Leticia had found herself in at E. O. Green, I had had to help my patient's school staff not make this boy into a paragon of brave difference, a position that he neither sought nor desired.

Speaking from my planet, I did not tell Ms. Boldrin that while resources may not have been plentiful in 2008, there were nevertheless resources available to help a school integrate a transgender child into its community. A quick Web search would have brought any interested adult to the Outreach Program for Children with Gender-Variant Behaviors and Their Families, a support network begun in 1999 by the physician Edgardo Menvielle. Or to the GLSEN (Gay, Lesbian, Straight Education Network) Web site, where information offered by educators could have been found.

But I did say to Ms. Boldrin that it did not seem out of place to me that someone like Joy Epstein could have set up a meeting with the teachers to offer some guidance and education, or perhaps bring in an educator who had experience working with transgendered kids. After all, Ms. Epstein was the liaison with Casa Pacifica, where Leticia's gender questioning was being taken up with greater respect. How were Leticia or her teachers supposed to bridge the differences between Casa and E. O. Green? Ms. Epstein encouraged Leticia's daring, and with a verbal pat on the back: "More power to you, if you can get through it." A verbal pat on the back that hinged on a dependent clause: "*if* you can get through it." Exactly what power did Leticia have? How exactly was she to exercise that power without a community upon which she could depend?

Outside of any way to speak, to debate, or to struggle toward recognition, the only power that seemed to be at hand was the power of "no." Leticia was left to undo and defy.

Ms. Epstein faced similarly limited options. Like Larry, she had the power of the law. But she did not have a community that stood with her, nor did they stand by the law. In an interview right after the trial, she said, "I did not make any decisions, I was only following the district's guidelines. And still I became the focal point because of my sexuality." When I asked her about teachers' complaints regarding Larry and about teachers' perception that she was granting him special rights, Ms. Epstein said, "Yes, teachers were upset. Not because anyone reported that Larry was doing things to other students or making them uncomfortable. No kid ever came to me and complained about Larry's way of dressing, acting, and somebody would have said something. Kids talk. And let's remember, it was only nine days! The teachers were upset because of the way Larry was changing—changing into somebody not of the norm. They wanted him to go back to being a normal boy."

Later in my interview with her, Ms. Epstein elaborated, "The teachers at E. O. Green were veteran, older, white, Christian. Larry made them uncomfortable. And I had to tell them that Larry's expression, just like anyone's, was his right, his civil right, and that he deserved to be protected just like anyone else."

Despite how well she understood the teachers at E. O. Green, Ms. Epstein was still shocked by their response to Larry and by their characterization of her defense of his rights as a "gay agenda": "These were people—these were work friends, people who knew my partner, knew my child. And this idea that I had a gay agenda is crazy." She laughed. "My sisters tease me: I don't even own a rainbow flag and have never been to Pride." Ms. Epstein's feelings of alienation magnified after the murder, when disagreement quickly turned to blame: "I was the rabbit in the lion's den. Blamed for something no one could have seen coming." She added tearfully and emphatically, "In nine days what could Larry possibly have done to elicit getting shot in the back of the head two times?"

After the murder, Ms. Epstein felt that she, too, had become a target "with a lesbian sign over [her] head." She lived for several years with "a lot of fear, a lot of fear." When Brandon was to be released from juvenile detention to attend his father's funeral, she called a friend, who was a police officer, to come and stay with her, because she feared for her life. She also absorbed the condemnation that she had somehow brought on Larry's death: "I what if-ed, what if-ed, what if-ed. What if

I had only let Larry go back to Casa the day before [the murder]? I beat myself a lot."

Like Ms. Epstein, Ms. Boldrin found her life unalterably changed—and frightening—after Leticia's death. Right after the shooting, she took a two-month leave and underwent treatment for depression. According to Ms. Boldrin, when she set about to return to E. O. Green, "the administration could not assure me that me or my students would be safe. They had made no security changes whatsoever." In the course of these safety discussions with the administration, she claimed that "they told me they no longer had a job for me. Bam! Out!"

At the time of the trial, and when we sat down for our interview, in late July of 2011, Ms. Boldrin had not yet found her way back into any school. She was working at Starbucks. She had been hospitalized five times for depression and post-traumatic stress. The police dragged her from her home in front of her children after she provoked a physical fight with her husband. Popping balloons still sent her into a cold sweat.

During her second appearance in court in late July, Ms. Boldrin took to the witness stand as one might take to the town square: she was there to speak her mind. Deputy District Attorney Fox objected fifty-four times, and Judge Campbell sustained the objections thirty-five times, ordering Ms. Boldrin's remarks "stricken." Ms. Boldrin persisted. Let them object; she spoke her words; she offered her trauma-riven mind as evidence.

Near the end of her cross-examination with Ms. Bramson on July 28, Ms. Boldrin spoke about the way in which the confrontation of the witness stand brought "it all back up." She said, "I work every day at living with what we've all been through. You don't recover from something like that. You simply live, and people don't like to deal with how uncomfortable it is, and so we all just simply pretend it didn't happen for the majority of everybody. And when we're confronted with situations like this, it brings it all back up, and it's very difficult to deal with, and people blame us for their uncomfortableness."

It was a commonplace to hear people blame Ms. Boldrin and Ms. Epstein for the shooting. After the trial, Susan Crowley told me, "Joy

Epstein and Dawn Boldrin are responsible for Larry's death; Brandon was just the conduit." Greg King, waving his cigarette at me in the first interview that I conducted with him and Dawn, said, "Joy Epstein is the one with blood on her hands. She was the alpha male in that school, and she had a politically motivated agenda; she was using Larry to start up a LGBT club at that school." His face reddening, Greg said, "She told me that he had the right to do it. Parents don't have the right to direct their own kids' behavior." Sitting with us at the same table, Dawn King chimed in, "And that Dawn Boldrin didn't know her head from her ass! What did she think she was doing?"

LIVING GENDER, ESPECIALLY AS IT blooms in adolescence, brings forth a host of emotions and counteremotions or defenses. When a group of people, such as schoolteachers, cannot consider those emotions, cannot discuss what is being felt and thought about gender, cannot learn together, then gender variance can be felt as too much, and reactive discipline short-circuits any building of community.

Without community there was no setting for negotiation and recognition, even in the face of differences of opinion—or especially in the face of differences of opinion. Without a community there was no way to speak about Leticia's gender as it undoubtedly intertwined with her well-known fragile mind. Gender is not only practiced by the sturdy and the steady among us.

Gender variance can only come into being and be practiced when fantasy and play are given the room to symbolize a body and to shape a gender into flesh and force. From that play space, from those fantasies, bodies are made and sexualities are found.

Leticia was outside the pack, but in many ways she wasn't up to that much more than the rest of her peers, as they were the first to tell us. They were fumbling through their first crushes. They were wobbling in their first pair of high heels. They were stealing cigarettes from their mothers' purses. But the anxiety of the adults left Leticia very little room to grow; her only option was defiance.

Employing diagnostic language, the sort that gets applied to problem kids, the defense team defined Larry (not Leticia) as "negative attention seeking." Repeatedly, the defense worked to shift the jury's perception of Larry from that of a kid with poor social skills, a kid who had trouble regulating his emotions, a kid who had trouble expressing himself, a kid who might blurt or talk out of turn, into a kid who was looking for trouble.

No efforts were made—again, short of those offered by Dawn Boldrin—to help Leticia pace and regulate her excitement, to practice her femininity, to reflect on her own behavior, and to recognize how those around her might be feeling, even if those feelings were not fair or just.

Like Jill Ekman, Shirley Brown asked the administration to "put an end to this." She bypassed Assistant Principal Epstein and went to Joel Lovestedt, the principal. Ms. Brown feared violence, even to the point of vividly imagining it. She told Mr. Wippert that she went to Principal Lovestedt and told him "that if something wasn't done soon that Larry would be taken behind the back shed of the PE area and beaten to death!"

During cross-examination, Ms. Fox returned to Ms. Brown's graphic prediction.

Ms. Fox asked Ms. Brown, "Who did you think was going to beat him to death?"

Ms. Brown replied, "To the best of my knowledge, I said, 'The boys are going to take him behind the PE shed and beat him to death.'"

"Did you mean that?"

Ms. Brown emphatically said, "Yes."

"Who did you think was going to beat him to death?"

Agitated, shifting in her seat, Ms. Brown crisply said, "Any boy that might have had difficulty with what Larry was choosing to do."

"Do you think that would have been a reasonable response?"

"Did I think that my response was reasonable?"

"No. Do you think beating someone to death for dressing in the attire he was dressing [in] is a reasonable response?"

Ms. Brown, incredulous, her voice shaking, said, "Certainly not, but I'm not a junior high student!"

"Well, I'll leave it. You didn't ever hear any student voice any intention to do violence towards Larry King, correct?"

"That is correct."

LARRY'S PEERS, ALMOST TO A kid, were not as aggrieved or brimming with violent visions as were many of his teachers. They readily spoke about how Larry had been teased and bullied. He was taunted, tripped, and shoved. In the last days of his life, it was also understood that he had begun to shove back. George, Jesus, Antwan spoke about Larry with agitation and titillation. But despite the stereotype of boys as aggressive, as killers, not one of those boys moved from agitation toward lethal aggression. When Brandon, the one person who did harbor such intentions, tried to engage them on the Monday before the murder, the boys backed away from him.

Larry was hardly the only kid with a lot on his mind and loud ways of expressing it. Larry was one among many emerging fantasies. As Victor put it, "It wasn't a hot topic. It was more like, kind of like, he stood out."

Others, like Jesus, spoke through a mix of taunting ("I smell queer!"). Mostly, they found it "funny." Sure, maybe Larry risked getting hurt. But who doesn't get knocked around a bit? Keith perceptively suggested that the idea of Larry as "funny" was a way for some kids to handle their anxiety about his gender transition. Still the few kids, like Kaj, who spoke about being bothered by Larry, all spoke about handling their distress by ignoring or avoiding him.

Ms. Fox asked every kid who took the stand, "Were you afraid of Larry King?" Every kid either laughed at the notion of Larry as someone to be afraid of, or seemed confused by such a thought.

She also asked every kid who took the stand, "Did you ever hear Larry King say anything that was sexually inappropriate or provocative?" Every answer was "No."

Ms. Fox took up these ideas with Keith, who was described by the defense as Brandon's best friend at school, but who showed no evidence of such a friendship in the court. Somber, perceptive Keith looked at his so-called friend and did not smile.

Ms. Fox asked Keith, "When you had the incident when Larry King passed in the hall, he made the comment to Brandon McInerney and Brandon was upset and you were upset, did you think about going and beating the crap out of Larry?"

Keith, his eyes darkening as he looked toward Brandon, said, "Absolutely not, no."

"Never entered your mind, right?"

"No. Never had a problem with Larry."

"So while it might have been disturbing, it wasn't disturbing to the point where—"

"—I wanted to fight him, no."

"Would there have been any point in fighting him?"

"For me, no."

"Does that mean it wouldn't have been much of a fight, right?"

"No, well, yes, it would not be much of a fight."

"You indicated that there were—were there others, other boys at school that Larry would also make comments to?"

"No. He would just make like facial expressions, like walk towards the boys, and the boys knew that Larry was trying to not really harass, but just bother."

In contrast to Keith's testimony and the testimony of every one of his peers, the defense steadily argued that Larry "targeted" Brandon through his gendered being and through direct and harassing expressions of sexual interest. Mr. Wippert and Ms. Bramson skillfully employed the teachers' phobias and ignorance to help make their case, even though the only teacher who spoke of seeing the boys interact, Arthur Saenz, bracketed his observation by talking about what he took to be Brandon's anger and alienation.

There was, however, one chink in this steadfast argument: a slip of the tongue, and by the defense psychologist, Dr. Donald Hoagland, no less, a slip that opens onto the question of who was the target and why.

Quoting from a 2001 study called *Hostile Hallways*, Dr. Hoagland told us that "among boys, the most upsetting form of sexual harassment was to be called gay." He focused on how some kids had called Brandon gay, and implied that this happened as kids observed Larry flirting with Brandon.

Dr. Hoagland did not speak to how often Brandon was called gay. Nor did Dr. Hoagland speak to the fact that "gay" has become the all-purpose put-down. The ubiquity of "gay" proliferates with meaning and meaninglessness; targets abound. You can be gay because you are suspected of being homosexual. You can be gay because you are wearing a pink shirt. You can be gay because you suck at sports. You can be gay because you excel at sports.

Advancing the argument about targeting, Ms. Bramson asked Dr. Hoagland, "Based on your review of the records, did you also additionally form the opinion that Larry King would provoke his peers?"

Dr. Hoagland said, "Yes."

Ms. Bramson fumbled, as she often did, in formulating her question: "Given those two—well, first—well, yes, well, let's combine them. Given the negative attention-seeking behavior coupled with the provoking of his peers, do those in any way support your opinion that Larry would, in fact, target Brandon?"

"Yes."

"Okay. Could you explain that without getting into the records?" (Larry's school records had been ruled inadmissible.)

"Okay. Well, I'm not sure what is records and what is not, but I will try. Brandon targeted Larry."

Ms. Bramson, her voice rising with urgency, repeated, "Brandon targeted Larry!"

Dr. Hoagland, looking flushed, said, "I mean—I'm sorry. I misspoke myself."

9

Dissociative State

Appearing for the defense, Dr. Donald Hoagland, a clinical psychologist, took the witness stand on August 12, a Friday. After taking the oath and spelling his name, he looked out upon the people in the room and smiled gently. That smile stayed with him throughout that Friday and throughout the following Monday, August 15, as well. Faced with a vigorous and critical cross-examination, he generated avuncular assurance. His round face and oval spectacles, his perpetual smile, even his rumpled tweed jacket looked friendly. Unlike the other experts who took the stand, Dr. Hoagland did not bring any notes with him. He spoke directly to the attorneys and to the jury. His manner of speaking was less like that of an expert and more in keeping with the ways in which a child therapist might speak with parents or teachers.

Dr. Hoagland began his testimony, directed by Ms. Bramson, by telling us that he and Brandon had met three times for "about seventeen" hours in March and April of 2010, two years following the murder. He explained to Ms. Bramson that he had devoted most of the time that he spent with Brandon to the administration of two standardized psychometric tests designed to assess personality traits and psychopathology, the Minnesota Multiphasic Personality

Inventory (MMPI) and the Millon Adolescent Clinical Inventory (MACI). Generally, these multiple-choice paper-and-pencil tests are self-administered and take anywhere from twenty minutes to a half hour to complete.

Dr. Hoagland told Ms. Bramson that he preferred to read the questions aloud to people with whom he met. He said, "That way, depending on the answer they give me, I may ask for, you know, examples or additional information. So, it's kind of a, you know, segue into the interview."

When asked by Ms. Bramson what the tests told us about Brandon, Dr. Hoagland said that they didn't tell us much: "It was all within the normal range." But, he added, he found Brandon to be guarded and reluctant to examine what troubled him. He said that Brandon held off any consideration of his inner life through denial, repression, and minimizing.

Dr. Hoagland made it clear that he was most interested in gathering the two-strand story of Brandon's life and the murder; from whence had the murderous impulse come? Speaking about how "we are all an accumulation of experiences throughout life," Dr. Hoagland told the jury that the murder was an "effect of abuse, passed on from father to son," and then from Brandon to Larry.

"Brandon was not only exposed to violence, but he was trained in violence by his father," Dr. Hoagland explained, a history of violence that went beyond father and son: "It's Brandon's understanding that his father was severely abused by Brandon's grandfather. So again, it extends it to multigenerations that, you know, violence and family problems through violence, be it verbal, emotional, physical, it's kind of the norm in this family."

Ms. Bramson asked, "Given this home environment, what was the impact that all of this had on Brandon's emotional state?"

"One key aspect of it was that it left him filled with rage," Dr. Hoagland said. "As Brandon told me, 'I really had an anger problem.'"

———

BEGINNING IN THE SUMMER OF 2007, Brandon had been withdraw-
ing from almost everyone, including his mixed martial arts class, which,
according to Dr. Hoagland, was "a kind of shelter, a home away from
home." Brandon boycotted school, doing no work, or sleeping in class.

Brandon's deterioration aligned, Dr. Hoagland posited, with Larry's
"cross dressing, which was not, uh, subtle or sedate." Brandon thought
that Larry was breaking the rules, or "mores," as Dr. Hoagland put it.

"It really kind of shook the foundations of the rules and the ways
things are supposed to go in a junior high school setting for a boy to be
dressing like a girl," Dr. Hoagland said. He kept his focus on the jury
as he added that it got personal: "Brandon was the object of sexual behaviors, the target of sexual harassment from Larry."

Ms. Bramson asked, "What specific emotions was Brandon feeling
as a result of what was going on with Larry at school?"

Dr. Hoagland said, "Well certainly one was, you know, intense
anger, which eventually reached a point of rage. There was a sense of
victimization. He also described it, I believe, as disgusting, kind of like
the worst thing that anyone had ever said to him. You know, the incident where Larry said, "What's up, baby?," that was like the worst thing
that anyone ever said to him."

Brandon, by Dr. Hoagland's account, grew more and more angry
on the evening of Monday, February 11, 2008. Brandon said that he was
"crazy mad," Dr. Hoagland told us. "After he left school, he remained
'pissed at Larry,' and said, 'I stayed mad the whole night. It was the mad-
dest I had ever been. I was frustrated. I didn't think about the consequences. I was mad at everything, my home life, school. I never felt that
angry at a person before when I was going to do something severe about
it.' "

Following Brandon's night of rage, Dr. Hoagland told us that the
"trigger on the following morning, Tuesday, February 12, 2008, was
hearing a female student say that Larry had changed his name to Leticia.
Brandon said, 'I just snapped at that moment.'"

Ms. Bramson followed up, asking, "Is there a term to describe what
Brandon, in your opinion, experienced during the time of the shooting?"

Dr. Hoagland said, "Yes. It's a psychological term that can be referred to as dissociation."

The trial came then to Dr. Hoagland's foremost assertion: that Brandon entered a "period of dissociation" for ten to fifteen minutes, beginning when Larry answered Jackie's question about his name change, saying "Yeah, Leticia," and continuing until Brandon was arrested.

Dr. Hoagland explained that "usually all of our awareness and functions are integrated and, you know, work conjointly, but dissociation is—it's a disruption of that integration of consciousness, awareness, memory, sense of self, and the perception of one's environment. So the usual integration of all the functions that work together get disrupted or fragment at that point, and so the individual is at least partly separated from the reality of their environment, and it can occur very suddenly or gradually, and it can be transient, very short, or chronic."

Several times during his direct testimony and cross-examination, Dr. Hoagland was at pains to clarify that Brandon did not suffer from a dissociative disorder commonly thought of as multiple personality disorder. Rather, Brandon suffered from a chronic pattern of intermittent dissociation. Dr. Hoagland ended his direct testimony by explaining that these "dissociated states" came over Brandon in stressful situations.

When Brandon reached "a level of anger and distress that could not be managed or processed in a normal manner, Brandon had to flee inward to escape the reality of the moment." According to Dr. Hoagland, Brandon had described these states as "like watching himself on a TV" and "going through the motions." Brandon knew that he was relating to real people but "not interacting or interrelating, and that's the disconnection or detachment." Dr. Hoagland again linked Brandon's psyche with his history of abuse, telling us, "People who have been significantly abused are particularly prone to dissociation."

MS. FOX STOOD UP AND WALKED toward the witness stand, saying, "You indicated that the defendant had to flee inward to escape, correct?"

Dr. Hoagland consented, "That was a statement, yes, I made."

Ms. Fox, turning to the jury, continued, "And luckily he just happened to have a fully loaded gun right in his pocket at the moment that he had to escape, correct?"

Before Dr. Hoagland could answer, Mr. Bramson objected to the question as argumentative, which the judge sustained. Ms. Fox, though, had made her point.

Making her way back to her desk, Ms. Fox asked Dr. Hoagland if he made a distinction between evaluating "a forensic client who's facing potential loss of his freedom versus a clinical client who comes in to seek relief from some psychological issue?"

Dr. Hoagland answered, "I do not make that distinction."

"So you don't think that for people taking tests multiple times [Brandon had been given these tests by two prior psychologists] that they might know or anticipate the questions, even more so if someone is reading the questions to them [a departure from standard practice], so they know how to answer to achieve a desired result?"

"I cannot answer that generically."

"I see, but perhaps you can tell us how it is that you saw Brandon McInerney in March or April of 2010, and here it is August of 2011 and my office has still not received a completed report? I have one incomplete report from May 21, 2011. Can you explain?"

Mr. Wippert interjected before Dr. Hoagland could answer, saying, "That was my mistake."

Ms. Fox shot back at Mr. Wippert, "You didn't finish the report? I want the whole file."

The judge ordered the file turned over immediately. But the cat was already on to her next mouse. Pointing to a note in the report that she did have, Ms. Fox read, "At lunchtime, Larry walked onto the basketball court and interrupted the game to ask Brandon to be his valentine; correct?"

"Yes," said Dr. Hoagland.

"And that information was related to you from the defendant; correct?"

"No."

"Oh, he never told you that?"

"I learned it later. He minimized it at that point."

"Isn't it true that the defendant told you about what we're calling the lunch incident when he read about it in *Newsweek*, and that he was adamant that *Newsweek* erred when they reported that Larry had asked him to be his valentine?"

"That's what he told me at the time."

"Earlier, didn't you indicate that the primary source of your opinion came from the defendant?"

"I don't recall my statement."

"Dr. Hoagland, did you lie to the court when you testified that Brandon was the source of the information?"

"No. Eventually, it was learned from him. At the time he was minimizing. I have learned now that he has acknowledged it."

"You have learned now from what source, Dr. Hoagland?"

"From his attorney asking him about it."

"His attorney told you that they had asked the defendant about it, and he reported that it happened; is that what you are saying?"

"After hearing the testimony from a number of witnesses that said that it definitely did occur, he now acknowledged that it did happen."

"Wow. Are you aware that no one, not one person testified that they saw Larry King ask Brandon McInerney to be his valentine? Not one."

"That is not what I understand."

"So, the defendant has been sitting here for almost two months, listening to witnesses, listening to hearsay. And *now* he stops minimizing—as you put it—and that is sufficient for you to draw your conclusion?"

"Yes. And the *Newsweek* article, and I don't remember what other sources," Dr. Hoagland added.

Ms. Fox shook the slim file at Dr. Hoagland, saying, "*Newsweek!* Do you believe that it is appropriate and ethical for you as a professional to come in here and base your opinion on hearsay, a *Newsweek* article, and sources you cannot recall? Is that the state of information upon which you base your conclusions?"

"I didn't base my opinion on it. It led me to inquire of Brandon about it."

"As you've said. Well, I'll leave it there."

ON THE FOLLOWING MONDAY MORNING, August 15, Ms. Fox was on her feet with the same pounce. She began by asking Dr. Hoagland what he knew about the literature on children who suffer abuse and about the likelihood that they will go on to commit violent offenses as adults. She said that the majority of abused children do not become criminals, barely 5 percent.

Dr. Hoagland, seemingly untroubled by the finding, smiled and said, "I'm surprised that he wasn't more aggressive than he was."

Seizing the doctor's assessment about Brandon's aggression, Ms. Fox challenged his conclusion that "it was all within the normal range" and that Brandon did not have a conduct disorder. She did so in order to try to establish Brandon's antisocial character. She reminded Dr. Hoagland that Brandon had described himself as "explosive" and as having a "real anger problem," one that often led to fighting both at home and at school.

Ms. Fox said, "You made a comment on page eleven of your report that prior to this offense there was little violence against persons outside of his family. But you are aware and, in fact, he even admitted to you that he was suspended from school five or six times for violence?"

"I don't believe it's that many."

"There was one incident where he held a kid down and tried to choke him. Are you aware of that?"

"He did not try to choke him. He was holding him. He said, 'I was just really holding him down.'"

"According to Mr. McInerney—his recounting—not according to the person who observed him who thought he was choking the other boy, correct?"

"Okay."

"There was also an incident where he was counseled or suspended after taking on one of the special ed kids. He told them that special ed is only for 'stupid retards.' Do you remember reading that?"

"I did not see that."

"Isn't it true that the defendant told you that on numerous occasions that he had called Larry King a 'faggot,' a 'fucking faggot,' 'what a fag,' starting in October or November of 2007?"

"If name-calling counts, then a lot of students would be included."

Ms. Fox, incredulity seeping into her tone, said, "I see. Well, what about the incidents where Brandon McInerney became upset and disgusted with Larry King. You indicated yesterday that you did think it was bullying when the defendant told Larry to 'Shut up, fag,' right?"

"Yes."

"So that would qualify as one of the features of a conduct disorder, right?"

Dr. Hoagland, for the first time losing hold of his placid manner, leaned forward and said, "No, it was not often, and was not a repetitive and persistent pattern."

"But we know that the defendant did that to Larry King on other occasions because he told you that he did, correct?"

"Yes, but I do not believe that name-calling qualifies as bullying here."

Ms. Fox pointed out that Brandon self-identified as "homophobic," and as early as July of 2007, if not earlier, had routinely referred to Larry as a "faggot" or a "fucking faggot."

Dr. Hoagland said that these incidents were commonplace "name-calling." "Fag," he told us, "is simply a name."

Ms. Fox rapidly shifted and asked Dr. Hoagland about Brandon's practice of shooting birds from trees when he was bored, noting that harm to animals is another criterion for conduct disorder.

Dr. Hoagland replied, "I don't know, but he did not abuse any, you know, dogs, cats, typical animals. Just shooting little birds."

LARRY'S SEXUAL HARASSMENT AMOUNTED TO Brandon being "beat up every day," Dr. Hoagland said.

Ms. Fox followed, "When you asked the defendant what was so upsetting about Larry King saying 'What's up, baby?,' he told you, 'It was super disgusting. It was extremely disrespectful. It got me all mad. No one ever said something so disgusting to me. It was the first time a gay person said, "What's up, baby?" Absolutely it was a gay person doing this to me, messing around with me. It's not like when you go up and say it to a girl,' right?"

Dr. Hoagland said, "Yes."

"That's a direct quote, right?"

"Yes."

"You asked him why it was so awful, and he described himself as homophobic and told you 'That's the way I was raised,' right?"

"Correct."

Switching tack, Ms. Fox questioned Dr. Hoagland about this assertion that Larry sexually harassed Brandon, asking a series of questions: "Because Larry looked at him?" "Because Larry said, 'What's up, baby?' " "Because Larry walked in front of him?"

In response to each of these questions, Dr. Hoagland answered, "It was more than that."

Ms. Fox persisted, "Larry never touched Brandon, correct?"

Dr. Hoagland said, "That is correct."

"He never was sexually aggressive toward him, correct?"

"Depends how you define it. I mean, to walk onto a basketball court and say 'Would you be my valentine?,' that's pretty sexually aggressive."

Ms. Fox, with a hint of girl in her tone: "You think that asking someone to be your valentine is sexually aggressive?"

"For a guy to do that to another guy on a basketball court? It was a rumor that quickly spread."

Ms. Fox approached the witness stand, taking longer than she normally did. She said, "So if there's enough rumors, if it's gay enough, and the level of your discomfort becomes such, then it's okay that you kill the object of your hatred?"

Dr. Hoagland narrowed his eyes and said, "That's not at all what I'm saying. It was disgusting to every boy in that school."

MS. FOX DID NOT DENY THAT Leticia had some fight in her. Nor did she minimize how Leitica enjoyed flirting with boys. But Ms. Fox did ask from whence had the harassment arisen? Had it come from Leticia herself, or was it coming at her, not only in the form of bullying, but also in the form of prejudice? And was prejudice at work in Dr. Hoagland's way of thinking about the murder?

Ms. Fox asked, "Based on everything you know about this case and everything the defendant has told you, if the person who did, as you call it, sexually harass Brandon McInerney was a girl, would he have killed her?"

Dr. Hoagland pondered for a moment and then said, "If it were a girl doing this, probably not."

"Even if the actions were unwanted, correct?"

"Because it wouldn't have the—the homosexual—a guy hitting on a guy. It wasn't having a gay student dressed as a woman approaching you and humiliating you in front of the school, in front of a large number of students with rumors spreading throughout the whole school. There's no comparison."

Ms. Fox, backing away from the witness stand and facing the jury, said, "But what Larry did was so much worse because he was dressed wearing high-heeled boots and he had makeup on, right? And that in your opinion is deviant, is it not?"

Dr. Hoagland asked, "What do you mean by deviant?"

"That's a good question because that is the word that you used in your report dated June 18th, 2011. You used the word 'deviant' in respect to Larry King's actions, and specifically I believe I asked you at the deposition hearing. And you tied it closely to his manner of dress, correct?"

Dr. Hoagland became flustered for the first time. "I was using the word to describe—it wasn't a judgment about Larry—his behaviors—well, they were very different, and went far beyond what was acceptable, or the norm I spoke about, the unspoken rules, and in that way it was deviant."

"Right."

Ms. Fox turned and walked over to her table, but sarcasm would not let go, and she turned back, facing Dr. Hoagland. "Deviated from the rules. Larry King was going through—and you are an expert, you know, about transgender dysphoria, right? It appears that he was going through a significant transformation regarding his own gender and sexual identity, correct?"

"It appears that way."

"Just as your client was undergoing a significant transformation of his own having to do with intolerance and hate in exploring white supremacy, correct?"

"No. He was exploring it."

"Hmm. Okay. So calling a transgender kid a fag is not as bad as what you believe that Larry King did to Brandon, correct?"

"It was simply a name."

"I see. Well, I don't. But, Dr. Hoagland, you got your clinical psychology degree from Fuller Theological Seminary, an evangelical Christian seminary, am I right?"

"Yes."

"Would it be true to say that Fuller Theological Seminary and the school of psychology frowns upon alternate lifestyles, particularly being gay, lesbian, or transgender?"

"I don't believe that's true."

"Well, in their mission statement—on their website—prominently—they do say that they legally discriminate against persons who engage in sexual practices which are not scripturally sanctioned, correct?"

"I don't know."

———

WHEN DR. HOAGLAND FIRST RETURNED TO the court on Monday, August 15, for his second day of testimony, after having appeared on Friday, August 12, he began to present a more definitive case for harassment and a more detailed account of Brandon's childhood abuse. He also offered more statements and recollections from Brandon.

Ms. Fox asked, "Up until February 11th, 2008, there were zero interactions between the defendant and Larry King, correct?"

Dr. Hoagland said, "That's what I knew at that time."

"Well, doctor, I'm going through your report. Do you have other information that you didn't include in your report?"

"More recent."

"Have you reinterviewed him?"

"Yes, I have."

Ms. Fox was approaching the witness, but stopped and asked him, "This weekend?"

"I did."

Ms. Fox took a moment, looked at the jury, looked at the judge, as if she were in need of orientation, and then asked, "At the request of the defense attorneys?"

Dr. Hoagland said, "Absolutely not. It was my decision."

Ms. Fox asked the judge if she and the defense attorneys could approach the bench. He granted her request. Ms. Fox demanded that she get a copy of the notes from the recent interview, then continued her cross-examination.

Ms. Fox said, "Isn't it true that Brandon tried to get others to participate in hating and hurting Larry King and all of those people declined?"

Dr. Hoagland pushed back. Looking at the jury, he said, "But none of them were being targeted like he was."

"Dr. Hoagland, that is inconsistent with what Brandon told you, and the report that you produced in June. You said that all of the boys were making fun of each other."

"Yes. He said that when he was among friends. But he was minimizing at that time."

Ms. Fox was at this point standing at her desk. She dropped her notes, leaned forward with both hands on her desk, and said, "Oh, he only told you the truth this weekend after he's watched the entire trial and heard all the testimony of all the witnesses and heard me cross-examine you for an hour on Friday?"

Ms. Bramson objected to the question as argumentative and compound. The judge sustained her motion.

Ms. Fox rephrased, "He told you the truth this weekend apparently?"

Dr. Hoagland said, "I received additional information."

DR. HOAGLAND USED HIS MIDTESTIMONY MEETING with Brandon to add to his opinion regarding harassment, but those additions were secondary to how he employed that midtestimony meeting to clarify the nature of the dissociation that he believed had informed the shooting. He focused on Brandon's new report of his experience when firing the gun. In responding to a question from Ms. Bramson, Dr. Hoagland, speaking, as always, without notes, quoted Brandon as having said, "The whole action had just happened. I did not know about it at all. I did not concentrate. It just happened. For a few seconds I didn't realize what I was doing. It was like I was on TV and not me doing it. It was like somebody else. It was like it was happening out of control." Dr. Hoagland also reported that Brandon had no recollection of pulling the gun out of his pocket or aiming at Larry or pulling the trigger.

Brandon, Dr. Hoagland explained, could not offer a motive for killing Larry. Dr. Hoagland told us that Brandon had said, "I don't know why. My brain made a connection that day. He triggered me. I didn't think about consequences. I felt like it would make everyone's life at school better. I felt like I was solving a problem and doing the right thing. I didn't even think of killing Larry, just of getting rid of him, and that's how I would get rid of him. It was not like I was thinking

I'm going to murder him and end his life, and that he's not going to be here anymore, and that's a good thing. My goal was to get rid of him and solve my problems and everyone else's."

When it came time to cross-examine Dr. Hoagland, Ms. Fox, referring to Brandon's new account of the shooting, said, "But something does not quite add up, right? You said that Brandon had no recollection of the shooting. Are you aware that the testimony in this case is that Mrs. Boldrin yelled at the defendant before the second shot?"

Dr. Hoagland, "I do not know that."

"Then, that is inconsistent with the information that you received, correct?

"I don't think it's inconsistent because it's consistent with the dissociative state, as I've described it. Because the disorientation, the disintegration of the normally integrated functions—and it happened so quickly, within seconds, I don't see that as inconsistent."

"But you still believe that he started to come out of it when he heard her voice, correct? He did tell you that, correct?"

"That is what he communicated to me, yes."

Ms. Fox said slowly, "And then he fired the second shot?"

"Okay, if that's the testimony. I didn't base it on that alone."

Ms. Fox, building on Brandon's account of at least some reality testing, moved to what she called Brandon's "criminal state of mind." She asked Dr. Hoagland if he would agree that shooting someone in the head, an effective way to kill someone, might also indicate a "good criminal presence of mind."

"Perhaps."

Ms. Fox pushed her point with grisly intent. "Do you think that shooting someone twice in the back of the head is an effective choice for ensuring that a person is not going to live?"

"Potentially."

Coolly, Ms. Fox asked Dr. Hoagland if he was aware of the precise spacing of the shots: "two to three inches apart at the base of Larry King's skull."

Dr. Hoagland said that he was not aware of that finding.

Ms. Fox had turned toward her table as Dr. Hoagland gave his answer, and her widening eyes expressed her doubt. She turned toward him and asked that he consider this finding to be true. And then she said, "Would such an ultimately fatal finding—would it in any way be inconsistent with your theory that the defendant was in a dissociative state when he delivered both of those wounds?"

"No, it would not."

A WEEK LATER, ON AUGUST 22, Dr. Kris Mohandie, a psychologist, appeared as a rebuttal witness for the prosecution. He would be the last witness to take the stand.

Dr. Mohandie had the look of young ambition in his well-tailored black suit ("Armani" was whispered in the hallway). He was tan and well groomed, and, unlike Dr. Hoagland, not somebody's cheerful uncle. He was a man of data and numbers. Then again, Dr. Mohandie was not there to tell a story; he was there to challenge what Dr. Hoagland had asserted as facts.

Unlike Dr. Hoagland, Dr. Mohandie came from a distinguished background of law enforcement experience and forensic psychology. He had served on the Los Angeles Police Department (LAPD) behavioral science unit for five years ("interviewing hundreds and hundreds of people involved in shootings") and was a consultant for the FBI beginning in 2003. He was the author of *School Violence Threat Management*, a book on how to assess the risk and management of school violence. He had testified as an expert witness forty-two times, for both the prosecution and defense. Ms. Fox reminded us that Dr. Hoagland had testified as an expert witness three times, and always at the request of the defense, two of those times for Mr. Wippert and Ms. Bramson.

Ms. Fox and Dr. Mohandie made a handsome pair. She wore a dove gray suit with a pencil skirt, and brown alligator heels. The courtroom could have been the suburban hotel bar where they had settled after missing the turn for the city.

They began by discussing Dr. Hoagland's claims about dissociation.

Dr. Mohandie dismissed the idea altogether, saying that he found it "highly inaccurate, misleading, and contradictory." The evidence that Dr. Hoagland cited as indicative of dissociation (forgetting the gun, for example), Dr. Monhandie saw as "normal fallout after a person has been involved in a shooting. So, it's a by-product of the shooting as opposed to the cause."

Dr. Mohandie maintained that Brandon's report about his experience of the shooting was a "normal, normal" kind of forgetting, following on a surge of adrenaline that moves a person into an "adrenaline tunnel." That which Dr. Hoagland was calling dissociation, Dr. Mohandie said, "was consistent with what I've seen in officers involved in shootings. It's consistent with what I've seen in regular citizens who have been involved in shootings, and it's consistent with what I've seen in offenders with shootings. It's like 'I don't even remember this.' They often describe a surreal quality but that's not dissociation. I just don't see dissociation as anything that occurred—'cause it's not, just no evidence for it."

Instead, Dr. Mohandie emphasized the nineteen hours of premeditation and how that showed "a criminal presence of mind." Brandon was "very much grounded in a cognitive—thinking plan, a thought out action plan." Dr. Mohandie went on to link the planning with a "cold-blooded" lack of affect.

"In affective states of violence [the passionate violence of voluntary manslaughter], the person is in a high degree of autonomic arousal that is very visible. You can see instinctual posturing, fist clinching, and jaw tightening. The person may be making sounds, like a guttural yell. There might be a variety of indicators that the person is tremendously upset. None of these behaviors were reported to have happened in this case. Many people saw the defendant beforehand, but they didn't notice that he seemed particularly upset."

When Ms. Fox asked, "What do you think drove the plan for Mr. McInerney?," Dr. Mohandie said, "Predatory violence is almost always fantasy driven. You'll hear the person describe how they've thought about it over and over again, sometimes with a lot of hate.

You'll hear their plans for revenge. In affective violence you don't see that kind of mental rehearsal."

Shifting back, Ms. Fox asked, "Do you think that the shooting was precipitated by Larry King's behavior?" Dr. Mohandie said, "In no way, shape or form would I characterize this as a victim-precipitated homicide. Even if some of the behaviors that were attributed to the victim were true, it still would not in any way be a normal reaction to those kinds of behaviors."

"What about sexual harassment?" Ms. Fox continued.

Dr. Mohandie: "Well, I think that that's a stretch. Does it meet the literal definition of what could be construed as sexual harassment? Perhaps. If, in fact, these events even occurred [the valentine, the lunch table clearing, the flirting]. If we say that they did, predatory violence as a response is not normal.

"Plus, in this case, there is a documented history admitted in the records of Dr. Hoagland by Mr. McInerney that he, unprovoked, was repetitively subjecting the victim to slurs of a disparaging nature, repetitively calling him 'faggot,' 'shut up, faggot,' et cetera. So contextually, the way that I would frame it would be that the victim's response to this bullying was his attempt to reclaim some of the power that was being taken away from him repeatedly by other people in the school environment."

"HAVE YOU EVER WORKED ON a reality show called *Paradise Hotel*?" Mr. Wippert asked as he began his cross-examination of Dr. Mohandie on August 23.

Dr. Mohandie said, "I consulted behind the scenes on that show years ago."

"I didn't see that on your lengthy CV."

"No. I don't list private consultations. That work is private and confidential."

Mr. Wippert persisted in asking questions about the show. What exactly had Dr. Mohandie done for the show? ("I conducted evaluations of participants for potential risk," Dr. Mohandie said.) What was the show about? ("It was based on a bunch of single men and women in a hotel. They had to form alliances by hooking up with the opposite sex," Dr. Monhandie explained.) Then Mr. Wippert asked again: What did Dr. Mohandie do? What was the show about? What were the contestants like? Finally, Ms. Fox objected, questioning the relevance of this line of questioning, and the judge sustained her objection.

Mr. Wippert asked about another reality show, *Moment of Truth*, for which Dr. Mohandie had consulted. Again, Dr. Mohandie indicated that he had screened potential participants for the show. Again, he said that he could not discuss the work because it was confidential. Again, Ms. Fox objected, questioning the relevance of the questioning. Again, the judge sustained her objection.

Mr. Wippert, though, kept going, laughing as he asked, "Is that the show where they hook people up to a lie detector and family members ask them questions to determine if they are telling the truth?"

Ms. Fox objected, and the judge sustained.

Mr. Wippert said, "I understand that you've been taken off the reality show circuit; is that true?"

Dr. Mohandie pushed back: "That is not true." He answered before Ms. Fox could object and before the judge sustained the objection.

Mr. Wippert repeated the question, relishing the accusation implied in the question, "Isn't that true?"

Ms. Fox objected, and the judge sustained.

In a hearing conducted outside the presence of the jury, we learned that a contestant on *Paradise Hotel* had committed suicide postproduction of the show. During the hearing, Mr. Wippert lost his bid to bring that alleged fact into testimony.

Judge Campbell chastised Mr. Wippert, telling him to "stop burning our time, and get on with it."

And so Mr. Wippert did, sort of. He asked Dr. Mohandie how much he was being paid to testify for the prosecution. Dr. Mohandie told him that his hourly fee was four hundred dollars and that he had worked on the case for about forty to forty-five hours.

Mr. Wippert looked at the jury while he did the math on a legal pad, and grinned as he said, "$18,000.00; is that right?"

Dr. Mohandie said, "That sounds about right."

Judge Campbell leaned forward and once again sternly warned Mr. Wippert to "move along to something relevant."

I imagined, if he could have gotten away with it, Mr. Wippert might have cracked, "That depends on what you mean by relevant, Judge." Later that afternoon, Mr. Wippert would refer to Dr. Mohandie as "Dr. 90210." Mr. Wippert wanted to make sure that the jurors understood that Dr. Mohandie was not one of them.

Finally, Mr. Wippert questioned Dr. Mohandie about the case, beginning, with a cagey move, by reading a passage from Dr. Mohandie's book about risk factors for adolescents, risks that included divorce, child custody battles, domestic violence, neglect, physical and emotional abuse, and substance abuse.

Mr. Wippert said, "Many of those factors were present in Brandon McInerney's life, and you would agree with that, right?"

Dr. Mohandie concurred, although he did not support Mr. Wippert's effort to move forward by arguing that Brandon's upbringing was the cause of his "risk for being violent." Dr. Mohandie explained that the kinds of risk factors that were at hand in Brandon's upbringing were "correlated with violence, but not causal, only 5 percent of children in high risk homes become violent."

Mr. Wippert walked toward the witness box as he said, "So what I'm saying is that what you wrote in your book conflicts with your testimony regarding Brandon McInerney and his abusive home. It shouldn't at all lead a person in his situation to commit a violent act?"

Dr. Mohandie: "Well, that's because most people that experience what he's experienced do not take a gun to school and kill people."

Mr. Wippert stopped his approach. "Okay."

He walked back to his desk, and Ms. Bramson handed him a neon orange Post-it, as if it were a stimulant.

Mr. Wippert turned back to the witness. "So you don't believe in the snapping?"

Dr. Mohandie said, "I don't believe that people just snap. You've got a violent thought process, and he engaged at that point in a series of behaviors that are in preparation for a proactive attack on the victim."

"Yes or no, you don't believe that people just snap? That's what you just said, right?"

"In cases of targeted predatory violence, I don't believe they just snap. There may be precipitating events that trigger them down that road. 'Leticia' was a trigger, not a snap."

Returning to Dr. Mohandie's book, in an effort to once again read him against himself, Mr. Wippert claimed that the doctor held that bullying and ridicule could push people toward violence. "You say, quoting from the book, 'The person perceives that the final straw pushed them to do what they did.' That's exactly what Brandon McInerney told Dr. Hoagland. Brandon snapped; it was the final straw."

Dr. Mohandie said he didn't consider what Brandon did to be "snapping." And "[I don't] agree with the part about bullying and ridicule because I really think it was your client finding the victim disgusting more than anything else."

Mr. Wippert returned to his desk and started looking through his many piles of papers. Ms. Bramson handed him another Post-it, this one neon yellow. He looked at it and said, not looking at Dr. Mohandie, "Oh, yeah, it is your opinion that it was improper for Dr. Hoagland to have that second interview, right?"

Dr. Mohandie said that, yes, he thought it was at best "irregular," or "unusual": "[It is] something that I've not really seen done, and he failed to take into account the reliability problems it created. Plus, your client modified his statements from the first interview to the second interview in a manner that better fit what he'd been observing in the trial."

Mr. Wippert and Dr. Mohandie drew the day and the witness phase of the trial to an end by talking about adolescent impulsivity. They concurred that teenagers are rash and often act without regard for consequence. They did not quite concur about the role that impulsivity plays in "violent problem-solving." Mr. Wippert asserted that adolescents often end up in violent scenes as a consequence of impulsive decision making. Dr. Monhandie said, "Yes, the decision can be made quickly, but the act is often revealed to have included a significant degree of planning, ultimately."

MINDS SHATTER IN THE FEROCITY of violence. Verifying that memory did or did not take hold in the roar of sudden deadly violence is a bit like trying to reconstruct a shattered glass. The glass is gone. It is only the shards that remain.

Dr. Hoagland's testimony unintentionally captured this dilemma: Near the end of his testimony on August 15, he said, "I put the pieces together," and at yet another juncture told us, "I had reached that conclusion before. There were a few details that I added—that were added." His first-person slip, "I added," suggested that he put the story together. In part, that was his job, but at the same time, one was left to wonder about his intentions in constructing the story as he did.

For instance, like Dr. Mohandie, I thought Dr. Hoagland should have been more precise about the "conclusion" he reached about the role of dissociation and "the few details he added." Unlike Dr. Mohandie, I did not dismiss outright Dr. Hoagland's propositions regarding dissociation. Brandon's state of mind during the shooting seemed likely to have been dissociative. How could it not? But dissociation is a broad phenomenon, and Brandon's report suggests that what he was experiencing was more akin to depersonalization ("I see what is happening, but I am not here") or derealization ("I see what is happening, but it is not real").

On the other hand, I thought that Dr. Hoagland could have made a stronger case for the role of chronic dissociation as it likely built Brandon's mind. Brandon's revised account links up with how trauma theorists describe the ways in which the brain, when flooded by acts of violence, fails to log what has happened. Perpetrators and witnesses alike are often left to deny what has happened, or to depersonalize it (as if it were on TV), or to derealize it (murder is a way to solve a problem, not the end of someone's life).

Dr. Hoagland's opinion linking abuse to violence was also in line with studies conducted by the National Institute of Justice (an agency within the U.S. Department of Justice) that correlate childhood abuse and neglect with the increased likelihood of juvenile arrest. Kids who are abused and neglected are five times more likely to end up in juvenile detention or jail. As well, Dr. Hoagland's perspective on violence as a transgenerational phenomenon was in keeping with data that demonstrate how familial violence is highly correlated with histories of adolescent and adult crime.

There is growing clinical insight that links child abuse to dissociation and to violent crime. Minds are stunted by abuse, reflection does not take root and grow, the ability to feel and to consider one's feelings falls mute, empathy does not develop, and language skills lag. The fist of violence not only bruises the body but creates cratered minds, marred by dissociation. Children who grow up in the midst of abuse not only are left emotionally mute but often resort to physical means of expressing themselves, left to repeat or refind the violence that they have not fully brought into their minds. Violence rushes forward from mental black holes and is refound in the haze of dissociation.

Perpetrators often cannot account for their violent acts. Then, in a way that seems contradictory, and indeed may be, the perpetrators almost always confess to their crimes with some knowledge of what they did.

As the psychologist Abbey Stein, who spent years studying violent criminals, found, abused children and adults have trouble with symbol formation; they are without language, they are mute, they cannot fantasize, they cannot draw, they cannot play. They react without the mediation of empathy. Yet, following their violent actions, they often fall, and fall quickly, into confused states of guilt and despair. As Stein describes them, these dissociator criminals are not without guilt, even when they cannot recount the violence they have perpetrated. Indeed, they are often plagued by guilt.

How, then, are we to make sense of Brandon's account of his experience during the shooting and his lucid descriptions of his dissociated experience? If we presume that dissociation rests on problems with the use of language or the ability to communicate with symbols, how can we account for Brandon's skill in communicating through drawing? How do we square Dr. Hoagland's claim that Brandon was dissociated with the ways in which his initial report included Brandon's recollection of a lot of what had happened, indeed, much of what happened at the murder scene?

How can we accept the claim that Brandon committed murder in a dissociated state when it is common for antisocial people to assert that they were dissociated as they try to maneuver around violations of communal ethics? How do we consider Brandon's seeming lack of remorse, even guilt? He told Dr. Hoagland that he "doesn't really think about Larry." He got "rid of him." How is it that none of his statements included a story of guilt or even the shadow of grief?

Dr. Hoagland's ideas about dissociation left me wondering whether his intent in foregrounding the claim that Brandon acted "without thinking" was to imply that we did not have to consider the role of consciousness as it informed his murderous act. Granting depersonalization and derealization during the murder does not mean that Brandon was not planning, thinking, feeling, and registering reality (however surreal). Minds regularly track multiple strands of thought and feeling. Brandon seemed quite clearly to have had some registration of reality, perhaps more than some.

Granting that dissociation helped to make and unmake Brandon's psyche does not mean that his inner world was wholly dark. To accept Dr. Hoagland's thesis of Brandon's dark, yet normal, nonpsyche is to stop short of considering the role that hate played in Brandon's life and how hate pulsed through the malice aforethought that guided Brandon's murderous intent.

Brandon was a haunted house made by his father's hands and his mother's vapor trail. Violence was left to lurk in dark hallways, secret passageways, locked closets. There was no mother, no father at the non-door. There was no one to oversee or lend a guiding hand. Violence came in and violence flew out with no mediation or recognition. Violence was dissociated (unnamed, split off, unlogged), yet it nevertheless remained alive and was refound through acts of aggression.

It was this last step, the step of haunted reenactment, the step of violence refound, that Dr. Hoagland posed but would not name. If he were to fully consider Brandon's acts of premeditation, would he have had to face questions about Brandon's culpability? Would Dr. Hoagland have had to consider Dr. Mohandie's description of how predatory violence moves from rage to plan, from hot to cold?

Did Brandon have any capacity to consider his thoughts, feelings, and actions? Could he reflect on how he collapsed anger into hate? ("He said that anger is hatred," Dr. Hoagland offered.) Did he at least have some facility to consider communal ethics, right and wrong? How did he monitor his impulses, granting, as we must, that adolescents struggle in this regard? Did he have room for remorse? If so, why had no evidence been presented to make that case?

What of the malice and hate that carried Brandon toward murder? Brandon had the ability to name his hate, to attempt to rally others through his hate, calling himself "homophobic." But did he have the capacity to reflect, even in hindsight, on the destruction that such hate wrought? Or had his hate been organized and upheld through white supremacist beliefs? If so, did he have an inkling that such beliefs stand in opposition to communal ethics and basic civil rights?

In framing Larry as the "problem," Dr. Hoagland looked out the same lens as Brandon. They moved together into what the British psychoanalyst Melanie Klein would have called a "paranoid-schizoid position."

Mrs. Klein, as she was known, held that we are all open to destructive primitive forces throughout our lives (fears of abandonment, annihilation, fragmentation, persecution, and corresponding rage and retaliation). We never fully outgrow these primitive states and ways of being; we only learn to better integrate and regulate those primitive parts of ourselves.

At the heart of Mrs. Klein's ideas about primitive life is the experience of "being in bits," being fragmented, disintegrated, dissociated, and plagued by fear. Her use of the word "schizoid" should not be confused with schizophrenia, or our common use of "schizoid" to refer to someone who is emotionally aloof and solitary. Instead, in keeping with the meaning of "schizo-," derived from the Greek *skhizein*, to split, Mrs. Klein proposed that we are always battling within ourselves and in our relations to others with the pull to split versus integrate. We are none of us as whole as we like to think.

The force of splitting is key to Mrs. Klein's ideas about how we live in bits, and how fragmented perceptions scatter into bits, leaving us unrealistic and unstable. In particular, she focused on how good and bad, love and hate, are especially susceptible to being split and rigidly distorted (she is all good; she is all bad) as opposed to the more realistic experience that goodness and badness inform everyone (she is both good and bad). But realistic views require a great deal of integration (being able to hold contradictory ideas in mind; to weather loss and disappointment; to acknowledge our own guilt and make reparations). Even then, we fail—daily—in our efforts to be realistic and even-tempered.

Paranoia, the best of guard dogs, exquisitely splits good and bad. Guards look out in order to find the bad, they do not look in. The world shrinks as the bad is pinpointed on the horizon. Unwanted badness, vulnerability, guilt, and injury are pushed out and into others. There is no loss.

And so there is no problem. Or, no problem inside. The problem was all on Larry's side. Problem solved. Except that paranoid solutions require vigilance and guard duty. The bad might creep back in. Brandon watched the door (with every click).

Brandon was left to live in bits, scrambling to defend against the possibility of attack. So long as ideas about dissociation were where the courtroom story began and ended, a fuller understanding of his psyche was not offered. And we were left with a disturbingly incomplete understanding of Brandon's mental states before and during the murder.

In the same spirit, when the expertise offered about gender was little more than common social convention, we had no way to see how both Leticia and Brandon were abused and neglected by social norms. Rather than offer the court any understanding of how both of these children were failed by what is considered normal, Dr. Hoagland attempted to bolster Brandon by an appeal to norms—and to blame Larry through an appeal to norms.

Gender conformity had been soundly questioned well before 2008, and not just in the rarified air of psychology (where questioning gender norms was, by then, routine). Larry and Brandon did not live in the world that was reported by *New York* magazine one week after Dr. Hoagland's testimony, in a cover story about Andrej Pejic, a transgender fashion model. Nor did they live in a world where feminism and its opposition to constricting gender roles seemed to have made much of a mark. But these kids did not live in a hermetic bubble. Nightly, as Brandon told Dr. Hoagland, questions about gender and sexuality came into their homes through the television: Brandon told Dr. Hoagland that he joined his grandfather, father, and brothers in hurling sexual and racial slurs at minority characters on television. Social change, no matter how it was mocked or debased, found its way under their doors and into their lives.

Shame also found its way under their gender doors.

Brandon's shame was told and retold as the valentine story and the "What's up, baby?" story. Any kid might be embarrassed by a valentine (of any kind), if, in fact, there was one. Any kid could be made anxious by clumsy flirtation, especially unwanted flirtation. Matters of sexual identity are fragile for adolescents. But Brandon was granted *the* valued heterosexual and imperiled identity; he was at risk.

Even Brandon's self-confessed homophobia was taken at face value, presumed to be the experience of a normal boy, in conflict with a gay boy, Larry. Brandon's irrational (anxious, phobic) fear and hatred of gay people was muted by the ways in which the defense team, their character witnesses, and their expert, Dr. Hoagland, accepted Brandon's fear and hate as normal.

Intriguingly, Brandon pointed to a more complex set of feelings than those that Dr. Hoagland and the teachers at E. O. Green could bring into mind. Brandon said something more precise than standard-issue homophobia when he talked about the "What's up, baby?" moment.

He said, "It's not like when you go up and say it to a girl."

We could understand this statement in a couple of ways. First, a gay person, Larry, should keep his "disgusting" desires to himself, not like straight boys who can rightfully approach girls and say, "What's up, baby?"

The second way that we could hear "It's not like when you go up and say it to a girl" rests on the way Brandon turned and looked over his shoulder as Larry passed by. Looking over his shoulder, looking with paranoid impulse, revealing his own vulnerability, Brandon reddened as Larry, or, more properly, Leticia, returned his gaze, saying something that included the word "baby." In that moment, Brandon became the object of Leticia's desire. In that moment, Brandon was a boy desired by a transgirl (Leticia), whom Brandon interpreted to be gay boy (Larry), and that desire, by Brandon's logic, made him the girl ("It's not like when you go up and say it to a girl"). In other words, Leticia had the upper hand; proper dominance was turned around.

No matter if we understand the "baby" exchange as homophobic or transphobic, Brandon's immediate response was rage, the blaze of going to bits. His wish was to bully Larry back into place. He tried to rally support. But when his friends did not join him, he was left with his own bullying mind. Such a mind expels vulnerability, injury, and dependence.

By suggesting that Brandon's actions were carried out in the name of preserving norms and "mores," Dr. Hoagland normalized Brandon. As if Brandon were acting like everyone else. As though Brandon had not alienated most of his peers, while also severing relationships with trustworthy adults, like his mixed martial arts coach, moving instead toward young adults on the Strand, many of whom had criminal histories and held antisocial worldviews. Brandon was a perfect target—not for sexual harassment but for a kind of hate, a hate that locked him in its grip. His mind, dark and fragmented by dissociation, was wide open for hatred and antisocial thoughts.

Antisocial worlds are built through keeping guilt, loss, and mourning at bay. The boys and men on the Strand were not losing. They were not lost. They were taking back their rightful land, their rightful place. If they had to resort to violence or sadism to keep their turf, so be it, and call it normal. If they had to cooly traffic in lies and stereotypes, so be it, and call it normal.

One of the sheriffs who transported Brandon back and forth from the juvenile detention center to the court told me near the end of the trial, "I have done this job for a long time, and I have never seen anybody this stone cold. Usually, a guy cracks, at least once. Come on, man, this is murder! Him, never; he talks about basketball like we was driving to school."

Murder, one could argue, is the ultimate turning away from mortal vulnerability. Murder is the ultimate paranoid solution. All that is bad is split off, put in another, and killed. Brandon pulled the trigger and accomplished the split.

I am not the baby. You are. I am not the baby screaming for a blacked-out mother. You are. I am not a girl. You are. I am not gay. You are. I am not guilty. You are.

10

Fourteen

"I'm going to give the instruction for voluntary manslaughter. I think it is for the jury to decide. There is potentially some evidence that might support that verdict, if they reach it," Judge Campbell announced on Tuesday, August 23, the thirty-sixth day of the trial. Ms. Fox bowed her head. Ms. Bramson turned and smiled at Kendra McInerney.

The judge's ruling came as a surprise. In bench discussions, beginning at least a month before this ruling, Judge Campbell had repeatedly warned the defense team that they had yet to make a case for voluntary manslaughter. Well into the final days of the trial, his impatience with the defense team, their procedural lapses and unorthodox conduct, had not waned. He had repeatedly chastised them for the ways in which they failed to provide the prosecution with witness lists and appropriate discovery.

Judge Campbell was impassive. Even as he chastised the defense, he did so in even tones, like a thoughtful, if weary, father guiding an errant child. But on occasion, even thoughtful fathers lose their patience. One day near the end of the trial, Judge Campbell upbraided Mr. Wippert, asking, "I have never seen a case of this magnitude handled in this way.

We have no witness list. Do you know who your witnesses will be? How, sir, are you building your case? Indeed, sir, where is your case?"

As Mr. Wippert began to answer, the judge held up his right hand and said, "I don't want any more of your diatribe. You may present this witness. Because, as you have pointed out, Brandon is on trial, not you."

Similar reasoning was apparently at hand two weeks later, at the end of the trial, when the judge decided to give the manslaughter instruction. His obligation was to the defendant, not the defense attorneys. And so, along with first- and second-degree murder, the jury would be instructed to consider voluntary manslaughter as they deliberated Brandon McInerney's guilt.

The judge did not specify how he came to his decision. It seemed to follow on the vigorous reiteration made by the defense that Larry had provoked Brandon. The decision was also probably influenced by the judge's belief that the verdict would surely be appealed if he did not include the manslaughter instruction.

The jury was brought in. Judge Campbell explained that they would be given packets that explained their work. He detailed and distinguished the charges Brandon faced: first-degree murder, an act of predatory killing without lawful excuse or justification; second-degree murder, the killing of another person or persons through reckless endangerment; voluntary manslaughter, most commonly thought of as a reactive crime of passion—lying in wait, looking for opportunity in the manner of an ambush.

He then explained the hate crime charge. The jury would have to find that "the Defendant committed the crime in whole or in part because of the alleged victim's actual or perceived social orientation—I mean, sexual orientation." Such hate, he emphasized, had to be a substantial motivating factor.

Through his "social/sexual" slip of the tongue, the judge drew our attention to the role played by society in the making of sexualities and genders. Sexualities and genders come alive between bodies and social customs, or norms that shape us even before we are us (It's a boy! It's a girl!). Social customs and values—or "mores," as Dr. Hoagland put it—that had reverberated around Brandon throughout the trial, and around Larry during those brief and rare occasions when he was allowed consideration, echoed once again in the jury's ears.

THE AFTERNOON OF THE JUDGE'S instructions, with its promise of deliberation, was colored by restless anticipation. The day that followed, the day of the closing arguments, was a far more somber affair. The courtroom seemed darker, as if someone had dimmed the lights.

The defense team was slow to gather at their table, and Ms. Fox, for the prosecution, was uncharacteristically even slower. She entered the room pushing her unwieldy cart. Her head was down, and for a moment she looked as if she had inexplicably walked through a rainstorm. Her hair was wet, towel dried, and hastily combed. She wore a wine-colored brocade suit that lay heavily on her small frame. Her clavicle protruded above the ill-fitting collar. Hallway chatter declared that she had lost ten pounds. ("Ten pounds that she didn't have to lose," as Dawn King put it.) She had applied a trace of makeup, but not enough to conceal that her eyes were bruised from fatigue and strain. Later she told me that she had slept the night before, what little she slept, in her office.

She looked like the weary widow holding it together for the guests who stayed too long at the wake. In the final weeks of the trial, her stamina had started to wane. Like her heavy suit, the weight of the fight and the anguish of grief hung about her.

She slowly made her way to a lectern stationed in front of the jury. After arranging her notes, she stood with her hands behind her back, and began by asking the jury to recall their experiences in junior high school, and in particular to recall the "odd kids," like "small, weak, socially awkward" Larry King. She projected the same image she'd used at the beginning of the trial. Once again, Larry smiled at us.

"He was possibly gay. He was effeminate. He was learning disabled. He was emotionally immature. He was very effeminate. He was possibly transgender. We don't know for sure. We will never know, but it appears that beginning in February of 2008 he began a transformation, and it appeared to his friends who knew him, some of the girls that came in and testified, that he was happy."

Then, just as she did in her opening statement, Ms. Fox pivoted to the crime: "No amount of revisionist history and attempts to paint Larry King as some kind of predator can ever change the fact of what occurred in this case, and that is that Larry King was executed for who he was.

"Cold-blooded execution by lying in wait: This case is a first-degree murder; it is only a first-degree murder. It never was and never will be anything else.

"Factually it won't be difficult. Emotionally it is a tragedy on all levels. But, this case is what it is.

"It is a murder."

THE JURY WAS FACED WITH untangling a two-month web of testimony offered by ninety-eight witnesses. Their job was not going to be easy, Ms. Fox forecast for them, and, making things even more difficult, she noted, was Brandon's age. During jury selection, they had been informed that Brandon was to be tried as an adult. They had been apprised of the law and had consented to participate, knowing the law.

"Sympathy," Ms. Fox held, "was going to be a huge distractor."

But deliberation could not be guided by sympathy, she reminded the jury; it must be directed by reason and by the logic of the law. This "cool headed" way of thinking was admittedly "weird, artificial, awkward." It wasn't "real life." But they could not let their feelings about Brandon's age "skew the evidence, or the facts." As she put it, "You have promised not to do that."

They would be helped by the clear-cut nature of the facts in this case. The evidence was plain. As Ms. Fox saw it, the story was best told by Larry and Brandon's peers: "They knew what was going on, and they told you straight up."

It was the kids' eyewitness reports that should guide the deliberations: "Who actually heard, who actually knew what was going on? The kids." The kids observed "firsthand," while the teachers were left to report on things they heard second- or thirdhand as "they talked about it in the lunchroom."

Ms. Fox reminded the jury that the teachers consistently had to admit that their accounts were constructed after the murder, and on rumor, not direct observation. The teachers, "in full-blown defense mode," reconstructed what had happened: "After the shooting, everybody is in a state of absolute shock, and they're thinking to themselves, how did this happen? How on earth, how under any earthly scenario could this possibly have happened?"

Over time, the rumors depicted a story of disturbance that, in reality, was never as "magnificent as the gossip," Ms. Fox said. "Where was all the disruption that we were promised to hear about, the complete breakdown of social order in school?" she asked. "Guess what? It didn't happen."

Many of the kids were not even aware of minor disruptions. All the kids reported that they were not afraid of Larry. They did not see him as a threat. Just the opposite: they saw Larry as the one who was bullied and threatened. Nor did they ever see him do anything aggressive or sexually provocative.

Keith, Brandon's best friend at school, was not aware of any of the stories (the valentine story, the chasing story, the lunch table story). He never heard Brandon being teased. As Keith recalled, it was Larry whom he saw being teased and bullied.

Ms. Fox said, incredulously, "I could say it ten more times, and I still wouldn't be happy. This is the defendant's close friend!"

Even when kids had observed Larry being "out there," as Mariah had phrased it, they did not report feeling disturbed. Victor saw Larry chase Jesus after he said, "I smell queer!" But as Victor put it, "The incident caused me no mental anguish."

Jesus did not hear the "What's up, baby?" comment. He did hear *about* it and "thought that Larry was messing with Brandon, not that he loved him."

Ms. Fox urged the jury to consider Jesus's reasoning: "That's an objective, reasonable interpretation of that comment, which pretty much every single other person except for the defendant was able to figure out."

Brandon's distortion—the distortion of hatred and rage—led to murder, not Larry's gendered being or behavior.

HOLDING A FEW PAGES FROM her notes, Ms. Fox reached toward the jury. "This case is not a voluntary manslaughter." Her tone shifted to outrage as she said, "And the defense theory in this case is gay panic. Let's just put it out there right now, because that's what it is. For the last six weeks, the defense has put up this giant smoke screen, correctional officers, family members, all these people talking about Brandon McInerney not being a violent person, growing up being abused, he's not a white supremacist, he's not a member of a criminal street gang, he's nothing. This was the biggest bunch of baloney!"

Ms. Fox reminded the jury that voluntary manslaughter rests on the idea that "objective provocation" would incite a "reasonable man" (an ordinary man of fair disposition, or in this case an ordinary boy) to act rashly. An emotional killer overwhelmed by egregious provocation, driven by passion and justifiable indignation, is partially excused by the law for the lethal actions he has taken.

"Would an ordinary person do what Brandon McInerney did?" Ms. Fox asked.

"No," she answered, "because what he did is so completely outrageous. It's not based on anything that a normal reasonable average ordinary human being would ever do. It comes from somewhere else."

"I'm telling you," Ms. Fox cautioned the jury, "if somebody in the deliberation room starts going down that road, the rest of you need to look at each other and have a discussion, and say, 'Who would do that? Who would do what he did?' Not any of the other students in the school certainly. *Not one of them.*"

In this particular case, a finding of voluntary manslaughter rested on the belief that a nonviolent homosexual advance, or that which was perceived as an advance, constituted sufficient provocation to lead an ordinary boy to lose self-control and kill in the heat of passion. In other words, the jury would need to be certain that the facts showed that Larry's short-lived flirtatious behavior had provoked his killing.

"Larry King never even touched Brandon McInerney," Ms. Fox said. "His 'crime' as the defense would have you believe . . . was sexual harassment. He said, 'What's up, baby?' Come on, people. Come on," she said with a mix of disgust and fatigue.

The problem had not been Larry's so-called provocation; the problem was "gay panic," she stressed, even as she described what could have been called "trans panic." Panic had been ignited by Brandon's "disgust" with the idea and the feelings set in play by Larry's wish to become Leticia. Even if one were to grant such disgust, even if one were to grant a state of intense feeling, we were still left to recognize, Ms. Fox pointed out, that "no reasonable person would—no reasonable person of any age—*any age*—would ever have reacted the way the defendant did."

Then she dropped her teacherly stance, turned off her PowerPoint, and cut to what she saw as incontrovertible: "Brandon basically confessed to first-degree murder when talking with Dr. Hoagland."

Standing ramrod straight, speaking in a measured tone, she told the jury: "He intentionally got that gun. He told people he's going to do it. He secured the weapon. He secreted it. He transferred it from his backpack to his pocket. He did it so nobody could see him, and he shot and he killed an innocent person. It's express malice. He intended to kill Larry King."

Moving on to the second hallmark of first-degree murder, Ms. Fox explained, "The killer decides to kill." This deadly deliberation need not follow on mature or meaningful reflection. It need not be a good plan.

Ms. Fox highlighted the moment when Larry had been called into the counselor's office, just minutes before the shooting. According to Dr. Hoagland's report, during that time, Brandon began to think that he shouldn't do it: "I wasn't sure if I wanted to do it. I started to worry about consequences. I knew it was not going to go well."

Raising her arms, as if to say "Come on!" Ms. Fox exclaimed, "This is not even close, people. This is a full absolute confession to the elements of deliberation. *Brandon McInerney decided to kill Larry King.* I don't know if I could ever say that enough for you. *Brandon McInerney decided to kill Larry King.* It's stunning in its clarity, absolutely stunning."

Not only did Brandon make a conscious choice, Ms. Fox argued, he had a conscious plan. Again, a plan to which he confessed in his discussions with Dr. Hoagland: securing the gun the night before the murder, going back into the house to get the gun on the morning of the murder (while his father waited in the car), hiding the gun from his father, lying about having it when questioned by Antwan, choosing a small lightweight gun that he had used many times before, watching for an opportunity, choosing a position of advantage.

As Ms. Fox recounted these steps, she reiterated, "There is a plan. There is a plan. There is a plan. He's ready. He is ready. He has made the preparations. He's taken the gun. It's loaded. He's ready to go."

IN SPEAKING WITH DR. HOAGLAND, BRANDON tied his readiness to take action to his "unceasing rage." Ms. Fox made a point of linking Brandon's "burning rage," as he put it, rage with which he lived for at least nineteen hours, to a mind primed by violence and hatred: "He knew how to live with rage. Dr. Hoagland basically said so. And, on the morning of the shooting, does anybody see him doing anything other than casually reading a book on Hitler? Is he so nervous that he's making sounds? Is he sweating? Is he making any guttural sounds? Is he shaking? Is he doing anything like that? He's not. All the other students, they said nothing. They had absolutely no idea what's going on in his head."

Brandon's mind was nursed by rage and violence, Dr. Hoagland and James Bing repeatedly told us so. But, as Ms. Fox reminded the jury, shaking her notes at them, "Still no one—no one!—would say he was violent."

"So let's talk about this," she said to the jury. "This was bizarre. For about six days, the defense marched up this group of people that worked in the "Juvenile Justice Center," correctional officers.

"I just have to ask you this, and I don't mean to be crass or inappropriate. But what the hell is wrong with these people?

"They were called to testify that the defendant was not a violent person, and we sat here and we watched the videos of the defendant attacking and assaulting people and beating them when they were not fighting back. And, these people think that he is nonviolent.

"And it got even weirder when the next week we spent about seven days with the defendant's family members who were brought in and described the most horrific, violent, abusive, assaultive, neglectful, horrible, bad family upbringing that I've heard in a while.

"And then we are asked to believe, again, that the defendant is not a violent person. It almost makes one's head spin. Given what we learned about how he was raised, what would you expect from him?

"This is not his fault. He is a violent person. This is an essence of who he is. This is how he deals with his problems. He's an essentially violent person through probably no fault of his own. This is who he is."

That the state of his mind was "not his fault," or that his violent nature was not of his making, did not release him from the law, Ms. Fox reminded the jury. He was responsible for his actions, even at fourteen years of age. And the jury was responsible for following and upholding the law that names such a killing as first-degree murder.

Don't be misled, Ms. Fox cautioned, don't get "suckered" by the idea that he did not know what he was doing, do not "fall for that load of bull" about dissociation.

"What does he tell Dr. Hoagland? 'I knew I had to get out of there.' He's completely and absolutely aware of what he did. Okay, so he doesn't remember dropping the gun. So he doesn't remember putting up his hood. Dr. Mohandie told you, shooting someone and killing someone is very stressful, and even police officers who are trained and who get in shootings frequently do not remember how many bullets they fired and what their actions were immediately in the aftermath of this shooting.

"So he doesn't remember these things? I'm sorry. He has clear presence of mind. And what does he do once he got 'out of there'? Is he in a dissociative state? Really? He takes his cell phone out of his pocket, and he hits the correct number, calls his father."

Running her hands through her hair, which had until that final day always been carefully styled, Ms. Fox asked the jury to reflect on what Brandon himself said as they looked for motive: "The defendant told Dr. Hoagland that he hated gays, again, based on the way he was raised. It doesn't seem like there's any doubt whatsoever that he hated Larry King because he was gay. He told Dr. Hoagland that he hated the victim and found him disgusting."

Ms. Fox told the jury she believed that Brandon's hate found a ready home in white supremacy, which "basically released the hatred that he already had." She readily admitted that Brandon "was not an experienced or knowledgeable white supremacist." He was "probably exploring—like Dr. Hoagland said." She went so far as to tell the jury that they could "throw out" Detective Swanson's testimony. Whether or not Brandon was a white supremacist, or simply on his way to becoming one, did not matter in the end.

What mattered was Brandon's hatred for gay people. Listen to what he told Dr. Hoagland, Ms. Fox advised. And look at the drawings, she urged the jury, look at them as they depict and express Brandon's fascination with Nazism and white supremacy. But, more to the point, "look at the feelings, and the hate that they convey."

Look, as well, she urged, at the way in which bias and hate had been reenacted in the courtroom. The defense was "nothing more than a character assassination of Larry King." The belief that Larry was guilty of sexual harassment was itself hateful.

"We are automatically charging him with sexual harassment? It's awful. It's awful. It's inappropriate. It's mean.

"This, ladies and gentlemen, is offensive: The idea that the worst thing that can happen to a boy is for a gay boy to hit on him. This is an intentional attempt to reach into you to a place where there is a deep cultural stereotype, and that is that homosexual men are sexual predators. That is where this is all going, and I'm just putting it out there because it couldn't be clearer.

"This is an attempt to paint this victim as some kind of sexual deviant. And therefore, when this fifteen-year-old, 125-pound, five-foot-four young man wearing women's boots approaches you and looks at you or, God forbid, talks to you, or says something so unbelievably outrageous as 'What's up, baby?' that is enough to drive the average ordinary reasonable person into a state of rage so intense that he loses all control, reason, judgment, and the only possible solution is extermination.

"Do not get sucked into this lie."

Brandon McInerney, Ms. Fox said, in concluding her final argument, was not "your average reasonable person. He perpetrated a murder where there was no fight. There was no fight. There was nothing.

"He's an extremist, and he did the most extreme thing humanly possible, and you should convict him of first-degree murder."

Mr. Wippert: Afternoon.

Jury: Afternoon.

Mr. Wippert walked toward the jury with his hands in his pants pockets, as if he were about to speak across a neighbor's fence. "That was a difficult morning. I felt like I was sitting through a different trial. I really did."

Shifting his tone (now, the incredulous neighbor), Mr. Wippert turned to the prosecution table. "Did it seem like anybody from this table wanted to hear the truth? This isn't a manipulation of the truth. This isn't supposed to be: 'Let me put on witnesses and manipulate what they say into the theory of my case.' That's not what this is supposed to be. I'm offended. I hope you are."

Ms. Fox objected, but Mr. Wippert kept going, despite the judge sustaining the objection and admonishing Mr. Wippert that "counsel's personal opinions are irrelevant." Mr. Wippert continued to assert that the prosecution had manipulated the truth: suppressing evidence, manipulating evidence, and making false accusations.

And, more important, he persisted in making it personal. Drawing the jurors into a patch of paranoid shade, the sort that casts long shadows, Mr. Wippert alleged that the unbridled prosecution would "charge *anybody* with a hate crime, lying in wait, first-degree murder. He was barely fourteen years old."

Look over your shoulder, neighbor, it could be you next. A boy, his family, and his neighborhood—your neighborhood—were being railroaded. This was a miscarriage of justice. "Every single fact in this case that could be twisted against Brandon McInerney has," Mr. Wippert exclaimed.

Again, Ms. Fox objected, her second in as many minutes. Again, Judge Campbell sustained the objection, instructing the jury to disregard Mr. Wippert's allegations.

But Mr. Wippert kept going, and soon Ms. Fox sat back, presumably grasping that repeated objections meant stepping into the roles that had gathered around them: She was the "bitch" lady prosecutor in her expensive suits and power heels. He was the everyman lawyer with a shingle and a heart.

Mr. Wippert, still with his hands in his pockets, spoke personally because, for him, it *was* personal: he was not only there to speak for Brandon; he was there to speak *as* Brandon. Referring to the red detention benches at E. O. Green, he said, "They had such things when I was a kid. I would be the one there all the time." Referring to the weekend Brandon spent on Matt Reaume's couch, Mr. Wippert laughed and said, "Wow. If I was affiliated with every couch I slept on and what criminal acts or organizations they might have been involved in, I would have been in trouble a long time ago."

Boys make mistakes; sometimes they make grave mistakes. Their judgment is poor. Their reasoning is easily overrun by impulse. Boys need adults who will speak up for them, offer a guiding hand, and the grace of forgiveness.

"Brandon took a life," Mr. Wippert said, in a tone of direct confession. And with equal directness, he asked, "Now the question is, are we going to lose another?"

Good neighbors come together. They do not slander. They offer sympathy and succor. "They counsel children. He's thirteen. He's fourteen. That is what you do," Mr. Wippert offered.

You do not envision irreparable corruption. You do not seek vengeance. Nor do you punish a child for the sins of the elders. Above all, good neighbors recognize that the case for retribution is not as strong with a boy as it is with a man.

Taking his hands from his pockets, Mr. Wippert made a sweeping gesture that took in the entire room, jury and gallery alike, including many of Brandon's neighbors and family members. (About midway into Ms. Fox's closing statement, James Bing had arrived. He didn't stay long, though. After less than ten minutes, he left, saying, "I can't stand this." Soon thereafter, Brandon's Aunt Megan wheeled Grandpa McInerney in. Dozing, his head lolling to the right, he sat near the front row of the gallery in a wheelchair, wearing an oxygen mask.)

Looking at Brandon and his family assembled behind him, Mr. Wippert pleaded, "This is someone's life we are talking about. This is a child."

"He was a fourteen-year-old boy," Mr. Wippert emphasized. "You heard over and over and over and over again Detective Swanson say context, context, context. You know what, when you evaluate this evidence and evaluate all of the circumstances of this, you need to keep one thing in context: Brandon McInerney was fourteen years old when he shot Larry King. He just turned fourteen. He had a fourteen-year-old mind. Not a mind like we do."

Thirty-nine times in the course of his closing statement, Mr. Wippert reminded us of Brandon's age at the time of the shooting. Mr. Wippert was not going to let this fact drop, despite, or perhaps in light of, the protracted and failed pretrial appeals to move the case to juvenile court.

The district attorney and the court may not have recognized Brandon's youth. But, Mr. Wippert insisted, the court's blind eye need not stop the jury from seeing a less culpable boy. Sentencing, judgment, and punishment for a crime should be graduated and proportional to the offense and the offender, he reminded the jury, "A court of law rests on the search for truth, and truth is relative, and must be relative to the age of the defendant."

The legal reasoning that led to Brandon McInerney being charged as an adult was open to a "common sense" ethical and activist challenge, Mr. Wippert implied: "Look around. Most of you are parents. You know what it is like." Defend a child, as any good parent would. Identify with a boy, as any good parent would.

"Think back," Mr. Wippert urged the jury, "think back to what some of us think was the hardest part of our lives. I couldn't imagine sitting here at fourteen or seventeen."

At this juncture, Mr. Wippert stopped rather abruptly and walked over to his desk. He rummaged about, looking through his notes, taking a swig of Diet Coke, and began again. While his opponent may not have slept the night before, he had the look of a man who hadn't slept for weeks.

But the meaning and idea of "fourteen" served to ground Mr. Wippert. It gave him strength. He returned to the theme over and over: "This is a fourteen-year-old boy. This is not an adult, whose mind is fully developed." Fourteen year-olds are impulsive, they take risks, and they don't always stop to think and reason. They are less attuned to the gravity of mortality: "They just restart the video game and the players reappear. That's how teenagers think. They don't understand the concept of death. Brandon wasn't thinking about taking Larry's life. He wanted this to stop."

Joking that he was glad that he had not had to pay Dr. Monhandie's "Beverly Hills fee," Mr. Wippert turned to the doctor's book, to his opinions in *School Violence Threat Management* about neurological immaturity, and our growing understanding of adolescent brain development; brains take longer to develop than we once thought. Or, as Mr. Wippert telescoped this complex phenomenon, "Adolescent brain development: you don't know what you're thinking."

Teens also want to belong; they want to be seen as having gotten it right. They want to "fit in and be accepted." Mr. Wippert went on to make the point that teenagers' social wishes leave them vulnerable to the opinions and the pressures of their peers.

Brandon wanted the rumors to stop; they bullied him. They harassed and provoked him. They drove him to kill Larry.

"You, as jurors, again need to think back to when you were fourteen. This was a fourteen-year-old boy in middle school, and all of a sudden a boy starts coming dressing in high heels and makeup, and everybody's talking about it, and everybody starts teasing everybody about it, and he starts targeting Brandon and saying, 'Hey, be my valentine' and these types of things. And you know what, nobody did anything about it. In fact, the administration empowered him. They sent out an email: 'Hands off.' "

Abused and neglected at home, Brandon was also neglected by the administration at E. O. Green. He was left on his own, Mr. Wippert held, to face Larry's harassment and the redoubling provocation of rumor.

"Let's talk about Lawrence King for a minute," Mr. Wippert added. "Larry was not the problem. His behavior was the problem. We haven't gone after Lawrence King, as Miss Fox claimed. He was a sweet kid, a troubled kid, confused and misunderstood. Larry was simply looking for friendship. He wanted to be loved." But in his quest for love, his behavior changed, and "he became a different person. He wasn't the same Larry they all had known."

Mr. Wippert did not name Larry's change as a question of gender. Mr. Wippert never spoke about gender. He never named Leticia. But he did describe how Brandon's rage increased as Larry changed: "It wasn't until Larry started dressing that way and his behavior changed that the problems started, and he targeted Brandon, and you know what's unfortunate is it's clear, of course, that . . ." Mr. Wippert searched the room, shook his head, and said, "I lost my train of thought."

Both Mr. Wippert and Leticia got lost in the vague distinction between Larry's behavior and his personhood. Mr. Wippert and Leticia got lost in the indefinite language ("*that way*"). To get back on track, Mr. Wippert named Larry a "problem" and left Leticia, the idea of Leticia, aside; inasmuch as Leticia remained in Mr. Wippert's consciousness, and in his closing argument, she was veiled behind the diagnostic language of "negative attention seeking." Over and over again, Mr. Wippert spoke about Larry as a problem boy who "acted out" and sought attention through negative behaviors: wearing makeup, donning women's accessories, clicking along in women's boots, chasing boys, blowing kisses, sassing, flirting.

To make matters worse, Larry, the problem, went unaddressed and undisciplined as a result of the poor decisions made by Joy Epstein. Mr. Wippert said that "Larry could do no wrong" in Ms. Epstein's eyes. Mr. Wippert said Ms. Epstein had "emboldened" Larry with talk of "rights," even as teachers were telling her that Larry, especially his way of dressing, was causing a disruption.

According to Mr. Wippert, Ms. Epstein, a "lesbian with an agenda, encouraged and empowered" Larry, when she "could have prevented it." She could have curbed him and protected him, instead of empowering him. Blame lay at her feet; blood was on her hands.

"You cannot blame Larry. You cannot blame Brandon. You can blame the teachers. Blame the grown-ups. They could have stopped this. Sometimes as parents you have to tell your children, 'No, you can't do that.' It's the same thing with an administrator or a teacher.

"The grown-ups knew about this. They all knew. And they did not protect these kids. That's what grown-ups are supposed to do: protect Larry, protect Brandon, protect all the kids. The grown-ups didn't do anything to Larry, and Brandon saw that. Everybody saw that. Larry became bold and confident in his behavior, and his actions, and the way he talked, and he was getting more and more attention."

"As Larry got more, Brandon got less," Mr. Wippert asserted. Brandon could no longer go to school and be a "normal kid," where "he could tease kids. He could play basketball. He could goof off. He could be the class clown. He could be a normal kid, and that was taken away from him."

Brandon was a "normal kid, not the monster" that Ms. Fox had made him out to be. He was not a kid with a long-standing history of rage and social isolation. He was not a white supremacist hater. He was not a lone wolf. He was not a gang member. He was "just a regular kid." All opinions and diagnoses offered by the prosecution and their experts were "scare tactics" or "propaganda designed to scare the hell out of you," Mr. Wippert told the jury. "Let's put up Detective Swanson and have him just go on and on and on and on and on and say Brandon McInerney is a monster. He's a white supremacist. He's a member of SSL. SSL is a gang. And you know what? Let's frighten you to put this young man away. Convict him of murder."

This was not murder. "This was a heat of passion crime. Brandon was pushed to his limit. For those last two weeks it was a buildup, over and over and over again, and it got to the point where he just felt so helpless that he had to do something about it.

Brandon was a boy driven mad, a boy pushed into an "extreme emotional state," prompted by disgust and rage in the face of harassment. Emphatically, Mr. Wippert asserted that Brandon's state was not one of panic, as the prosecution held. The "idea of gay panic was absurd," yet another "manipulative move" made by the prosecution.

Brandon was not intent on killing Larry as a homosexual, Mr. Wippert told us. Yes, Brandon was repulsed by Larry's desire, a disgust that was in keeping with how normal boys respond to gay desire, as Dr. Hoagland had testified. But it was not that Larry was gay. It was the harassment and how the harassment resounded with the rumored implication that Brandon was gay.

"Brandon was consumed by rage and he had no thought. It was an action. It was straight-out emotion. It was a quick action," Mr. Wippert argued, continuing to build the foundation of his case for voluntary manslaughter. Brandon acted rashly under the influence of intense emotion, in a state of dissociation, vacant of deliberation: "He wasn't thinking of any consequences, like the arrest or anything, he wasn't thinking about killing him. He just wanted this to stop."

Pointing again to Brandon's age, Mr. Wippert asserted, "This is a fourteen-year-old boy. This is not someone who is an adult, whose mind was fully developed." As he was reiterating this point, he put a photograph on the overhead projector. There was Brandon, right before the murder, with his mother. Brandon was lifting a little cousin into the air. The sun was shining (the photo was over-exposed), the colors were fizzy, and they were all laughing.

The image hovered, a snapshot; the edges were curled, a corner was bent, a photo that had never made its way to a scrapbook, an image of a childhood life that was rarely graced with such order. Mr. Wippert reiterated, "It's a tragedy. Absolute tragedy. The grown-ups have failed both Larry King and Brandon McInerney over and over and over again. We've already lost one life; let's not lose another."

"Remember this young man," Mr. Wippert said, as he rested his hand on Brandon's shoulder, "remember how he grew up." Mr. Wippert paused for a moment, looking down at Brandon, who, wearing a lavender shirt, was gazing at the table's horizon, as he had done throughout the trial.

"The law says that you can't vote out of sympathy or passion," Mr. Wippert concluded, "but what it doesn't say is that you have to leave your heart at the front door or leave your conscience in the hallway. Use your common sense, use your heart, use your soul, use everything that you have as a person in making this decision, and if you do that and you remember this is a fourteen-year-old child, then you're going to do what's right, and you're going to agree that he is guilty and he should be held responsible, but he's not a murderer. Follow your heart. Remember that he was fourteen."

MS. FOX BEGAN HER REBUTTAL STATEMENT even before she had gotten up from her seat at the table, telling the jury, "Mr. Wippert basically without saying it just asked you to violate the law. You know, use your heart. Thirty-nine times he reminded you that the defendant was a fourteen-year-old boy. Thirty-nine times. And as if you didn't know that already."

Brandon's age and the course of his life were not to figure in the jury's deliberation; that was the law. What should figure in the jury's work was its consideration of the facts, especially facts that were offered for the "truth of the matter asserted"; that is, the jurors were to pay special attention to the testimony that was offered upon direct observation, as opposed to testimony that was offered as hearsay.

"You are going to have to be very careful," Ms. Fox instructed, "as you parse the evidence" because much of what the defense offered "was hearsay, or what we commonly call rumor." She directed the jury to the testimony of two key defense witnesses, the psychologist Dr. Donald Hoagland and the seventh-grade language arts teacher Jill Ekman, saying much of what they offered "was hearsay, not fact."

Despite what Mr. Wippert alleged, the defense was trying to cover over the hate that compelled a murder spurred by gay panic: "Do you really buy Mr. Wippert's characterization that there was this continuous pattern of torment, of harassment that was so completely torturous to the defendant that he had no other choice than to kill Larry King? Really? Really? It is an attempt to reach somewhere down inside you, into some dark place that speaks to that stereotype."

And if you need any further evidence of the paranoid push-and-pull of panic, Ms. Fox argued, "Look at what just happened to Joy Epstein: the lesbian thrown under the bus." The lesbian, the witch, "the liar, the pariah, the person who could have averted this tragedy. Yeah put it on her. She did it!"

Ms. Fox walked toward the jury but stopped, as though reconsidering. She turned and walked back to her table, where she rifled through three stacks of paper and pulled out a shingle sheet. She took hold of the paper and walked toward the jury. As she walked, I could see that it was a photocopied picture of Larry. It was the picture Leticia had requested, the photograph that Dawn Boldrin had taken, a picture taken on the last Friday of Leticia's life.

Ms. Fox held the photograph by its top corners, as if it were a rare document. We had seen this image before, when defense attorney Robyn

Bramson put it into evidence. Then, it had been a grainy black-and-white projection, shining from the old equipment that rested on the defense counsel's cluttered table.

Now, as Ms. Fox turned the paper toward the jury, I saw the green.

The dress flashed, lime candy green, in this incarnation. Not the bilious yellow-green of accusation and incrimination. Not the Kelly of the circus midway. Here was the dress before it was evidence. Before it was buried in a brown paper bag. Before it had to prepare its skeleton on an evidence shelf.

The dress, as Leticia held it, bisected the photo and created a horizon line. A landscape. Looking over the green hillside, Leticia smiles broadly, happily. The dress suits her. The American flag hangs in the background.

"This is the picture," Ms. Fox said to the jury. "This is the picture. He actually has some makeup on. You can see it. Does he look like a clown? This is the dress. This is the guy that you are supposed to believe was a sexual predator who tortured the defendant into a state of complete despair so great that he completely snapped and lost his mind."

I strained to see the photograph better. It seemed that everyone in the courtroom strained to see. We were looking for the carnival queen. But she wasn't there. I saw a boy who wished to be a girl, practicing. In this photo she was wearing makeup applied with a steadier hand. Makeup was not caked on, it had been applied with a more practiced eye.

Leticia stood in front of a mirror to find this face. With little instruction, she had been learning femininity on her own. It looked as if she was learning fast. No matter the opposition, derision, humiliation, torment, and threat, Leticia kept practicing.

Pointing to the ways in which there was no place for Larry or for Leticia's practice, Ms. Fox said, "Poor Larry King never had a chance because he was washed over and swept away by a tidal wave of hatred so immense that he never saw it coming."

Ms. Fox looked down and could no longer speak. She turned toward her table, choking back tears.

As she turned, the lime candy ghost hung in the air; the future cannot and will not unfold.

Recognize Larry, look at him, Ms. Fox implored, look upon him (already three years dead), look upon him and recognize that his life mattered enough to speak of its end as murder. Name it, and name the hate that ended his life.

11

Too Hard

"Was that an earthquake?" Marta Cunningham, the documentarian, asked me as the courtroom floor shuddered.

"No," I said, disbelieving.

"Yeah. Yeah, it was," Marta replied.

In fact, at 1:47 Pacific Time on Thursday, September 1, 2011, a 4.1 earthquake shook Courtroom F51.

In another era, we might have spoken of it as an omen.

Earlier that morning, both Marta and Zeke Barlow, a reporter from the *Ventura County Star*, had called me to say that Judge Campbell was calling the court back into session at two o'clock that afternoon. The attorneys had received a note from the judge; the jury was deadlocked.

The note sent to the judge, after the jury had been deliberating for about fourteen hours, was not the first note he had received. On Tuesday, August 30, after the jury had deliberated for about six hours, the judge received a note from a disgruntled juror, asking that the foreperson be relieved of her elected position.

The jury never settled into deliberation. Beginning with their opening vote, they split. They never found a way to begin. In a post-trial interview with a reporter from FOX-LA, Rosalie Black, an alternate juror, declared, "We were very divided: polar opposites. The people who believed one way were passionate. They were equally passionate on the other side, even before we went into deliberation."

The deadlock was confirmed when the jury was called into the court-room. Judge Campbell asked the foreperson if she thought it was "likely or unlikely that the jury was going to come to a decision or agreement?"

"With the conversations we were having today, it does not seem likely," she answered.

The mood of the group mirrored her assessment. They had always seemed an amiable lot. Smiling, chatting with one another on their way into court, exchanging comforting glances during moments of disturb-ing testimony, laughing at the few moments of comedy that had come our way. They had gathered in small groups for lunch in the jury room and sat together outside during breaks.

But at the end, they avoided eye contact. They looked dulled, used up, and brittle. Two of them seemed to have been crying. Most of them stared into the middle distance, as if looking for a way out.

The judge asked a different juror if she felt a decision could be reached. She shook her head "no." She was done with talking.

Another juror, her arms folded across her chest, asked the judge to clarify what was meant by "average disposition." The judge told her he would discuss this question with the attorneys and sent the jury back to the deliberation room.

There ensued a back-and-forth between the attorneys that reverber-ated with the mood of the jury; no agreement could be reached. After twenty minutes, Judge Campbell interceded, saying that he was going to define average disposition as "a person of ordinary temperament and self-control."

As the judge wrote out the definition for the jury and closed this por-tion of the proceedings, he said, "I think they are going to stay hung."

THE STORY SEEMED ON THE verge of a hard stop. I could feel myself slip-ping beyond my own capacity to bear witness. I felt adrift, and as though time were not adding up. I chalked up my feeling to the fatigue of the two-month ordeal and my frustrated desire for the closure that a verdict is supposed to render.

A week earlier, on the day after the case went to the jury, Friday, August 26, I had left the court, gotten into my car, and headed north to Santa Barbara, the place I went to swim on the weekends. Along the way, I had stopped in Oxnard. I had driven to E. O. Green. I had peered through the chain-link fence at Classroom 42. Desks were stacked in front of the windows, a barricade. I stood there for a long time, as if I might see something I had missed before. But the scene had not wavered. It did not waver. Nothing moved. Not even the wind. Nothing unsettled the gap between what had happened and what we could know.

I got back in my car, back onto Highway 101, and was soon on the Ventura Highway, the Pacific churning outside the driver's-side window. I opened the window and breathed in the briny air as I passed Carpinteria and Summerland, beach towns, sirens actually, that seduce you into fantasies of hippy escape (the bungalow, the bearded boy, the mutt). I arrived at the hotel just in time to see the rabbits that came out every night at sunset. I could have been Alice: I might have fallen down the hole, only I was too tired to hallucinate. I went to bed instead.

On the following morning, Saturday, I got up early and went to the pool. I ran into Alex Ramirez, my young friend. "It's such a long time," he said. I didn't know if he meant that it had been a long time since I was last there (I had not been there the prior weekend), or that the trial had taken a long time.

My eyes must have registered my question, because Alex said, "You know, life in prison, can you image?"

There it was, the time about which I could make no sense. I had effectively split off thinking about retribution. I could not bring it into mind.

I recalled a moment from my interview with Detective Swanson, when I had said to him that I found it very difficult to think about a fourteen-year-old as a murderer. He replied, "Good. It's not your job."

I remembered feeling grateful for the exemption, even as I knew that I had still to do that work, to think through and to imagine my way into the act of murder.

Across the weeks of witnessing the trial, steadily assessing what I heard and what I saw, I had come to think of what had happened as murder, not voluntary manslaughter. I had also come to believe that there was an important distinction to be made between the motive and the mind of a murderer, and the motive and the mind of one who commits voluntary manslaughter. Naming this distinction named the crime.

I felt it was important to preserve reason. Reflection, recognition, mourning, and the work of going forward rely on reasoning. How else were we to help the families or help Brandon? How else were we to learn to see and apprehend—when we could, if we could—such persons before they moved toward paranoid and murderous action? How else were we to grasp the role of hate as it festers into violence?

Yet, like Alex, I could not wrap my mind around retribution, especially vengeance devoid of rehabilitation. What was it going to achieve?

"Yeah, it is like time killed," I finally said.

Alex said he thought that Brandon "did it." He was guilty of first-degree murder: "Man, he *said* he was going to kill him. He planned it. He brought the gun to school. He *knew* he was going to do it."

At the same time, Alex thought that the punishment was too harsh: "He may never get out. Or he will be like an old man. That's not right."

"Yeah, I agree. I think he did it. I think that he is guilty of first-degree murder. I think hate played a role. I think that Brandon was a boy who grew up violently, a boy who was made violent. And, like you, I find it hard to think about the punishment."

I went ahead to say that I did not think it was unfair or unjust that we ask people who murder to contemplate their guilt and atone. Still, what should that atonement look like?

Alex was busy stacking white towels on a table. A yellow warbler lit on the iron fence that guarded the pool. I was so far away from Courtroom F51 in Chatsworth, farther than the literal seventy-six miles.

"Maybe," I suggested, "it has something to do with how a person like Brandon comes to terms with his culpability, you know, his guilt. So far, I have not seen anything that would suggest he has done that."

"Yeah, I haven't read anything in the paper about that. He hasn't said anything. Right?"

"Yeah, that's right. We spent a lot of time talking about Brandon, his life, his world. But really little was said about the murder. It was so hard to think about. Murder is blunt."

Is there anything more blunt? I wondered. Later, I looked up the origin of "blunt." It is related to the Old Norse *blunda*, "shut the eyes"—blot out, block out.

Talking with Alex, I could see that the way I had held off thinking about the sentencing was willful. I had thought that if I considered the sentence, somehow I could not stay focused on naming the crime and the hate. I could also see that I had been holding back thoughts about sentencing because I could feel the mood in the courtroom shifting from the crime toward Brandon's future, two phenomena that are separate, but also not.

I explained to Alex that, by law, the jury is not supposed to be thinking about sentencing when they are deliberating.

"You mean they can't think about what is going to happen to him? How does that work?" Alex asked.

"Right," I said, "The law is all about reason. You know, 'Just the facts.' But of course people's feelings are going to get mixed in. There was a lot of emotion in that courtroom—mostly about Brandon, because, you know, he is the one on trial. He is alive. He will live. Larry wasn't there very long, and when he was there he was 'trouble' or a parade float."

"A parade float?" Alex asked.

"Exaggerated. Seen only as a kind of clown or crazy kid running around disrupting the school," I clarified.

"But it sounds like that did happen," Alex held, as he started to use a pool sweeper, a net, to gather leaves that had fallen into the pool during the night.

"Yeah, I think it did, a little. Larry was a troubled kid, psychologically. He had it rough, and his mind could run ragged. Sometimes, a lot of times, people react to people like Larry with aggression. Trouble gets stirred up. Still, I think the disruption was exaggerated. The kids at the school didn't report nearly as much disruption as came out in court. Also, it was such a short period of time. Like nine days, or parts of those days, like lunchtime."

I realized I was so lost in my thoughts that I had begun following Alex around the pool. I consciously sat down at the edge of the pool.

"You know," I said, my thought shifting a bit, "murder is actually very rare. It doesn't really happen that often."

"What do you mean? It happens all the time," Alex said.

"Sure, you're right, of course, you're right," I said, "any time it happens is too often. And it does happen all the time. Still, if you look at the numbers, it is rare. And it is really rare that a kid kills another kid. What Brandon did is so far from the expected. It is rare in that way."

"Yeah, he killed him, like point-blank killed him," Alex said, stopping his sweeping and looking at me.

"Yeah. I guess we are talking about how important it is to name what happened. How else are we going to learn? Right?"

Recognizing that I had likely already waxed a bit too abstract—and as if to make up for what I could not give—I offered Alex an apple.

"Too hard," he said, smiling and pointing to his braces.

A waiter from the café next to the pool came by. I ordered an espresso. Alex had by this time circled around the pool and was back, near where I was sitting. He talked about how many kids he had seen go to juvy or prison, and how he wanted to go to college: "They got nowhere to go, man." I encouraged him to apply. I was so grateful for the optimism of his wish that I wondered if perhaps he was giving it to me as a kind of gift; surely, he must have seen how distraught I felt.

I headed back to Chatsworth on Monday, August 29, only to learn that the jury would deliberate for just two hours because the young woman juror, a college student, had to return to class. More lost time.

I went to a movie, *The Help*. It was based on a novel written by a southern white woman, a journalist, from the perspective of her mother's maid, in an effort to expose the racism that the maid and her friends had faced. The movie was set in Mississippi in 1963. With broad performances and brightly lit sincerity, the film pulled for tears and social justice. Any real consideration of the scars of race, gender, and class, however, were neatly remedied.

I sat there despairing, even as I cried. Almost fifty years beyond the time period of the film, there I sat, as I had been sitting for the past two months, as a transgirl's gender went unspoken and her race was deemed inadmissible in a hate crime.

After the movie, I went to a diner and ate a slice of carrot cake the size of a snow shovel.

On Tuesday afternoon, I drove to the courthouse. I walked upstairs to the courtroom, but the door was locked and the lights were off. I peered through the door's small vertical window into a murky gray box.

I went downstairs to the cafeteria and ran into Greg and Dawn King. Greg was heading outside to talk to a reporter, and I sat with Dawn for a while. She played solitaire on her cell phone, clicking the cards with her long, manicured nail. As she played, she spoke of how glad she was to have been thrown out of court.

"I never wanted any of this," she whispered, nodding in Greg's direction outside the door, as if to suggest that the trial was his idea, not that of the district attorney. She couldn't see "any good that was going to come of it. 'Cause ain't nothing going to bring Larry back."

Then she told me a story about the death of a woman who was not her mother but whom she called "Mommy." It seems that, upon this woman's death, neighbors descended upon her house and took everything—"*every* single thing!" Dawn exclaimed. Many of those things, keepsakes and appliances, Dawn claimed, had been intended for her. But "they were gone," and there was nothing she could do: "That there house was picked bare."

Greg came back. "Nothing to report. The reporters don't know anything."

Greg and Dawn gathered themselves together in order to head home. Dawn struggled with the weight of the medical boot she wore on her right ankle. She scrounged her hand in a clawing gesture, her way of waving good-bye, and, speaking of the jury, said, "They'll soon be done."

As I watched them walk away, I noticed for the first time that the benches we sat on spelled "the." I had noticed the large bronze "we" in the entryway of the courthouse on the first day of the trial. I followed the trail and walked upstairs, where I saw the grid of photos that I had been looking at for weeks: "people." Forty-eight grainy black-and-white photographs of old women, young men, boys, black men, babies, girls, brown women.

I may have said, "We the people" out loud, laughing at myself. And at the same time ruefully laughing at the idea that the idea of "the people" was somehow settled. Who got to be the people? No one who looked like Leticia was to be found in that grid of photographs.

I headed out of the court and walked through the main door to the parking lot. There I saw a juror, one of the two older men, He was pacing, worrying the asphalt. I thought he looked angry, or at least distressed. I got into my car and watched until he reentered the court-house. I would later learn from Maeve Fox that this fellow and another juror had been called into the judge's chamber that afternoon, to see if they could help bring calmer minds to prevail in the deliberation.

I got up on Wednesday and packed a box of books to send home. I took down the magazine photo of tennis player Rafael Nadal that I had taped over the pastel print of two peaches. I cleaned out the refrigerator, admiring the orange mold that the yogurt had cultured. Then I walked out into the ninety-four-degree day and wandered the small streets behind the hotel. No one was there, not a single person. Nor could I see signs of life in any of the buildings. The only sign of life I saw was a little white dog depicted on tattered signs affixed to light posts: FOUND DOG. He sat on a large chair. He looked happy. There was a number you could call if you wanted to be reunited with him.

I stood for a long time at an intersection where there was a triangular rock garden. At the center of the garden stood a flagpole with a colossal American flag. It did not move in the still heat.

"GET BACK IN YOUR SEATS," Deputy Sheriff Mike Anton, the bailiff, called out, as he stuck his head around the door of the courtroom. It seemed that we had just left the courtroom on that Thursday, September 1, after the judge had excused us so he could provide the jury with his description of "average disposition." We could not have been standing in the hallway for more than a few minutes.

As I came back into the room, I overheard a sheriff's walkie-talkie: "We're looking for him." They were trying to locate Mr. Wippert. "He is coming up, Your Honor," said Kathryn Lestelle, the defense investigator, as she came breathlessly through the door.

The King family took their customary seats. Larry's grandmother was wiping tears from her eyes. The Kings looked as if they had shrunk, faded, had already been forgotten, in contrast with the growing anticipation that filled the other side of the room.

Kendra McInerney came in with various family members, one of them pushing Grandpa in his wheelchair. They were followed by a number of Kendra's Silver Strand neighbors and trailed by Mr. Wippert.

Kendra took a seat to my right. She looked over, alarmed, struggling to breathe. "What's happening? Can you tell me what's happening?" she asked.

I told her I thought they were about to announce the verdict, or rather the lack of a verdict. It seemed that the jury could not come to a verdict; the jury was hung.

She was trembling and gasping for air. I told her to breathe, to lower her head and take deep breaths. She did not listen. I am not even sure that she heard me. Frantic, she asked me, "Is that a good thing?"

At which point, Judge Campbell entered, took to his bench, and said flatly, "The jury has informed me that they still have not reached a decision. I think we need to bring in the jury and alternates, and declare a mistrial."

Mr. Wippert pushed away from his table, as though he wanted to stand but checked himself. Ms. Bramson put her arm around Brandon, leaned into him, and wept.

Brandon did not move. Minutes before, he had been doing his geometry homework in his holding cell. Now, judgment was fore-stalled. His neighbors were leaving the courtroom to celebrate in the hallway.

Ms. Fox rested her head in her hands and stared at her table. She did not move either.

As the bailiff called the room to order, two deputies ushered the jury in. The judge asked the foreperson once again if the jury could reach a decision, and once again she said that they could not. He asked her for the final vote.

"Five for first-degree, seven for voluntary manslaughter," she tersely replied.

With that, the judge told the jury that they could stay if they wished to speak with the attorneys or the media, but they were under no obli-gation to do either. He thanked them for their service and said, "I am sure it is frustrating to have spent all of this time and not come to a decision. It was a difficult case, difficult issues, people saw it differently. I want to thank you again."

As the judge stood, the King family quickly left the courtroom and the courthouse, without comment and without looking back.

Brandon stood with his defense team, who had their arms around him. He turned and faintly smiled in the direction of his mother and of his girlfriend, Samantha Criner, who leaned in to hug Kendra. The hip-high wall that separated the gallery proclaimed its punitive function with more emphasis than usual; Brandon was still in jail.

Amid the commotion, I did not see Ms. Fox leave. When I turned back, she was gone.

I made my way outside to where the local television affiliates were setting up their cameras. I sat on a bench for a while with Marta Cunningham, the filmmaker. We both kept shaking our heads, as if to shake off the feeling of being stunned, even as we had been aware of the seismic shifts that culminated in this sudden release of energy.

Media folks were scrambling. People not connected to the trial, people who were not thinking about death or repudiation, people who had just come to pay a parking ticket, were going about their annoyed day. The palm trees threw off their ragged shade.

But material reality—what I could see and hear—was not what held my mind. Rather, a feeling of unreality gripped me, an undertow; this story would always resist comprehension.

Abruptly, I got up and said good-bye to Marta. Surprised, her cameraman asked, "What about the attorneys, what about the jurors?"

"I've already heard them," I said.

I DROVE TO LAX. THERE was little traffic, and the drive was fast. I turned in my rental car and bought a ticket for the next flight east, leaving for Boston with a connecting flight to Provincetown, the last town at the tip of Cape Cod. My closest friends gather there every Labor Day to celebrate summer's end.

My ticket allowed me access to a lounge where there were private bathrooms with showers, an amenity for a foreign traveler, one who had come far. The shower was tepid, the soap dispenser spat foam. I persisted. I cut the palm of my hand pushing at the dispenser, but I washed every bit of me. I stood in the spray for a long time. The water turned cold, but I stood there, letting it wash over me.

I was about to throw away my shirt when I caught myself. I stood for a long time staring at an ordinary blue T-shirt, trying to decide what to do, trying to determine its fate. But I knew that I could not bring it home. So I folded everything, except for one change of clothes, and stacked my clothes near the trash can.

The phobia in my flight did not escape me, even as the underlying anxiety propelled me. The clothes memorialized the endless impact of murder, *not* its escape.

I boarded the plane. Soon I would be gone. As though I could fly into another possibility of being. As though I could fly away from the ethical burden of survival. As though I wasn't left to tell a story of murder and failed deliberation.

The plane lifted off. I sat looking out the window for the waxing crescent moon. My mind turned toward one of my favorite passages in American literature, Harper Pitt's monologue near the end of Tony Kushner's *Angels in America*. In that passage, Harper is flying from the East Coast to the West Coast, chasing the moon. I was headed east with the moon on my tail. She was flying toward. I was running away.

Harper dreams of flying beyond the high, calm stream of air in which we cruise cross-country, and crashing through to the ozone, where she sees souls rising from the earth below, "souls of the dead, of people who had perished, from famine, from war," and she watches as they come together, forming "a great net of souls, and the souls were three-atom oxygen molecules, of the stuff of ozone, and the outer rim absorbed them, and was repaired."

"Nothing's lost forever," Harper thinks. "In this world, there is a kind of painful progress. Longing for what we've left behind, and dreaming ahead."

"At least I think that's so," she ends.

Looking for the moon, out of my plane window, I longed for Harper's optimism. Was progress out there? I knew that progress had called the rigid necessity of the social order into question; psyches need not be fenced in the same old cage. But had Leticia found a net of souls? Could she dream forward, the resurrection of mounted butterflies? And what about Brandon's soul? Were his molecules rearranging and repairing? Could he find a highway up from darkness? Could he dream backward the memory of murder?

I took a blue pill and fell asleep. I did not dream. I didn't even recall sleeping. It was as if my mind could not dream, could not make up anything it hadn't already experienced.

12

His Hands

"Hung jury" clangs eerily, uneasily; the jury could not agree, and the case was suspended, hung up. The case remained open, and the charges against Brandon still stood.

One way to look at this impasse is to say, as did Judge Campbell, that people did not see what had happened in the same way. And surely, they did not. There was a choking difference of opinion; deliberation could not breathe.

From outward appearances, it might be accurate to say that seven members of the jury agreed with the case made by the defense, while five agreed with the case made by the prosecution. A verdict could not be reached. But the suspension of decision was not the prevailing mood in the courtroom on September 1.

The jury's nonverdict was hailed as a victory for the defense.

As I left the courtroom that afternoon, a young woman who looked as if she might be Samantha Criner's sister sat on a bench with a little blond boy, a toddler. He had a toy radio that was playing the old Carpenters song "Sing": "Sing of happy, not sad." They were swinging their joined hands to the beat.

Later that afternoon, Karen McElhaney, one of the seven jurors who voted for voluntary manslaughter, and Rosalie Black, an alternate juror, also sat on a bench outside the courthouse, with Christina Gonzales, a reporter from the FOX LA affiliate, KTTV. The sun shone behind the women; a light breeze ruffled Ms. McElhaney's feathered hair and Ms. Black's flowing blouse.

With her hands folded in her lap, Ms. Black said, "The enormity and the severity got us, and there were a lot of tears. There was a lot of 'Oh my gosh.' This is it. We have to make a decision. We have to decide this child's fate, and we can't forget the victim either."

Ms. McElhaney, holding her hair against the wind, interrupted, "I saw a very damaged young man. I saw a very intelligent young man, and I think he would give anything to take that day back."

Ms. Black said, "I don't want to discount the young man who died, but I don't think Brandon should have been tried as an adult."

Ms. McElhaney, gesturing toward the ground from the bench on which she was seated so as suggest a small child, said, "Yes, he was so young, so young. He was only fourteen."

Near the end of the short interview, the women spoke about how, as Ms. McElhaney put it, "They [the district attorney] are considering retrying the case."

Ms. Black waved her hand as if to say 'No, no,' or to caution the viewer, and said, "What a travesty. It's a tragedy to do that. What are they going to accomplish?"

The less dramatic Ms. McElhaney spoke plainly and forewarned, "There were more people who were thinking voluntary manslaughter than murder one or two, the evidence is the same."

Ms. McElhaney and Ms. Black were the first jurors to speak, but soon four other jurors joined them. Five of the seven jurors who voted for voluntary manslaughter, along with Ms. Black—an alternate juror who shared their point of view—came together to decry the fact that Brandon faced a retrial as an adult. Wearing SAVE BRANDON bracelets, these six jurors attended the October 5, 2011, pretrial hearing that was to inaugurate Brandon's second trial.

They spoke to local news affiliates, reiterating and emphasizing their belief that a new trial was an abuse of power. They also went national, appearing together on ABC's television magazine *20/20*, holding up their SAVE BRANDON bracelets, proclaiming that they were raising money to support Brandon's defense. During that interview, they repeated themes from the defense argument, naming Larry as "the bully" and Brandon as a boy with "no way out." The *20/20* producer, Jim DuBrellie, and his reporter Juju Chang readily repeated and reinforced these claims, referring to Larry as a "troubled child with behavioral issues," while referencing Brandon, in voice-overs, as "a typical eighth-grade boy," and a "boy who wanted to do everything right."

Above all, these six activist jurors drew attention to the fact that Brandon was a kid who had been tried as an adult. One juror, who identified herself as Lisa S., wrote a letter to Judge Campbell and copied it to "Maeve Fox, Scott Wippert, ABC 20/20, Ventura Star, FOX-LA, and GOD": "Brandon was a juvenile and is a juvenile. In my humble opinion, you are wasting taxpayers' money trying Brandon McInerney as an adult. Brandon McInerney made a horrible mistake when he was 14, and there is a consequence. He has been paying for it since seven minutes after the shooting. You want him to pay for the rest of his life. Are we not a society that wants to rehabilitate our youth?"

At first there was no dissenting voice. No one publically challenged the activist jurors. The district attorney did not counter them, declining to discuss the case. Judge Campbell took his time in responding to Lisa S. The five jurors who voted for first-degree murder all declined interview requests, including my own. They still have not spoken publicly.

In light of the silence of the five jurors who voted for first-degree murder, I made a decision to hold off on interviewing the activist jurors. I began to think that the story might be more productively understood as it did or did not become part of the public discussion.

The one person who did speak out about the activist jurors was Detective Jeff Kay, the lead detective on the case. I met Detective Kay one afternoon in November of 2011, not long after the pretrial hearing that was held to initiate the second trial. We met at his office at the

Oxnard Police Department. He had recently separated from his wife, and we talked a bit about the trials of being a single parent. We talked about kids and divorce; he was eager to make things right with his young son. I was struck by his remorse and his seriousness, qualities that matched my impression of him when he had appeared in court at the beginning of the trial.

When we turned to talking about the case, and the ongoing campaign being waged by the activist jurors, Detective Kay said, "Man, I've never seen anything like this. Have you?" I told him, no, that I had not seen this kind of activism, although I was aware of jury nullification, juries that refuse to convict because they perceive some injustice either in the law or in the way the law is applied to a particular case.

Pushing away from the table in the small, well-organized room in which we sat, Detective Kay said, "Yeah. They are worried about Brandon. And look, I feel sorry for the kid, I really do. He made some bad choices, some bad mistakes. He did. Should he spend his life in jail? I don't know. But I do know that he shot a kid in the back of the head at point-blank range. Not only that; he premeditated it."

Looking toward a sliver of a window squeezed between a phalanx of black file cabinets (they seemed to be the true occupants of the room), Detective Kay said, "I was at that school. I saw those kids. I saw the shock. I saw the blood. I never want to see something like that again, and you see a lot in this job.

"But man, how have they [the activist jurors] made the victim the cause of his own murder? I've never seen that before. I saw those jurors on the news the other night, wearing Free Brandon bracelets. What if it was their kid, what if Larry had been their kid? . . . If you've got me at your door in the middle of the night to tell you that your child is dead, man . . . the news you never ever want to hear. How are you going to feel then? Are you going to keep that bracelet on?"

THROUGHOUT THE TRIAL, I HAD been aware of the uneasy truce I had made within myself about the fact that Brandon was being tried in an adult criminal court. Clearly, he was not an adult, and the decision to try him as one struck me as a legal misstep and an ethical lapse. At the same time, I was aware that children's capacities to relate, to reason, and to live within commonly accepted ethical bonds were consistently simplified or overlooked outright in the court and in the claims made by the activist jurors.

It is a false generalization to presume that youth automatically negates empathy, reflection, and responsibility. In fact, recent neuropsychological research demonstrates that teenagers may suffer, if anything, from an abundance of empathy. Teens, we are learning (slowly), are more complex than we give them credit for. They are more adaptive and functional, in many ways highly functional. They are inconsistent, notably so. Their prefrontal cortex is 20 percent less developed than that of adults, and they may be somewhat less capable of complex reasoning, especially in pressured situations. Still, they almost always reason their way through problems as well as adults do. And, contrary to common wisdom, they recognize the fact of mortality, both in themselves and in others.

Youth does not always override culpability. And murder moves beyond the kinds of risky or irresponsible behaviors we typically associate with youth. The brutality and cold-blooded character of premeditated murder is an act of madness of grave proportion. To minimize the degree of mental illness that propels this most serious of crimes is dangerous to us all, including the youthful offender. His is a mind set apart and should be understood as such.

At the same time, his is a mind made in a social and familial world. Where does the murderous impulse begin? When everyone is young, the categories of guilt and innocence do not hold with the assurance we desire. As the prince of Verona cries out at the end of *Romeo and Juliet*, "All are punish'd."

I found myself admiring the way in which the activist jurors pushed back at the fact that Brandon had been charged as an adult, a charge that did not follow on principled reasoning. The charge ensued from a systemic problem, one that stood on weak ethical feet: what do we do with a fourteen-year-old who murders another child?

The district attorney felt that the evidence in this case was strong enough to charge Brandon with first-degree murder and a hate crime. He and his staff, including Ms. Fox, believed that the juvenile system was not prepared to address such a vicious crime. California law, along with laws in thirty other states, has sought to redress violent crimes committed by juveniles by trying them as adults, as the district attorney's staff chose to do with Brandon, bringing his case to the Superior Court.

The activist jurors' pushback against the prosecution was, in part, a rejection of the prosecution's case against Brandon, but it was also a refusal to participate in a system that was failing. The fact that the American penal system has given up on rehabilitation did not mean that this jury was going to sit by and accept how participation in such a system kept them awake at night and, as they saw it, unfairly determined Brandon's fate.

I parted with the activist jurors, though, as they rallied around Brandon as a "typical" fourteen-year-old boy who made a "mistake," or, as Juju Chang, the *20/20* reporter, put it, "did something a little unexpected." The gravity and the unreason of murder slipped away when the jurors spoke about their feelings and perceptions, while defending their finding of voluntary manslaughter and their rejection of the hate crime charge.

By their account, an ordinary, reasonable boy killed an unordinary, unreasonable girl. And this reasonable boy did so because he was provoked, not because he hated. The category of "reasonable boy" appeared to include a boy who would shoot someone in response to what the jurors variously called "teasing," "bullying," or "harassment."

In a scene from *Valentine Road*, Marta Cunningham's documentary about the trial, juror Karen McElhaney said, "None, not one of us, saw him as a white supremacist."

Rosalie Black, the alternate juror, agreed, "Never."

Gathered together in Ms. McElhaney's kitchen, the women, joined by a third juror, Diane Michaels, ate pastries and drank wine. Ms.

Michaels complimented Ms. McElhaney on the wine. "This is delicious, and it came from Trader Joe's?"

"Yes, $4.99 on sale. Everybody is talking about it," Ms. McElhaney said, as she tapped her manicured fingernail on the glass bottle.

The women talked about how difficult the jury deliberation had been, and in particular how hard it had been to sit in judgment of a child.

"Oh my God, he is fourteen. It was the first thing I thought," Ms. McElhaney said.

"He was such a kid. My heart broke for him, as a mom," Ms. Black added.

"Yes, and you know, they are just figuring things out," Ms. Michaels offered. "Like, he was figuring out symbolisms, you know, with the doodles.

"They love to draw at that age. And he's combining symbolisms."

Ms. Black laughed. "I doodle now especially when I'm not happy about what I'm hearing. And my hands go faster and faster!"

Ms. Michaels set her wineglass down and said, "Where are the civil rights of the one being taunted by another person who's cross-dressing? They have to address that."

"Clearly that wasn't addressed," Ms. Black said.

"No, it wasn't," said Ms. Michaels. "He had no one he could turn to because the school was so pro Larry King's civil rights. But where were Brandon's civil rights?"

In similar spirit, Lisa S., another of the activist jurors, raised the rhetoric in the letter she wrote to Judge Campbell, calling the trial "a tragedy and a propaganda-filled witch hunt!" Lisa S. maintained, "This was not a young man acting as a 'lone wolf' or shooting Larry King because he was gay. What I can't understand is your unwillingness to correct your mistake. You all know that this was not a hate crime. You all know that the victim had a long history of deviant behavior. Yes, I said deviant."

In the grip of the overbroad and unsubstantiated claims, like those made by Lisa S. and Ms. Michaels, the jury deliberation seems to have been less one of reflection than fraught, personalized argument. One of the jurors who voted for first-degree murder told Maeve Fox that the discussion never even got to the point at which they could discuss the hate-crime charge. Consideration of Brandon's direct expressions of hate and homophobia were overwhelmed by ideas about Larry's deviancy. Deliberation about the charges was overshadowed by ideas about Brandon's "fate." Such sentiments negate the explicit instructions to the jury to deliberate "free of bias" and to set aside any consideration of sentencing. The jury's task is to name the crime. Sentencing falls to the judge.

The jury could not take up, or so it appears, a reasoned consideration of evidence that pointed to Brandon's malice aforethought and premeditation. The rhetoric in Lisa S.'s letter to Judge Campbell suggests that she, at least, saw the prosecution's claims as conspiratorial and suspicious. Such paranoia, coupled with outrage over Brandon's age, seems to have led some of these jurors to a distorted view of the charges.

Ms. Michaels, talking with Ms. McElhaney and Ms. Black in *Valentine Road*, offered, "I do not think it was first-degree murder. However, it was premeditated. He had a plan to resolve this terrible problem. Because nobody was taking care of this problem." Seemingly unaware, Ms. Michaels identified two of the hallmarks of first-degree murder (planning and premeditation), but she called it something else. She called it something less.

The activist jurors responded to Brandon's youth and his pain, as good citizens must.

But they could not think about his will to murder or his hate, as good citizens must.

They accepted the assessment of the damaged, yet normal, non-psyche Dr. Hoagland attributed to Brandon. They renamed Brandon's explicitly stated hatred as "a reaction to provocation." They accepted the idea of Brandon as a vague, unknowing, dissociated actor, as opposed to an antisocial boy with a deeply troubled mind. "Normal" became a defensive label for Brandon. "Trouble" was Larry's.

ON NOVEMBER 21, 2011, WEARING A standard-issue blue jumpsuit and ankle shackles, Brandon pleaded guilty to second-degree murder and voluntary manslaughter. As part of the plea deal worked out between the district attorney and Brandon's defense team, he would serve time for the lesser charge of manslaughter, twenty-one years.

How much impact did the activist jurors have on this deal? They certainly kept alive the idea that a retrial would likely face another hung jury, as reflected in a written statement released by the district attorney's office: "The district attorney is keenly aware that many in the community feel that McInerney should have been tried as a juvenile. The McInerney case has resulted in strong and unprecedented emotional and philosophical outpourings, both in the community as well as the trial jury."

At the same time, speaking to reporters, Gregory Totten, the district attorney, said, "Mr. McInerney will be labeled for the rest of his life as a murderer. He murdered Larry King, and that cannot be overlooked. For us, this was always a murder case."

Everyone spoke of the plea as a compromise. Even the structure of the plea, which, in an unusual move, spread guilt over two charges (second-degree murder and voluntary manslaughter), spoke of compromise. As did the sentence: charged with second-degree murder (killing that follows on willful negligence), Brandon would serve twenty-one years, in accord with the sentencing guidelines for voluntary manslaughter.

Looking tired, his shoulders rounded by years of battle, Greg King spoke of accepting the plea, with Zeke Barlow from the *Ventura County Star*, saying, "Twenty-one years is a long time, and we are satisfied that justice has been done."

Mr. Wippert, also speaking with Mr. Barlow, said something similar:

"I think it's an appropriate sentence given all the circumstances and the evidence that came out in the trial."

Notably, the hate-crime charge was dropped, and this too was seen as a compromise.

"Dropping the hate crime moved this along," said Jay Smith, former executive of the Ventura County Rainbow Alliance, an advocacy group for the lesbian, gay, bisexual, and transgender community.

The perfunctory sentencing hearing took place a few weeks later, on December 19, 2011. I flew back to California to attend the hearing and to conduct further interviews. During the fall of 2011, I had set about to do more background research (on white supremacy, juvenile justice, trauma, parental drug addiction). The thought of returning for another trial was not a place my mind wanted to go. The announcement of the plea deal, while complicated, as I saw it, relative to the facts of the case, as I saw them, nevertheless seemed a small mercy, another compromise.

I flew back to California during the day on December 18, with no moon to chase. I stayed in Los Angeles, with a friend—no Extended Stay this time. On the morning of December 19, I woke to the first cloudy day I had experienced in California during the entire period I spent there. For the first time, I understood the affection my friends who grew up in California have for cloudy days, a fondness I had always considered perverse. The clouds felt like shelter. Sunglasses could be left on the bedside table. I headed out of LA, skirting the valley and Chatsworth, toward Ventura, which was another change. The hearing was being held at the Ventura County Courthouse, a rambling glass and red-cedar campus that could have been a small college.

I walked to up to the courthouse, where I found myself greeted by the unexpected sentiment of reunion. Everyone was hugging and catching up. Dawn King rushed to hand me a big JUSTICE FOR LARRY! button, with Larry's picture on it (his cheeks round, his smile wide). She implored, "Come sit with us!" Kendra, visibly distraught, stopped to shake my hand, breaking free of five of the activist jurors, all women, wearing gray shawls, who were surrounding her. Kendra was also draped in a shawl. When I asked Rosalie Black about the meaning of the shawls, she told me that they "symbolized protest and mourning." It also seemed clear that this group of women was intent on offering Kendra protection. (She would later tell me that she found the women and the shawls frightening. Referring to her shawl, she said, "I lost it.")

In the throng of the crowded hallway leading to the courtroom, Dawn Boldrin told me that she had finally gotten her "sorry ass out of Starbucks" and had taken a job at a library. Averi Laskey and Mariah Thompson shyly said hello and asked me how the book was going. I commented on how the sentencing seemed like a "strange party." Averi, her inflection ironically rising, said, "Right!" Mariah started to giggle but then said, "Everyone is talking about 'closure.'" Averi, again ironically, said, "Yeah, right."

We crammed into a much smaller courtroom than the one in Chatsworth. I sat next to Dawn Boldrin and Mariah. When Brandon entered, he looked out at the gallery in a way he had never done during the trial. His hair was buzzed—no more Eton boy. He wore an oversized white T-shirt, blue cotton sweatpants, and white canvas slip-on shoes. His eyes, a gray blur, were set in a scowl. He looked worn and thin. He slouched into his chair. He had never slouched, not once, during the trial.

As the trial began, so too, it ended: no gavel fell. There was a back-and-forth between Ms. Fox, Mr. Wippert, and Judge Campbell about how Brandon's eventual probation would be structured and about the financial restitution Brandon would eventually owe the King family.

My mind wandered as they debated the terms of the probation that would greet Brandon at a prison gate when he was thirty-eight years old. I seem to recall that it was set at ten years. But what was the amount set for restitution? Was it $10,000 or $20,000? I couldn't stay focused on numbers. I was too busy looking around the room. It felt stuffy and claustrophobic. Was it all that trauma and grief, pushing up against the idea of an end?

Once they'd settled the matters of probation and restitution, the judge asked if anyone from Larry's family would like to speak. Greg King made his way to the front of the court and sat at a table next to Ms. Fox. He apologized as he did so, saying, "I am too nervous to stand." He read from a prepared statement and began with statements from Larry's grandmother and mother, who spoke of a future lost, not only Larry's but their own as well.

Clearing his throat and choking back tears, Greg went on in his own words, which were less sentimental than those of his mother-in-law and wife: "This is not manslaughter. It is murder, plain and simple. And this case was not about saving Brandon, it was about seeking justice for Larry.

"An incompetent jury provided the convicted felon, sitting in court today, with a great opportunity. They gave him the opportunity to stay out of trouble, and get on with his life in twenty-one years.

"The convicted murderer, sitting at the defense table, did much more than simply kill our son. He robbed us of one son and stole from his brother a lifetime of companionship, leaving instead a lifetime of griev-ing. He subjected his own family to guilt, shame, and a profound level of remorse, emotions he has yet to display.

"My family was not the only victim on that fateful day. The other victims in this senseless act of violence were the students that were forced to witness it. In the aftermath of the murder, I asked the Oxnard Police Department why there were no charges brought on behalf of the students in the classroom. I was told, 'They were witnesses, not victims.' I disagree. Watching some of those students testify made it very obvi-ous that they were scarred."

Greg King called on the California legislature to enact a law that would allow prosecutors to bring charges against anyone who dis-charged a weapon in a classroom. He asked that defendants be charged with one count of assault for every child in the classroom.

Speaking of schoolchildren's need for safe classrooms, Greg charged the E. O. Green school staff with negligence and poor judgment, point-edly naming Dawn Boldrin and Joy Epstein. He went on to blame the media for focusing "on the plight of the defendant," overlooking the failures of the school system, but most of all overlooking the fact that his son had been senselessly murdered.

Ms. Boldrin did not flinch as Greg leveled his accusations at her; she had heard them before. Mariah, two seats to my left, had begun to cry, and Ms. Boldrin was searching her handbag for tissues when Greg turned his wrath to Brandon.

"McInerney, I can only hope that one day I can forgive you for the pain and loss you have inflicted upon our family. Perhaps when you finally face punishment for your crime, my family can move on. For three years, endless delays and despicable defense tactics almost worked, but after everything was said and done you've shown who you are: a murderer."

With that, he rose, shaking, from the table, his head bowed, and made his way back to the second row of the gallery, where he sat down next to his wife.

The attorneys made brief statements, beginning with Mr. Wippert, who remained seated. (Had he ever spoken from a seated position during the trial?) He held that Brandon "felt deeply remorseful. If he could take back what he did, he would do it in a heartbeat. He lives with this every day."

Again, he said, "If he could take it back he would. He wanted everyone to know how remorseful . . ."

His statement trailed off. In the silence, likely not as long as it felt, I wondered if perhaps Mr. Wippert was overcome. I also wondered why he hadn't prepared a more formal statement. And why didn't Brandon finally speak?

Mr. Wippert never finished his sentence about remorse. Instead, he said of Brandon, "He realized that he can never take it back."

Forty-seven words, twelve of them repeated.

Ms. Fox also remained seated while she spoke. She read from notes, her head bowed, saying that she stood by everything that she said in her closing statement. She added, though, that she thought Brandon had it in mind that he could "get away with murder" as a juvenile and that he would "do a few years in juvy."

She confessed that the "extent of the hatred and stigma that is attached to being gay" stunned her. "The jury," she alleged, "blamed Larry King for his own death." She spoke of the verdict as "cruel justice," saying, "He didn't do anything, he didn't do anything."

Ms. Fox ended by saying she hoped that Brandon could lift the burden of hate under which he labored, and turn his life around: "He was wrong about eliminating 'the problem.' For Larry King was loved. Mercifully, that love did not die."

With little ceremony, Judge Campbell said, "This crime is about as serious as it can get." He asked Brandon if he understood the terms of his sentence and the obligation of the restitution. Brandon replied, "Yes" and "Yes."

Judge Campbell then ordered Brandon remanded to the Ventura County Juvenile Center, from which he would be transferred, at age eighteen, to a facility under the authority of the California Department of Corrections and Rehabilitation, for a "total of twenty-one years."

The judge then ordered the gun destroyed. And said, "We are in recess."

Everyone filed out, somber, no longer fizzy with reunion. The media was right outside the courtroom door as opposed to outside the courthouse as they had been in Chatsworth. They felt bigger, more in-your-face, even though, I think, there were actually fewer journalists. Five of the activist jurors swept around Kendra, shielding her, and moving her down the hall and into the refuge of a women's restroom. The Kings pushed through the crowd to a nearby elevator, making no comment.

Ms. Fox left by a back door. Mr. Wippert faced the cameras alone, saying over and over again, "Now he has a date that he can circle."

I walked out into the cool day, buttoning my wool coat. Cirrocumulus clouds flew across the gray sky, like white dwarfs chasing a star that had supernovaed. The climax had happened out of sight.

IT WAS JUST BEFORE CHRISTMAS 2012, and the street in Oxnard on which Kendra lived was well known for its Christmas decorations. The street snowed lights. Blow-up Santas billowed, mechanical reindeer sluggishly bowed their heads, plastic Nativity figures glowed from within. "Jingle all the way" rang down from a palm tree.

A few doors down from Kendra's house stood a little white bungalow with two windows set off by green shutters. The peaked roof and windows were trimmed with white lights. Minus a sprinkling of snow, it looked as if it could have come out of *It's a Wonderful Life*. I stood in front of the little house, realizing that that movie, which inspired my midwestern childhood fantasy about Christmas, had probably been filmed a short drive from where I was standing. Later, I read that the movie had been filmed on a ranch in Encino. And the snow that fell on George Bailey was a new kind of chemical snow, not the noisy sort they used to make out of cornflakes.

Kendra met me at the door, laughing. "Welcome to Christmas Lane!" Her house offered only a modest string of colored lights around the doorway. She explained that they had a blow-up Santa, but he was now a "pancake." ("Maybe James can fix him," she said.) Three dogs bounded to the door, two elderly dachshunds, grizzled and gray, and a lively black mutt with a white-tipped tail.

I was visiting Kendra for the second time. A year earlier, in January of 2011, I had met with Kendra along with James. Then, as now, the dogs wagged for my attention, as Kendra ushered us toward the dining room table. Eight years sober, Kendra had played the role of Redemption in this tragedy. There were times when I thought the defense had cast her expertly. There were times when I thought that the grace of recovery was too easily taken for "truth." But there were other times— many—when she was gasping for air, looking like a woman washed onto shore, when it seemed to me that it didn't matter whether or not she was playing the role of redeemer; her grief was profound.

During this meeting, I better understood Kendra's compound of grief and repentance as her effort not so much to change the past, for that was beyond her reach, but to try to change the effects of past happenings. Possibly some good could be found; perhaps painful memories could be healed. As Emily Dickinson might have it, "Remorse is memory awake."

Kendra offered me some iced tea or pop. I told her I missed hearing the word "pop," from my childhood. I could hear her laughing in the kitchen when I told her that I had "graduated to 'soda' when I moved east." She came through the kitchen door with a plastic glass of diet cola and a green glass bowl of Christmas pretzels: bells, angels, and trees.

I was taken aback by the change in her appearance and mood from when I last saw her. I told her she looked well. She thanked me and told me she had been slowly regaining some of the weight she'd lost during the trial. "Was there anybody who didn't just about fade away?" she said. "Every time I looked at Scott or Miss Fox I thought, 'Oh my God!' They were both so skinny."

She proudly brought out pictures of Brandon, including pictures from his high school graduation at the Ventura Juvenile Center. There was Brandon wearing a mortarboard and a light blue gown and hugging his grandfather, who sat in his wheelchair. Then Kendra showed me some more recent pictures of Brandon, standing with Ryan in the visiting room of the prison where he was then housed. In the later pictures, he too looked different. I blurted, "Wow, he looks so much bigger."

Kendra replied, "Yeah. He has put on like forty pounds. He always said they starved him in juvy. He has unlimited access to peanut butter and jelly now, his diet of choice." She laughed her husky rattle. Then she said, "But, you know, he is doing okay, I think. Not like it isn't hard. But it is okay. I go to see him every weekend."

We spoke a bit about her work as the intake coordinator at the rehab center where she got clean. She told me about a particularly difficult intake she'd had to handle that morning. "But, you know," she said, "I'm good. Maybe the best I've ever been. The first time I have been single since I was fifteen. I'm not *gone*, like I used to be. I'm good."

I smiled and said, "Welcome back."

She laughed so hard that she scattered some pretzels across the table, picking them up with one quick motion of her right hand. Still laughing, she whisked them into the trash while straightening the candy cane tablecloth with her left hand.

"Okay," I said. "I am just going to cut to the chase. What do you think happened between Brandon and Larry?"

"Oh boy! Okay. Well, I don't know if I have an answer for you," she said. "I learned just like you did. I knew nothing. Alls I have is what you heard. What's rumors, what's not rumors, what's real, what's not. That's why, when sitting there, I was like, 'What?' You know, I was learning it just like you guys were."

Looking past me toward the window that fronted the street and the Christmas outside, she said, "And Brandon won't have a conversation about it."

I told her I had heard something similar from Kathryn Lestelle, the defense investigator, who told me that "Brandon never talked about the shooting."

"Yep," Kendra said.

Ms. Lestelle had told me in a phone interview that Brandon's silence "drove [her] nuts": "I kept telling him, you have to talk about it. And he refused. Once, he said, pointing to his head, 'It is here in a box, with a string tied around it, and it will never be opened.'"

She offered that anecdote as evidence of the impact of dissociation. I suggested that dissociation would not be so clearly articulated. What she was describing sounded like plain old refusal. Ms. Lestelle had continued to argue for dissociation.

I asked Kendra if she thought Brandon understood that it was not a good idea to keep silent, to keep it all in.

Kendra said, "Do I think he understands it's not good for him? I almost want to say that because everybody tells him it's not good for him, he's just going to keep it that much closer to home and show people that he doesn't need to deal with it or think about it or talk about it."

Thinking about Brandon's refusal to talk, Kendra associated to the phone call Brandon made to her early on the morning of the shooting. Kendra had been dropping Ryan off at preschool and missed the call.

She explained that she didn't see the "missed call" message until

Brandon would already have been in class. So she had it in mind that she would call him back later in the day.

"Well, obviously, that didn't happen," she said. "You know, I keep telling him, Brandon, it kills me that you called me that morning. Do you think it would have changed anything if I picked up the phone?"

"'No. No. No.' He always says," she said. "But I'm like, well what were you calling me for?

"And all I get is 'I don't know. I don't know.'" Her voice trailed off as she looked toward the empty living room.

Then she returned to my question. "Does he know it would be good for him to talk about what happened? I just get a lot of I don't knows, and he changes the subject. You know, he doesn't even push it away; he just straight skips over it."

I said, "You seem to be describing defiance or a kind of stonewalling, right?" I added, "So I guess he only talked to Dr. Hoagland."

Kendra leaned back in her chair and rolled her eyes. Was she looking at the ceiling? Or were her eyes closed? Eventually she looked down at the table, as she shook her head "no."

Confused, I said, "What do you mean?"

"Well, he maybe told him some things about the shooting. But not much," she said softly, leaning in.

I began to track the pattern of candy canes in the tablecloth with my eyes. They ran in parallel lines, in groups of five, as if marching in formation. It took me a moment to call myself back from what I recognized as an old obsessional defense I'd employed as a child: count, figure out the pattern, solve the puzzle, get out.

"I see," I said, continuing to note the tablecloth's pattern. There were bunches of holly, three green leaves, two red berries, at equal intervals between the candy canes.

"I often wondered about what Dr. Hoagland was saying," I finally managed, "or was saying in Brandon's words. It sounded too sophisticated for a kid, especially a kid who everybody said did not talk that much."

"Yep," Kendra said.

"So, wait a minute, what do you think it was like for Brandon to sit there and listen to Dr. Hoagland tell 'his' story?" I asked.

"Surprised?" she guessed. "Brandon, when he was sitting there, when Hoagland came back on Monday and had gone to see Brandon over the weekend . . . Brandon was sitting there [in the courtroom], and was like, 'What the fuck?'"

"Brandon said that he was trying to tell them what they wanted to hear. He doesn't even know how they got those stories over the weekend. He can't even explain it. 'Cause when he was hearing the testimony, he was like, 'What?' He was lost in it as well."

I momentarily fought the urge to return to the pattern in the table-cloth. Slowly I said, "So we have no idea, no idea at all? No idea what was on Brandon's mind, no idea what led him to shoot Larry?"

"Yep," Kendra said again.

"Nothing. Nothing," I said, as if repetition would help heal the gap.

"Yep," Kendra said for the third time.

"Kendra, I think you can see that I wondered if this had happened, but what you are saying leaves me a bit speechless . . ."

She did not speak, and finally I said, "For you too?"

Kendra still did not speak but sat across from me rhythmically nodding her head "yes."

We sat in silence for a while. Noises from the street, the sound of a car, a kid shouting, another kid answering, found their way in through the window.

My thoughts were moving faster than I could articulate them. Brandon had admitted killing Larry. He said, "I shot him," when he was arrested. But it seems to have stopped there. He admitted the shooting, but he did not confess to the killing. Confession implies a story, along with a set of feelings, usually the intertwining of rage and guilt.

I said, "So I guess Brandon did not exactly confess. Right? There is no story. No motive. No feelings, perhaps beyond anger. He reportedly told Dr. Hoagland that he was angry, angrier than he had ever been."

Kendra looked again in the direction of the empty living room. I wondered: Who or what was she looking for? James? (He showed up later, right as I was leaving, and after greeting me, went into the living room and sat on the large overstuffed sofa, to call his girlfriend.) I remembered that when I had met with Kendra and James, they told me how they sometimes would all gather to watch football in the living room and put Brandon on speakerphone so that he could be there with them.

"I don't know what to think, I really don't," Kendra said, still looking toward the living room.

Again, we sat for a while, in a silence that felt more protracted than the gap on my tape managed to record. There was, in this silence, a kind of opening, perhaps even relief. We moved out of the stories that had been told, the arguments that had been made. We departed from knowing and understanding toward the traumatic fact that Brandon refused to speak and perhaps could not speak. The weight of such witnessing had dragged us all down, but perhaps no one more than Kendra.

I began to talk with Kendra about my frustration over the ways in which the signs of Brandon's distress were dismissed as "a boy being a boy." I told her how it seemed to me that he had been growing more and more disturbed, beginning in the summer of 2007 and throughout that fall and into the early winter of 2008. There had been plenty of signs at school that something was wrong: his grades were falling, his attitude was sullen, and he was basically checked out.

"Yeah," Kendra concurred. "You know, Billy was going to the school. He knew something was wrong. My biggest thing is that Brandon was so angry at everything and everybody in his whole life that that's the way he thought. Larry just happened to be there at the wrong place at the wrong time. Either doing or saying the wrong things at the wrong time to a kid that was about to freakin' lose his freakin' mind."

Again, my thoughts moved outside of speech. Kendra apparently believed that what had happened was first-degree murder. Crimes of passion are relational, whereas this planned act of abnegation was asocial, random, by her account.

I reminded her that when we last met, she spoke a lot about how isolated and unrelated Brandon was. I also brought us back to something James had told me, a theory of sorts, a theory of paranoid perception: "Brandon was obsessed with this movie, *Boondock Saints*. It is like a vigilante movie, about these two Irish brothers [abused and abandoned], and they basically go around and whack out mafia guys. [They kill thirty-four people in 140 minutes, a little over four per minute.] They are like vigilante saints, killing all the bad guys that had messed with them or people in their neighborhood."

James had suggested that Brandon felt "messed with" by Larry, saying that he, James, was not sure if, in fact, that happened, " 'cause I don't know Larry. But if Larry was capable of doing this [of sexually harassing Brandon] . . . what was he capable of as an adult, you know what I mean? I honestly think that Brandon thought that he was doing the right thing. He was executing the problem and saving somebody else from a future problem, like some crazy vigilante executing the problem."

Kendra said, "Yeah, I remember that too. But the only thing Larry did to Brandon was some teasing. It was just a lot of rumor. It was grade school."

I said, "I agree. Like you, I don't think the teasing and the rumors amounted to sexual harassment. But that is what we understood. The question is, did Brandon see it that way? I don't think so. I think what we are both saying, and James too, is that Brandon's perceptions were distorted. He was paranoid. He was, as you said, 'freakin' out of his mind.' "

I looked at my pop. I hadn't touched it. I drank some. It was flat.

Kendra watched me. I wondered if she could see that I was anxious. Perhaps, because she soon reassured me, saying, "He was messed up, that's for sure. He had to have freakin' lost it. How else can we explain it?"

But she didn't stop there, saying, "I knew it was going to happen sooner or later. We all knew it was going to happen, because he was always flying into a rage, always, his whole life."

At that point, I was so absorbed in my own thoughts that I startled when her phone rang. It skittered across the table, and she quickly grabbed it, flipped it open, and said, "Hey, Bubba." Her voice was suddenly sunny.

She mouthed to me, "Brandon."

"How you doing?" she asked. There was a brief exchange, during which she mostly listened, saying only: "Good." "Okay." "Yeah." "Okay."

She asked, "Do you have enough money?"

"Good," she said.

"Listen, Bubba, I'm here with Dr. Ken. You want to talk to him?" she said.

"No. Okay. Okay. I know. I know," she said.

"Okay, yes, I'll have James call you when he comes home." She hung up.

She looked at me and tried to smile. I smiled in return, meeting her will as she struggled to persevere, stemming the tide of grief.

She said, "He is not going to talk. Not now. I don't know." Her tone shifted toward despair.

I said that I thought it had to be hard to remain hopeful, in the face of Brandon's refusal.

"Yeah," she said, flatly, looking past me.

The abrupt quality of Kendra's response led me to think about how we both knew that Brandon had grown mute long before the murder and the trial.

Neglect and sorrow are often muted by rage and destructiveness: I have not lost. I have rendered loss. Even as the action of mute murder insists, if only for a passing moment, that others become mired in one's own devastation.

And there Kendra and I sat mired.

I remembered that she had told me, when last we met, about a time in the fall of 2007 when Brandon was so angry he punched a tree, bloodying his hand.

"Yeah, the tree in front of the house on Tiller . . . And I'm so used to that with him." Again, the despair surfaced. "You know, like James wears his heart on his sleeve. James will spill his guts to me. Jeremy will spill his guts to me. Brandon is just," she struggled to inhale, "since he was a kid, a little kid, he was either really happy or really mad a lot of times."

Kendra began to weep. "I remember looking at his hands, a lot. You know, just like looking at those hands, those hands had a gun in them. I looked at his hands a lot. And I couldn't look at his hands for a long time."

Hands she had washed, hands she had held, hands she had watched grow, hands she had bandaged. Hands that now symbolized how her son had failed our collective ethical charge to not take away the life of another.

What was it like to hold the guilt, the confession that her child refused? Perhaps the fact that Brandon consistently refused help could be read as the most damning detail. I said that I thought that it "must be so hard to recognize—in a way, to see—the rage and ruin that Brandon still refuses."

Kendra took off her glasses, grabbed a paper napkin, and wiped her eyes and her forehead as she pleaded, "If only he would talk to you, or someone like you, even his cellmates. I keep asking him if he talks to them. No. No. No. But I keep asking, because how much worse could it get?"

I understood that Brandon was not going to talk with me. His lawyers had advised him not to speak with me. "It's not going to happen. And there is no good reason for it to happen" was how Scott Wippert replied to my request to meet with him and Brandon.

Brandon had also called when I met with James and Kendra. James took the call and went into the back of the house to talk. When he came back into the dining room, he said, "Dude, he needs to talk to someone like you. But he won't do it. He won't do it. I don't even think he talks to any of the guys in there."

Kendra said, "No, he doesn't. He gets along with everyone. But I don't think he talks to anyone."

James said, "No, he doesn't talk to anyone. And he is not going to. He is not going to."

When Brandon turned twenty-one, I wrote to him and asked if he would like to speak with me. He did not respond to my letter. His continued secreting of the murder was the way I would know him.

Kendra, though, was still seeking help for her child and spoke about how her own shame and guilt could make it difficult for her to accept help. "It's hard, sometimes, to accept a lot of the support, too, because my son did something horrible. Horrible. Just like this shooting in Connecticut. [The Sandy Hook Elementary shooting had happened five days before our conversation.] Oh, my God . . ." She began to sob, and just like so many times in the courtroom, the paper napkin came apart in her hands.

Recovering a bit, she said, "You know, I called Robyn [Bramson] right away, and I was like, 'This is so fucked up, it just all goes back.' And she's like, 'It's not even relatable to Brandon's stuff.' But it is to me. To me, it is. It's a school, and there's kids that are shot multiple times, dead."

Kendra covered her eyes, put her elbows on the table, and held her head in her hands, but she kept talking. "To me, it is kind of similar. I mean, so far apart, but very similar for a mother, you know. That mom, his mom, you know, thank God in some ways, she doesn't have to go through it, because she's in a better place. And the dad, who wasn't in the boy's life for two years, you know, just watching on TV one day, and here's your kid. You're seeing your kid's name in the paper every fuckin' day . . . every day, the news . . . every day."

Now it was I who stared into the living room. Was I trying to summon a family scene? Was I looking for others to help hold the grief, the guilt, the despair that Kendra was struggling to hold against the hate and revenge that her son was refusing to name?

It was Kendra who kept us going at that moment, telling me it was a newspaper that first brought her face-to-face with Larry. "The first time I saw Larry's picture, I was walking into a store. It was on the *Ventura County Reporter*. He was on the front page, and I didn't even read the heading. I knew exactly, you know, that it was him. It was the picture when he was a little bit younger, you know, the little boy, and I lost it.

Lost it. Because I had no idea who he was or what he even looked like for a long time."

I said, "Yeah, we haven't really talked that much about Larry."

She took a sip of iced tea, picked up a pretzel, and set it on a napkin next to her glass. She said, "I felt so sorry for him. I felt so sorry for him. Still, to this day, I don't understand why, if Brandon was so mad, why he couldn't have just beaten him up. Or whatever—whatever! Anything. Anything! But to do what he did. What the hell was he thinking? I just can't . . . can't wrap my brain around it. 'Cause, I mean, how hard would that have been? How hard would that have been to say, you know, I'm gonna beat your ass if you don't leave me alone. Or, whatever."

Kendra told me that she "identified with Larry." Like him, she was adopted, and like him, she enjoyed the company of gay people. She had a lot of gay friends. Brightening, she said, "Well, you met Nancy. She was my rock. Love her!"

My mood lifted as well, and I told her that I found a kind of delight in the way that Nancy, the dignified Mexican Indian, sat at Kendra's side every day. I said, "It was like you brought Larry's queer ancestor to court."

We both started laughing and coughing. Kendra reached for her tea, me for my pop.

"I gotta catch my breath," she said. But soon she was telling me about her best friend, Louie, who "was always at my house. We were never without each other." Cackling, she described him as flamboyant and "completely obvious! I loved him. He was a sweet guy. And Brandon knew him, knew him well.

"That's why it is hard for me to think that it had anything to do with that, with Larry being gay. If it did, I don't understand it," she said. Then she added, "Billy was not a big fan of Louie at all. Constantly bashing him. Same thing with Troy, another gay friend of mine. We'd be hot-tubbing, and Billy would go up in the top bedroom and throw M-80s in the Jacuzzi. He constantly tortured this guy, made fun of him all the time, and it was horrible."

Kendra returned to the idea that Brandon had been around a lot of gay people in his childhood. I interjected, "But it seems he was also around gay people who were being tortured."

"Yeah, I can see what you are saying. But I still don't get it," Kendra said.

Kendra didn't "get it" because she was busy doing the work of sympathy, identification, and reparation that her son had refused or had yet to find. Through identification and acts of sympathy, we work out our feelings of guilt and loss; we make reparations.

I wondered if Kendra wished that she could offer her sympathy, her identification as an avenue that Brandon had yet to find. But staying with Larry, I told Kendra that I wasn't sure that Larry was gay, and that I thought Larry may have been trying to come out as transgender.

"There was never anything dissected or really defined in court, was there?" she responded. "I don't think anybody understood it. 'Cause they didn't want to. That would have been just a whole other thing. It's easier to talk about white supremacy than transgender. And a lot of people probably don't even understand the difference between gay and transgender. And if people don't want to understand, they don't even try.

"Just like the school," she continued. "Was there a special person that was brought in to talk to kids that were having a problem? Was there someone brought in to help the teachers understand Larry? No.

"Now, the school people that talk about it say they are going to do something about it. It's been, oh, five years already, have they implemented anything over there? No. So they just wait for the next disaster to happen."

Just then Ryan came out of his room and joined us in the dining room, grabbing a handful of pretzels. Kendra said, "I think it is bedtime. Right? Take some more pretzels. But then, you're brushing teeth."

After he headed off with two fistfuls of pretzels, Kendra told me about how worried she was for Ryan. She explained how she "didn't tell him for several months. I told him that Brandon hurt somebody really bad at school." In light of her worries, she got him into therapy: "He still goes. We both go."

She said that she worried about their future. She was happy with the little local elementary school he attended. But junior high would be here soon enough, which brought her to E. O. Green: "Putting my kid at E. O. Green school? Hell no! Hell no! No. It's not gonna happen. He'd be home-schooled before that would happen. There's no way I would put him there. Or any kid. That school has done nothing but sweep all of this under the rug. Has anything changed at that school? Not a fucking thing. Not a thing. And putting in metal detectors and stuff like that is not what we're talking about."

"No, metal detectors are not the answer," I said. "I think that what you are trying to get at here are the ways in which we are all, all of us, bound to the lives of others. We need people, not metal, at the doors of schools—people who can ensure the bonds through which kids grow—people who can help kids negotiate the trouble they have in relating to kids that are 'other'—people who can pull up the rug and grieve."

Kendra looked at me quizzically, and I had to laugh at myself. I apologized for my rant.

She said, laughing, "You're the doctor."

I laughed, and took her comment as teasing kindness. We were separated by marching candy canes, but we were at the same table. Life had taken us to different worlds, but there was the plain recognition of the social bond—the opposite of the splitting paranoia plaguing this story—that made both of our lives possible, a bond that tragically had gone missing at E. O. Green and in the Superior Court of the State of California.

We like to think that we can mourn and achieve some coherence. But we are transformed by loss. Mourning changes us forever. It hits us at the grocery store. It hits us when we see our child's hands. We come undone, and if we are lucky enough to come back, we come back together. That is, we come back with others; we need them to bind us to life but also to bind our sorrow and our rage.

In a similar way, we like to think that gender guarantees some coherence. We live with the common idea that masculinity and femininity are tidy, organized categories. They bind us. Some people even speak of gender as a core, a solid state. But gender, even when lived in its most "normal" fashion—the "boys' boy," the "girly girl"—is anxiously postured and primped. No one escapes gender's tyranny.

I didn't say much of what I was thinking. But I did say that it had been a comfort to speak to her, and to hear the reason that she was bringing (finally) to a story that had slipped the knot of reason and the guiding hand of common ethics. I also told her that it was a comfort to me to listen as she grieved for Larry through her identification and sympathy. I said that I thought Larry's life had not been seen as a life that warranted grief, and that had been painful to witness. In the same way that it had been painful to witness the ways in which Brandon's mental illness and destructiveness had been disavowed.

I told Kendra I thought that mourning can allow us to recognize together not only what we have lost but what social forces helped put the gun in Brandon's hand. Or what social forces led her community to "sweep all this under the rug," as she put it so well.

"When we get over grieving, we clean the house. Right? We pull up the rug," I said. "And that way we can at least we see what has happened. We can, at least, try to right the wrong. We can put the room back in better order."

"God, I remember those first few days," Kendra said. "Oh, months, really months and months. Oh, hell, years. At first, I couldn't go home, you know, to Prototypes. It was crawling with media people. They put me in a hotel. I sent Ryan to stay with his dad. I didn't have him back with me for at least a month and even then only for a day or two. I remember being with James in that hotel room. I couldn't sleep the night of the shooting. I was afraid to take anything. The phone kept ringing and ringing. I let the battery run out. And then when we heard that Larry died, you know, on the TV, we heard the news. I thought I would never stop crying, crying, and crying, and crying. I could not leave that hotel room. I could not even get up off of the floor. I could not eat. I could not sleep. Those days, those months it seemed it would never end. I thought it would never end.

"And it hasn't. It won't." She paused, catching her breath. "But now, I don't cry every day.

"Well, I probably do," she added. "But, you know, not as bad, not nearly as bad. And I can say more. And I hope I am learning. I hope we are learning. We have to. Right?"

Ryan and Beau, the eager black mutt, returned, each wagging in his own way. No teeth had been brushed. More pretzels were requested.

Kendra laughed and said, "Okay, one pretzel, then teeth, then bed. Come on, I'll help."

ACKNOWLEDGMENTS

I begin by thanking the community of Courtroom 51, who graciously allowed me to live among them during the summer of 2011. To the extent that I have not fully captured their stories or their grief follows on my limits, not theirs.

I could not have written this book outside of my friendships with Judith Butler and Gayle Salamon. My ability to think this book and to survive the trauma it tells rests on the kindness and brilliance of their good company.

This book gathered with the help of many research and clerical assistants, whom I wish to thank: Pascale Boucicaut, Kathy DeLaO, Ted Dodson, Jessie Gaynor, Meg Giles, Christian McCulloh, Stella Tan.

I especially want to thank my "Agatha," Kris Clarkin, for her local sleuthing and her steadfast generosity.

I benefited greatly from trenchant readings offered by Frances Coady, David Hopson, AB Huber, Daniel Kaizer, and Adam Moss.

I thank Sarah Burnes for her faith, and Barbara Jones for her determination. It has been my good fortune to have them in my corner.

Michael Cunningham's devotion has made mine a richer life. His eye, his poetry, his persistence have made this a richer book. I am forever grateful.

I want to recognize Laura, Linnie, Leora and Linda, my mother, my grandmother, my aunt and my cousin, who loved beyond the expected. As well, I wish to honor my late father, James, the reader.

I dedicate this book to Sasha Vorlicky, who found his way from fourteen to see anew.

ABOUT THE AUTHOR

KEN CORBETT is clinical assistant professor at the New York University Postdoctoral Program in Psychoanalysis and Psychotherapy. He maintains a private practice in New York City. He is the author of *Boyhoods: Rethinking Masculinities*.